BETWEEN
THE CROSSES

Catherine Moore

of the Flynn Family

from the famed Bouboo.

Best Wishes

Just Sullivan

March 2017

BETWEEN THE CROSSES

A JOURNEY ALONG A COUNTRY ROAD

JACK BUTLER

Cover image by David Clarke.

First published 2010

The History Press Ireland
119 Lower Baggot Street
Dublin 2
Ireland
www.thehistorypress.ie

British Library Cataloguing in Publication Data.
A catalogue record for this book is available from the British Library.

ISBN 978 1 84588 994 4

Typesetting and origination by The History Press
Printed in Great Britain

The author's royalties will be donated to Console,
a registered charity supporting and helping people bereaved by suicide

CONTENTS

CHAPTER 1

INTRODUCTIONS

I am living away from Clonboo, from 'home', for the best part of thirty years. After my Leaving Certificate in Templemore CBS, I made my way to college in Limerick in 1979. Going back and forth over weekends, it was not until I started working full-time in 1984 that you could say I had finally 'left home'. Whichever way you look at it, the fact remains that I am living longer away from Tipp than I lived in 'The Premier' county.

Like everything else nowadays, just living is a busy job, with time being a scarce commodity. As someone pointed out to me recently, 'We are wealth richer but time poorer.' The years go by at a frantic pace. Kids grow up and it gets harder and harder to keep up with our ever-changing world.

I am lucky to have family, relations and friends back at home but as the years go by, it is hurling matches and funerals that bring me back more regularly than the earlier years, when it was still hurling but also cutting turf, thinning turnips and going to Hayes Hotel on Saturday nights. As I keep telling my friends from Lucan, Sarsfields and anywhere else, Tipp is the 'Home of Hurling', but little do they know that there was often other things on our innocent minds on a Saturday night in Hayes Hotel at around 1.30a.m., than the vision of Michael Cusack, Maurice Davin and Archbishop Croke founding the GAA on that famous day in 1884 upstairs in the same hotel. Before Hayes Hotel became the regular haunt for us, we had the Premier Ballroom in Thurles, the occasional céilí in the Brothers (CBS) or Tighe Mhuire for a 'hop' in McDonagh Terrace, Templemore. Thank God for the Lee brothers of Shanakill, Tim and John, and their red Vauxhall Viva car, as Thurles is fourteen miles from home. Templemore is walkable, being about five miles away, and it was walked too many times, especially on wet and dark winter nights and often alone. There were no mobile phones and not too many cars either, but we survived.

Funerals are a necessary part of human evolution. We are born, we live our lives as we pass through whatever time we are given, then we die. We are gone but we are not forgotten, we hope! There are no practice runs. When I go to a funeral, especially to a funeral of someone I know in Tipp, I always try to stay around after the removals or the burial, to hear some of the conversations about the deceased. As I get older, I now find myself knowing more about the person who died, but I could never know or remember as much as the people who lived in the same community for fifty, sixty or seventy years.

Before the years have gone, and for my own children (and for myself too), I would like to put down on paper some information about the people who lived near home in Tipp. The information is a combination of my own memories of the people and the houses, together with the information I could get from the 'Elder Lemons' of the area and the information I got from the families.

'Between the Crosses', as most will recognise, is the road between the Cross of Clonboo and the Cross of Toher.

TOHER SCHOOL

I must make a short mention here of Toher school, which is located about halfway up the road, about halfway 'Between the Crosses', and which was the centre point of our lives growing up in Clonboo at primary age. My youngest child, Sarah started school in Scoil Mhuire, Lucan, in September 2005, around the same time I started this book! Sarah is now in third class, where there are two classes of approx twenty-eight pupils in each class. Every class in her school has between twenty-five and thirty, just like every classroom around the country these days.

My kids can't believe that when I was going to primary school, we had a total of twenty-eight children in Toher National School, with two teachers. We were lucky to get such a great education and most of my friends who grew up in various places around the country cannot believe it either. Late one night, as we reflected on life, one of my friends, Matt Kelly, in an affectionate way, coined the phrase 'La La Land' for his view of the unreal place we lived in.

A funny incident occurred after Pope John Paul II died, God rest him. A lady rang in to the Gerry Ryan radio show from a hairdressing shop in Nenagh, claiming that the image of the late Pope had appeared in a towel in the Hair Salon. When Gerry asked her what the local reaction was, the lady said that they had contacted a local radio station and local press, but, 'ah sure you know yourself some people think we live in La La Land, down here'.

Most people who went to school in Toher National School lived 'Between the Crosses', but due to the distance from Clonmore and Templetuohy schools, others outside the Crosses also attended. It was a good school with very good teachers. I was taught by two main teachers, Mrs Fogarty from Baby Infants to Second Class, and Mrs Bergin from Third to Sixth Class. During the years we also had substitute teachers while the permanent teachers were out sick or took time off while pregnant. In this regard, Mrs Everard (Josephine Costigan) would be the teacher I remember.

I just barely remember starting school for a few days in June 1966 in the Old School and then officially starting in the New School in January 1967. The school closed in June 1998 due to lack of numbers, having been reduced to one teacher a number of years earlier.

But we will come back to the school later.

PREFACE

My original idea of recording the houses and families who lived in them 'Between the Crosses' started to wander a bit as I recalled related childhood memories along with a passion for hurling. Hopefully the wandering does not diminish the original idea.

The original idea, as noted at the start, was to put down on paper as much information as I could about the people who lived and the houses that were 'Between the Crosses'. The accuracy of the information is based on my own rec-ollections along with the information that my mother and father have. Some of the information has been passed on from previous generations. Other people will have the same information and others will have different or conflicting informa-tion about the same house or the people who lived there. Along with all this, the enclosed information has taken a bit of time to put together and events have overtaken the details. New houses have been built, people have moved in and out of the area, sadly people have died, and happily there have been new arrivals with family extensions.

At the very start, I will apologise for any error or mistake in any of the details or any assumptions that I have made, which are not correct. Nothing has been included that I know to be a deliberate mistake. I would also hope that nobody would take offence to any matter or description or comment or recollection of a story or yarn that might be included which might upset anyone or bring back sad memories.

The short memories of *Between the Crosses* is intended for my own family and my children as a record of my recollections, but it may be of interest to others also. I hope that the reader will appreciate and acknowledge the context in which the information was compiled. I would also hope that further information about vari-ous houses, people and families can be added by others who read this: maybe we could put it all together at some stage in the future?

The other deviation from the earlier idea was the putting together of a compre-hensive family tree for the Butler Clan, along with the maiden names that 'added value' throughout the generations. In this regard, additional documents have been added to accompany the written information. It is often easier and simpler to understand the various combinations and relationships when you see the whole family tree. You may have heard the saying, 'he couldn't see the wood from the trees'. From my own children, Aoife, Sean and Sarah, I have gone back eight generations of Butlers and picked up as much information as I could along the way, including the Doolans, Whelans, Farrells, Shanahans, Delaneys, O'Maras and Dwyers.

This book has been a labour of love for me. The more you look for information, the more avenues open up and you go after other information and into a different direction. Working long hours in the construction business is not conducive to sustained and regular research, so I have decided to stop searching and put this book to print.

I hope Aoife, Sean and Sarah, along with my nephews and nieces, will some day read the book and add new chapters of their own, for future generations.

REFLECTIONS

When embarking on a journey and a task like this, you must research and spend many hours thinking about what to write. You are constantly finding new information, but at the same time, you also get a great sense of those that have gone before you: the past generations who made life, entered our daily lives and passed on so many gifts and benefits to us just by their very presence in the world. As I wrote these pages I was constantly reminded of them, all the people that I know that have gone ahead of us and more, thank God, still with us. Many of them are mentioned in the preceding pages, but many more that did not live 'Between the Crosses' still made their mark and touched our lives.

I am reminded of some sound advice, received from a very good person and a great friend, in a message that was passed down through the generations and which will remain permanently embedded in my heart and mind. People come along and stay a while. Some stay too short a time, but that does not diminish their impact. We are fortunate to have met them. Never lose an opportunity to enjoy and appreciate them while you have them, tell them how you feel about them. Life can be so short, do your best, have no regrets, we will meet again. The piece is simply called 'Normal Day':

Normal Day, let me be aware of the treasure you are;
Let me learn from you, love you, savour you, bless you, before you depart;
Let me not pass you by, in quest of some rare and perfect tomorrow.
Let me hold you while I may, 'cause it will not always be so.
One day, I will dig my fingers into the earth, or bury my head in a pillow,
Or stretch myself taut, or raise my hands to the sky,
And want more than all the world, your return.

T.G.J.

FOREWORD

BY PAT BUTLER

Clonboo Road. It's a road that comes from nowhere and goes nowhere, but it's a very important part of the world to the people that are part of it. Whenever I think of Clonboo I think of the great neighbours, past and present. The short stretch of road has unique people, which I believe would not be matched anywhere else. Could anywhere else claim to have had a bigger character than the late Billy Grimes (Banjo)? His legend is known the length and breadth of Ireland. Could anywhere else claim to have a better tradesman than Billy Grimes (long), who looked after all our household emergencies over so many years? I'd say you could travel the world and not find a farmer more proud of his farm than the late Martin Deegan.

These are just a few examples of the tremendous people of Clonboo. However, the best way of knowing how great your neighbours are is in times of great sorrow. I can remember when sorrow visited our door with the tragic death of my brother Ned. All the neighbours, young and old, rallied around in support. I know that our family was never so glad to be from Clonboo than when we saw what the people of Clonboo did when it was most needed. Tragedy has visited many doors on Clonboo Road and the response of the neighbours has always been tremendous.

I have a lot of vivid memories of growing up in Clonboo. One such memory is of our annual card game in our house on Christmas night. I can remember when I was very young, looking forward, with a certain amount of fear, to Toby Maher (RIP), Patrick Clarke (RIP) and Neddie Guilfoyle (RIP) arguing continuously about the playing of the cards. Toby used to always say that if you got a red four in your hand you would never have luck. I'm not sure what the logic was behind it, but maybe someone will be able to throw some light on it.

Clonboo also has some great focal points. Tommy Deegan's bog was a hive of activity during the summer months for a long number of years. It offered a great opportunity of employment for us kids and offered a social outlet to the elderly people of the road. The other focal point of the road was Toher school, were we got our early education. One of my memories of my school days is having the dubious honour of being the first pupil to break a window with a wayward football. My only consolation was that only a few days after the window was replaced it was broken again by T.J. Maher (Lisanure).

I think it's great what Jack is doing with this book. It's a lasting memory to the people who lived on the road. My parent's generation are a goldmine of information and it's great that it is documented forever more and not lost to history. I hope you all enjoy this read and it evokes great memories of times past.

WHERE ARE YOU FROM?

As part of any conversation, the question often arises about where you are from. Most people introduce the topic into a conversation when introduced to a stranger, to try and make a connection in some way or another. Ireland is a small country and everyone knows someone from almost every corner of the country.

When I am asked, I usually say Tipperary and as the county is long in geographical size, I usually emphasise the North Riding part of Tipp. It is the only county with two County Council Authorities. When asked further or as often volunteered, I will say that I live about five miles outside Templemore and if the stranger shows any knowledge of the area then I will get into the Clonmore parish and keep going all the way to the townland of Clonboo. But usually the mention of Templemore gets a response about the Garda Training College and a question about why I did not become a Garda. However, on one occasion a good few years ago, I was on a train and the conversation started about where I was from. We got as far as Tipperary and then the North Riding distinction and then Templemore. But on this occasion, instead of the Garda connection, the reply came back, 'Oh that's where the bleeding statues were.' It was years since I had previously heard that connection, and yes, the 'miracle' of the 'Bleeding Statues' did indeed happen in Templemore and it is worthy of mention, lest we forget it and not pass it on to the younger and more sceptical generation.

THE STORY OF THE BLEEDING STATUES

On the night of 16 August 1920 violent scenes erupted in Templemore as the Northamptonshire Regiment carried out attacks in response to the killing of RIC Inspector Wilson by the IRA. Shots were fired, houses attacked, shops robbed, the town hall set on fire and other premises damaged during the rampages.

Next thing that happens is that 'Our Lady saves Templemore'. Immediately after these deaths, supernatural activity was reported, accompanied by 'cures', in Templemore and just outside the town in the townland of Curraheen. It was alleged that religious statues at several premises, including the RIC barracks in Templemore, were shedding tears of blood. It was alleged that local farm labourer James Walsh was experiencing Marian apparitions, and that a holy well had appeared in his bedroom floor. It was reported that after the outburst on that night, some of the statues, from which blood had been oozing, were taken by Walsh to Templemore, and it is believed that it was this that saved the town from destruction. Divine intervention was believed by many to have occurred to prevent the town being destroyed in revenge for the Wilson killing. Soon after the alleged 'miraculous apparitions' the word spread, and by early September 1920, it was estimated that more than 15,000 people a day visited to see the bleeding statues. Extra trains were put on from

Kingsbridge (now Heuston) Station in Dublin. People described how they saw statues with streaks of blood flowing down the faces, necks and bodies. Pilgrim numbers increased and many people claimed to have been healed either by direct contact with James Walsh or by exposure to the bleeding statues. The official position of the Catholic Church was one of extreme caution and reserve. Walsh travelled outside Templemore and it is said that while he was a guest of the Monsignor in Cashel, that statues he had touched began to bleed. Cashel then experienced the arrival of new pilgrims. Back in Templemore, the police and military had disappeared off the streets and the IRA had stepped in to take over. They acted as stewards and marshals but did not appear on the streets in uniform and took advantage of the absence of the military and police. However, money poured into the IRA coffers by way of charges been imposed on cars entering the town and the local IRA lads getting tips from all the visitors. All of a sudden, the 'cause' of freedom and the 'struggle' lost its focus and importance among the IRA men on the ground. This upset the IRA leadership.

The local IRA commander Jimmy Leahy interrogated Walsh, who told the IRA lads that in a recent conversation with Our Lady, that she indicated her approval for the armed struggle and supported the intensification of the campaign. The IRA lads were not able to keep a straight face, and concluded that Walsh was not the 'full shilling'. Leahy then informed Canon Ryan and asked that the apparitions be denounced from the pulpit to stop people and pilgrims coming to Templemore. The Canon declined to say anything. Leahy then told Michael Collins, who instructed Dan Breen to question Walsh. Breen reported back that Walsh was a fake and the miracles and apparitions were not genuine.

The IRA resumed the war at the end of September 1920, and the town returned to normality. Collins sent a courier to Templemore to get one of the statues, as he had been given information by a local Catholic Churchman that local IRA Volunteers had engineered statues that would regularly bleed at specific times. The internal mechanism of an alarm clock had been concealed inside the statue, connected to fountain pen inserts which contained a mixture of sheep's blood and water. When the clock mechanism struck at certain times, it would send a spurt of blood through the statue, giving the impression that it was bleeding. When Collins got the statue he banged it off the side of a desk and sure enough, the internal works of a clock fell out.

James Walsh left for Australia and in 1947 he was granted Australian citizenship. By the way, prior to the IRA getting involved in the commercial part of the venture, it was said that Walsh used to use a small needle to prick the inside of his lip or his gum prior to kissing the statue and then, as the calcium or chalk of the statue absorbed the blood, it reacted and the blood streaked down the statue's body.

So that was the end of the 'Bleeding Statues' of Templemore!

THANKS

I'd like to thank my Mother and Father, Mary and Johnny Butler for the tremendous amount of information that they gave me. My Mother unearthed a great deal of 'hard evidence', including original documents, remembrance and memory cards, books, newspaper articles, historical records and religious details. Along with this, she also wrote out a comprehensive record of each family unit for every branch, down to children's names and maiden names of cousins' wives. For this information alone it was worth putting the book together, as nobody that I know of would have known so many details.

Over the past few years it has been interesting to fill in some of the missing details about various families and concerning various events, etc. I would often go down to Tipp on a Sunday afternoon, have the dinner and then pull out my list of queries or questions about conflicting information or blanks to be filled in. My Mother and Father would not always agree on the answer, but usually the finding of the answer would invariably lead to another question or some new information. During their respective digging for other information with neighbours and people, other information was discovered.

I hope I have done justice to all their hard work and I hope that they look at this book as largely their work, which I was very happy to put together. I would also like to thank them for giving me the gift and interest for doing this type of thing. It is a bit like farming, hurling or politics, it is in your heart and soul, that's why we enjoy it. Sorry it has taken a bit longer than expected, but I hope some day my own children, grandchildren and maybe future generations of Butlers, along with all their spouses and offspring, will remember the people that have gone before them and take time out from their busy lives to live a bit in the past.

That's what I have done!

Jack Butler, Summer 2010.

CHAPTER 2

THE PARISHES

No man will love his land and race
Who has no pride in his native place,
Nor will traditions linger long
Where local poets make no song.

The area of land between the Cross of Clonboo and the Cross of Toher forms part of two parishes, Clonmore and Templetuohy. There are also a number of townlands between the two crossroads. The length of road has a strange and unique border between the two parishes. From the Cross of Clonboo, both sides of the road are in the parish of Clonmore all the way up to the stream at Clarke's. After the stream, the left side of the road is in the parish of Templetuohy, while the right side of the road remains in the parish of Clonmore. The parish of Clonmore actually extends all the way up to the Cross of Toher and towards Templetuohy, all the way up to Shelly's house on the right-hand side. It is a difficult parish boundary to understand. In effect some houses further away from either village are part of the opposite parish. It also means that parts of the Toher townland are in both parishes.

The townlands themselves have changed over the years. Nowadays there are four townlands overlapping the length of road: Killavinogue, Clonboo, Toher and Lissanure. At the start of the twentieth century the townlands included Killavinogue, Ballysorrell Little, Clonbough Lower, Clonbough Upper, Togher and Lissanure.

In the pre-twentieth-century Toher school roll book entries, families such as Prendergast, Keenan and Pyne were registered as living in Sorrellhill. Those houses would currently be in the townland of Killavinogue. Nowadays Killavinogue extends from Clonboo Cross up to the ruins of Skehan's house. Today there are no houses along the lane that goes into Deegan's bog, where originally Will Cormack lived. This house was located in the townland of Ballysorrel Little. Clonbough Lower starts at Stamps and extends up to Guider's at both sides of the road and then up to Deegan's on the right-hand side only. Clonbough Upper originally started at Myren's and included Morrissey's, Greed's, Doolan's and Ryan's, which was where the school teacher lived next to the school. Togher started at Tom Butler's and went up past the Cross of Toher when you turn left. Lissanure started at Darmody's, now Bowe's and extended up past the Cross of Toher turning right. The main change from the turn of the last century to now is that Clonbough Upper was changed to Toher.

KILLAVENOGH, KILLAVINOGUE OR CLONMORE

Samuel Lewis's *Topographical Dictionary of Ireland* (1837) defines Clonmore or Killavenogh as:

> ...a parish in the barony of Ikerrin, county of Tipperary, and province of Munster, 4 miles north-east of Templemore, on the road from that place to Rathdowney; containing a population of 3,000 in 1831 and 3,557 in 1841. Houses 569 number and 5,946 statute acres, including a considerable quantity of good land interspersed with bog. The seats are Sorrel hill House, Foxborough Lodge, Dromard House and Clonbough. The chief antiques are the ruins of Clonbough Castle and St Anne's church. The parish is a rectory and vicarage, in the diocese of Cashel, forming part of the union with Templemore. The tithe composition, £369 4s 7½d; and there is a glebe of 36 acres. In 1834 the Protestants amounted to 11, and the Roman Catholics to 3,146. There were two private schools with about 130 children attending. At its size the parish was approx 5¼ miles long by a width of ¼ mile to 3¾ miles.

TEMPLETUOHY

In the same publication by Lewis, Templetuohy is described as:

> ...a parish, in the barony of Ikerrin, county of Tipperary, and province of Munster, 4 miles east south-east of Templemore, on the road by Johnstown to Kilkenny; containing 2,653 inhabitants, of which number, 602 are in the village. This parish which is separated from the parish of Callabeg by a small stream which also separates the baronies of Ikerrin and Eliogarty, comprises 6,193 statute acres, as a plotted under the tithe act. The land is generally of good quality and principally under tillage; there is a large proportion of bog, which might be very easily reclaimed. The principal seats are Cranagh, the property of J. Lloyd, Esq. But now in the occupation of Revd M.N. Thompson, a handsome mansion attached to a circular tower in the rear, the remains of a very ancient castle; and Long Orchard, the residence of Richard Lalor Sheil, Esq. The village has lately been much improved, and several new houses have been built; a penny-post has been established; nine monthly fairs are held in the year, chiefly for the sale of pigs; and the constabulary police force has been stationed there. The living is a rectory, in the diocese of Cashel, united to the rectory and vicarage of Callabeg, together forming the corps of

the prebend of Kilbragh, in the cathedral of Cashel, and in the patronage of the Archbishop. The tithes amount to £501 10s; the glebe comprises 13¾ acres, and the gross value of the benefice is £749 10s 9d per annum. The church is situated in the village. In the Roman Catholic divisions the parish forms part of the union or district of Moyne; the chapel, a neat building, is situated in the village. About 340 children are taught in four public schools, of which the parochial school is supported by the rector; and there is a dispensary. There are remains of several old castles in the parish.

The Civil Survey records the name 'Tampletoughy' as that of the civil parish, indicating that the name had by then supplanted the earlier name of 'Ballyvissin', which, however, continued to be popularly used. The use of the name Templetuohy for the parish appears to have come into being in the early part of the sixteenth century. Templetuohy, Teampall Tuaithe, 'the church of the tuath' (district or remote place) was used for the parish church long before it came to denote the parish as well. The use of the word Teampall, one of the ancient names for a church, appears to have gained a revival in the later medieval period, and it is notable that the parish churches of Moynetemple, Templeree and Templemore, which also owed their origins to Anglo-Norman patrons, have the component Teampall in their name as well.

IRISH TERRITORIAL DIVISIONS

The administrative divisions in Ireland consisted of a variety of land units in descending order of size: province (4), county (32), barony, parish and townland. It is worth having a look at the different types and their significance in years gone by, along with how they originated in the first place.

PROVINCE

This is the earliest and largest administrative division in Ireland, dating back into prehistory and early historic times. There were originally five provinces in the island of Ireland, with provincial 'over kings' who were supported by the kings of the smaller local kingdoms within them. However, by the seventeenth century, this had been reduced to the four modern provinces of Ulster, Connacht, Leinster and Munster.

COUNTY

A territorial unit equivalent to the English shire, it was created by the English administration in Ireland as the major subdivision of an Irish province, and dates back from the thirteenth to the seventeenth centuries. The counties as they are today were planned in 1584 but many existed long before this date.

BARONY

Originally the landholding of a feudal baron, the barony is now an obsolete administrative unit that is midway in size between a county and a parish.

PARISH

An ecclesiastical unit of territory that came into existence in Ireland in its present form in the twelfth and thirteenth centuries and was continued by the Established Church of Ireland after the Reformation. It was then adopted as a civil administrative area, but over time the boundaries of some civil and ecclesiastical parishes came to vary from each other. Roman Catholic parishes, for example, when reinstated, were often redrawn to suit the needs of their parishioners. Because civil parishes may extend across rivers that were often used to delineate the boundaries of counties and baronies, civil parishes can be in more than one county and in more than one barony.

WARD

This is an area used in District Electoral Divisions. They were originally established under the Poor Relief (Ireland) Act, 1838, as Poor Law Electoral Divisions but their present names up to 1972 were fixed under the Local Government (Ireland) Act of 1898. They formed the territorial units in rural districts for the election of members of Rural District Councils. The ward is the equivalent territorial unit for the purpose of elections in county boroughs, municipal boroughs and urban districts.

In larger urban areas there will be a number of wards but in the smaller areas the entire urban district acts as a ward. In 1973, new district councils were set up and these 26 districts were subdivided into 526 wards which were in turn grouped into 98 District Electoral Areas for local government elections.

TOWNLAND

The townland is an ancient unit, dating back to pre-Norman times, and it is the smallest administrative division throughout the island of Ireland that is still in use. Variations to the townland and smaller local divisions were in existence and had different names in different parts of the country.

TOWNLAND MEANINGS

Returning back to Between the Crosses, two townlands overlap the mass of land between these two crossroads, Clonboo and Togher, along with Lissanure and Killavinogue. Toher is from An Tochar, which means 'the causeway'. Lissanure translates to Lios an Iuir, which means 'the fort of the yew-tree'. Clonboo is from Cluain Buach, which means 'pasture or meadow of victory'. (I have to say that I always thought that Clonboo meant Cluain Bó, meaning 'meadow of the cow' or 'the cow's meadow', but this is the translation that was found.)

PARISH PRIESTS

My mother, some time ago, sent me up a list of all the parish priests who ministered in the parishes of Templemore, Clonmore and Killea going back to the 1700s. She often sends me up newspaper clippings and lots of other interesting articles to keep me up to date with the local news.

1704:	Very Revd Cornelius Guilfoyle
1740-1755:	Very Revd Patrick Ryan
1755-1761:	Very Revd William Maher (native of Killea), Very Revd Stephen Wall was his successor for a short time.
1763-1793:	Very Revd Walter Morrissey
1800-1809:	Very Revd John Fogarty
1809-1814:	Very Revd Jeremiah Morrissey
1815-1847:	Very Revd Patrick Fant
1847-1872:	Very Revd Thomas O'Connor
1872-1882:	Very Revd Thomas O'Connor (nephew of late Parish Priest)
1882-1912:	Canon William Meagher PP, VF (native of Killea)
1912-1925:	Canon Daniel Kiely PP, VF
1925-1926:	Canon Michael Bannon PP, VF
1926-1948:	Canon Denis O'Brien PP, VF
1948-1974:	Canon Philip Fogarty PP, VF
1974-1988:	Canon William Noonan PP, VF
1988-1999:	Canon Augustine O'Donnell PP, VF
1999-2008:	Canon Liam McNamara PP, VF
2008-present:	Fr Eugene Everard

CHURCHES

ST ANNE'S CHURCH, CLONMORE

The church in Clonmore was our regular Sunday excursion for ten o'clock Mass when I was growing up. In my latter teenage years, a quarter past twelve in Templemore was a rush due to a different type of excursion on the previous Saturday night.

In my younger years, getting up around 8.30a.m., or maybe a bit later, say around 9a.m., was the norm, as you had to be fasting for one hour before Mass. If you left it until after nine, then you would have to go to Mass hungry, as the one hour rule was extremely strict. I remember my father would only drink a glass or cup of water on a Sunday morning, no matter when he got up. Even if he had more than an hour to spare, he would still only have the cup of water before Mass.

But my very earliest memories of going to Mass in Clonmore would have been from a very young age. At that time, a few memories stand out, like the pennies and the very odd shilling coin that would be left beside the Holy Water font in the porch to the side aisle. As you dipped your finger into the Holy Water, you would leave your Mass offering on the shelf beside the Holy Water. In later years the basket collection was introduced, but I remember the few coins next to the Holy Water in the porch. The other very early memory was one that stayed with you for a few hours after Mass. That memory was the soreness in your two knees. First of all, you knelt a lot more during Mass, secondly there were no padded kneelers, and thirdly I had short pants on. So bare knees on solid timber. The worst thing was if someone walked on the kneeler and left a bit of grit there. When you knelt down the grit would be buried into the skin of your knee. I suppose I wore short pants until I was five or six, but the real luxury was the arrival of the padded kneelers. Another memory would have been the waist-high railings that surrounded the priest and the altar. These were removed in the 1970s.

As you look down from the altar, our pew was in the side aisle on the left-hand side, the third one back in the third row. Matt Ryan and his family prayed in the first pew, while Philly and Ina Martin and their children sat in the second pew in front of us. Other people who had pews in that side aisle included: the Marnells, Paddy Martin, Eugene Martin, Andy and Joe Maher, the Doyles, the Delhauntys, Ryans (Shanakill), Jimmy Clarke, Tommy and Maggie Skehana, Timmy and Sara Hennessy (who sat in the pew behind us), Willie and Margaret Fogarty, Pat Martin (Moyners) and Jimmy Maher, 'Feathers'. Pews in both side aisles were generally occupied by the same family every Sunday as they had been allocated that particular pew going back to the time the church was built, as recognition for some financial contribution that was made at that time. Directly across, at the opposite side aisle, you would see the other regular occupants sitting and kneeling in their pews, such as Deegans, a few different Maher families, Bourkes, Codys, Guiders, McGraths, Bohans, and Ryans, among others.

Soon after I made my First Holy Communion, I started to serve Mass as an altar boy, and I was on duty every second Sunday. For that Sunday when I was serving, we would always try to go a bit earlier because the jobs you could do serving Mass were allocated on the basis of 'first up, best dressed" The first altar boy in the sacristy got the pick of the jobs. The top job at that time was the holding of the patten, that is, the holding of the flat plated metal trowel type with a handle under people's chins who were receiving Holy Communion. At that time, of course, Communion Hosts were only handed out by the priest and placed on the person's tongue. The idea was that if the Communion Host fell out of the person's mouth that you would catch it on the patten. If a Communion Host ever fell on the floor of the church, it was a major incident, with the floor having to be thoroughly washed. Holding the patten was the top job because you were walking around after or before the priest during the whole Communion period of Mass.

The next top job was ringing the bell. In Clonmore church the bell was a large, solid, inverted dome-shaped bell, a smaller version of the large church bell. The only way I can describe it is that you had a drumstick with a padded bulb at the end. Then when you hit the inverted dome-shaped bell, it vibrated and sounded a 'bong'. As it happens, my father told me that the Butler family donated this very piece to the church when it was built or refurbished at one stage or another. The bell was rung four times during Mass and you did it on your own, which was always a benefit. Now the problem with the bell job was that the ringing was often split between a few altar boys, usually into two parts. One person would do the Consecration, when there were two thumps at the changing of the bread and at the changing of the wine. The other two times was usually left to one person, at the start of the Eucharistic prayers, just when the priest took the consecrated wine and started Communion. The next job was serving the last wine at the end of Communion and the other job was the presenting the water and wine at the offertory along with the water and towel for the washing of fingers, also at the offertory. This job was shared and took two people to carry out.

The altar boys were divided into alternative weeks based on geographic spread and townland. Usually, we in Clonboo were linked in with Dromard, while Graffin and Dareens and the village areas were in the other group. I often remember tearing across the gravel yard into the sacristy after jumping out of the car 'at the pump', as Pat Delaney's car was behind us and Pa Delaney had the same thing in mind as me, to get in first and get the first pick of jobs.

Of course there was no scarcity of altar boys, and it was an exclusively boys' club at that time. The big gigs were always financially worthwhile, including happy and sad occasions such as weddings and funerals.

When we started Paddy Martin, the sacristan, trained us. We generally started off with the easy jobs but soon progressed on to the top jobs. It was a different experience at Mass watching from the altar, down the chapel. You always had to watch your kneeling and sitting times as you didn't have your mother or father to nudge you. Generally you followed the crowd. There was the odd deviation of jobs during funerals such as the incense, and giving out palms on Palm Sunday, and it was an enjoyable way to experience religion. I think it also gave you a better appreciation of the life a priest had to lead with loads of highs and lows. Paddy Martin was a great help and served his church and his community well over many years. Before the bell was automated, the bell had to be rung twice a day: for the Angelus at noon and at six o'clock. Either Paddy or his wife Maire did this every day. Willie Fogarty is the current sacristan, and goes about his job very efficiently and respectfully.

St Anne's church was built in 1832; the foundation stone was laid on 26 July that year, on the feast day of St Anne, the mother of the Blessed Virgin Mary. A Latin script on the foundation stone records that it was laid by a curate in the parish, Fr Denis Ryan. St Anne was the patron of the medieval church in Killavinogue, the name of the original parish now represented by Clonmore. Fr Ryan had been curate in the parish since 1828. He died of cholera the same year the foundation stone was laid. The parish priest at the time was Fr Patrick Fant, who built the first Catholic church in Templemore in 1815. He died of cholera in 1847.

The site for the church was provided by the landlords of Clonmore, the Lidwells of Dromard, which showed the good interdenominational relations in the area. The church in Clonmore was built at a time of boom, when a rush to religion had followed a general surge in the population, but it was also hot on the heels of the increasingly confident Catholic Emancipation movement. The passing of the Catholic Emancipation Act in 1828 granted Catholics the right to sit in parliament and to hold senior government offices. This gave impetus to the building of more imposing Catholic churches, such as St Anne's in Clonmore. The abolition of the prohibition against Catholic churches having belfries, included in the 1828 Act, led to the inclusion of belfries on the cut-stone facades of the new churches. The design of several churches in North Tipperary were based on the design of the 'Big Chapel' in Thurles, and St Anne's church draws its inspiration from this church. A well-crafted belfry was added to the church in Clonmore in 1879 in honour of the Sacred Heart. Clonmore church is cruciform in outline, having a very short projection at its sanctuary end. A low-roofed sacristy was added to it later.

A major refurbishment job was carried out to the church in Clonmore in the 1970s, including work to the facade, where two side doors were converted into windows, and internally the altar rails were removed. At the time there were major discussions on their removal. Clonmore was following other places where the altar rails were removed in an effort to give the general church a more open and transparent image. Before the rails were moved, the priest was isolated or corralled within the altar area, with an apparent barrier around him. When you went up to receive Holy Communion, you had to kneel down at the altar rails to receive the Host, whereas nowadays you walk up to the edge of the altar area and stand to receive the Host. At this time a new mosaic of the Holy Family was put on the wall behind the altar.

In 2002, further restoration work was carried out to the external façade and floodlighting was added, which greatly enhanced its appearance by day and by night. It is a church that has been well kept over the years and a church that the community can be rightly very proud of. Long may it continue to be a place of community gatherings and a place of devotion and worship for all parishioners and visitors.

Like all churches, in every country village, this building is a very important focal point for the people who live there. Gathering around the old pump outside the church was a weekly ritual for most of the men folk, and the women too. Mostly the men stayed around for a short while after Mass to talk about the weather, local news and politics, along with recent or upcoming GAA matches, both at club and county level. During election time the pump was the 'stage' for prospective councillors and TDs to deliver their message. Friend or foe, supporter and opposition, all speakers got a respectful hearing. Of course, country people always tend to vote in a predetermined way, and usually from a traditional perspective that has been carried from past generations, but more and more exceptions are developing in the changing political world.

Before I get away from Clonmore church, I have to mention the other churches that the family has been associated with and which were part of their lives back through the generations. The churches included here are St Mary's church in Moyne and Loughmore church, although the churches in Templetuohy and Templemore were also and still are often visited.

The Butlers came to Clonboo in 1820 from Cloghereally More (The Islands), Loughmore, but along with their association with Loughmore church they also must have regularly gone to Moyne church, as my ancestors were buried in Moyne graveyard. The Islands in Loughmore were only a field away from Moyne parish and as the crow flies, or in this case, as the pony and trap went, the journey to Moyne was nearer than Loughmore.

MOYNE CHURCH

The catholic parish of Moyne–Templetuohy consists of the medieval parishes of Templetuohy, Moyne (An Mhaighean) and Kilclonagh. The three parishes have been combined for Catholic administration purposes since the latter part of the 1600s. The parish has two churches: the church of the Sacred Heart in Templetuohy, dating back from 1877-79, and St Mary's church in Moyne, dating back from 1902-04. The church in Moyne is built alongside the medieval church ruins. The Butlers had left Loughmore and also their association with Moyne church by the time the new church was being built in 1902. The church, as mentioned earlier, was built on the site of the old chapel, which in turn was built on the site of an earlier chapel erected about twenty-five years earlier. The nave of the 1812 chapel ran parallel to the street.

LOUGHMORE CHURCH

The Catholic parish of Loughmore consists of the medieval parishes of Loughmore East, Loughmore West and Templeree. For Catholic administration purposes they were combined since around 1700. From the 1720s up to 1761, Templeree was attached to Templemore but since 1761 it was reattached to Loughmore, and this remains the same to the current day. The modern church in Loughmore was built in 1977. This church, that of the Nativity of Our Lady, stands on the site of an ancient cruciform church built in 1825. It overlooks the old church ruins and is surrounded by its graveyard. The Latin-inscribed foundation stone of the former church, built by Fr James Mullally, who was parish priest from 1798 to 1833, has been inserted into the new church.

On 11 May 2008, the parish of Loughmore and the wider community commemorated the 150th anniversary of the death of the Cormack Brothers. A pageant re-enacting the 1910 homecoming of the brothers and their burial in Loughmore was a tremendous occasion and a great success.

The two brothers, Daniel and William Cormack, natives of Loughmore parish, were sentenced to death on the charge of murdering a land agent named John Ellis in 1858. They protested their innocence up to the last moment on the public scaffold outside Nenagh Jail. They were buried in the jail grounds after the highly controversial sentence of death handed down to them. They were hanged outside the entrance to the jail, which was the last execution to take place in that jail, and indeed in North Tipperary. Dudley Byrne from Sorrillhill House was nominated as a juror originally, but he did not sit on the eventual jury.

When Nenagh Jail was closed down in 1910, the remains of the Cormacks were exhumed from the jail grounds, and brought to the newly built mausoleum in the Loughmore churchyard. On 11 May 1910, one of the greatest nationalist demonstrations of its time took place, when the remains of the Cormack brothers were triumphantly brought back to Loughmore.

It was a very impressive occasion in Loughmore on a sunny day in May 2008, when the re-enactment took place. People dressed up in costumes of the 1910 period and all modes of transport used at that time were in evidence for the procession behind the horse-drawn hearses containing the Cormack coffins. All modern cars were banned from the village. It was a great day. Monsignor Dooley celebrated a Tridentine Mass in the church. This was a Latin Mass and it brought memories flooding back to an older generation. My father, who was with me at the commemoration on 11 May 2008, told me that he served Mass in Latin. Another difference with the celebration of Mass from that time compared to today was the priests' location in the church. At that time, the priest celebrated Mass with his back turned to the congregation.

At the conclusion of the Mass, the coffins were carried to the mausoleum and placed in the vault. Monsignor Dooley delivered the same address that was given by the then parish priest, Canon Hackett, in 1910. This was followed by Tim Meagher's stirring delivery of the speech given by John Dillon MP. The pageant concluded with John Egan's emotional rendition of 'The Ballad of the Cormack Brothers'. Food, drink and all sorts of refreshments were provided all over the village, with open-air music and craic being the main ingredients late into the night. It was great to be there with my father and see it all.

PARISH SIZES AND POPULATIONS

The parish of Templemore, Clonmore and Killea is situated partly in the barony of Eliogarty and partly in that of Ikerrin. It embraces the old civil parishes of Killea, Killavinogue, and Templemore in Ikerrin and Templemore in Eliogarty. The overall area of the three parishes is approximately 21,500 acres.

Clonmore has undergone a few changes of association with the other two over the centuries. Clonmore temporarily gained independent status as a parish during the period 1800-1815. During 1815, Clonmore was again placed in the care of the parish priest of Killea and Templemore. However, the new parish priest, Fr Patrick Fant (1815-47), was never formally appointed as pastor of Clonmore.

The special status of Clonmore was again noted when Dr Thomas O'Connor was appointed parish priest of Templemore and Killea in 1847. Archbishop Slattery's letter of appointment noted that Clonmore was placed in Dr O'Connor pastoral care *ad beneplacitum* (at pleasure). The archbishop and his successors reserved the right to detach Clonmore or any part of it from Templemore and Killea, 'as is deemed expedient to do'.

To complicate matters even further, the parish of Killavinogue (Clonmore) was attached to Moyne until *c.*1758. When Dr James Butler I visited Clonmore on 3 July 1754, the report noted that 'the chapel of Kiloton [Killavinogue] is built of new by Mr Crusheen [Cashin] of said parish'. Fr Cashin was administrator of Moyne at the time.

The population has fluctuated over the centuries. In 1766, the combined population of Killea, Templemore and Clonmore was estimated at 1,640 Catholics and 231 Protestants. By 1841 the total figure had risen to 11,049, including personnel at Richmond Barracks. A decade later, famine, emigration and death had reduced the figure to 9,077.

During the century following the famine, population decline continued. By 1961 there were 3,030 people in the parish. The population of the parish has stabilised during recent decades. Today, there are 3,140 people in the parish, a figure which includes the Garda Training College personnel.

The Christian Brothers had a long association with the area, from 1932 until 1987. The lack of a second-level school for boys in Templemore led to an approach to the Irish Christian Brothers in 1932, and at the same time, the Brothers also formed a primary school in Templemore. During their fifty-five years of dedicated service to the area, the Christian Brothers made a significant contribution to several aspects of life in the parish. Due to declining membership, the Brothers withdrew from Templemore in 1987. In 1985 Our Lady's Secondary School was formed, representing an amalgamation of the former Christian Brothers' secondary school and the Sisters of Mercy girls' secondary school.

The parish of Moyne–Templetuohy has changed over the years. In 1841, the population stood at 5,857, while a decade later it had declined to 4,366. By 1901, the figure was 2,025, and by 1971 the census figure was further reduced to 1,406. Nowadays the population is approximately 1,500, and the area of the parish is around 18,700 acres.

The parish of Loughmore–Castleiney had a population of approx 1,060 in 2008, which is about a sixth of the pre-Famine figure of 6,500 as recorded at the State census of 1841. The area of the parish is approximately 15,100 acres.

CHAPTER 3

VALUATIONS & RECORDS

GATHERING INFORMATION

Apart from the first-hand and invaluable information available from people directly, there are several sources of information available in researching family roots and information particular to your locality. As time goes by, the task becomes all the easier as documents and new information comes available online and is there to be seen on screen at the touch of a button. Most of the drudgery is replaced by search engines, but it is still a buzz when you come across a reference to a topic you are looking for. What generally happens, of course, is that while looking for some connection to a name or a place, you stumble upon some other 'lead', which takes you off in a totally different direction, and by the time you have washed out this new piece of information, you forget what you were looking for in the first place. Also these new leads often arrive at dead ends, delays and frustration. That is the downside, but there are also great feelings of satisfaction when you uncover a gem or follow a successful trail that verifies a previous piece of evidence.

In relation to the local townlands, parishes and the Butler family searches, I have contained the information to relevant documents as follows:

Tithe Applotment Books: These books were compiled between 1823 and 1837 in order to determine the amount occupiers of agricultural holdings should pay in tithes to the Church of Ireland (the main Protestant Church, and the Church established by the State until its disestablishment in 1871). The Tithe Applotment Books for Civil Parish of Killavinogue for 1824 can be found in the National Library of Ireland. There are entries there for Clonboo and Lissanure.

Hearth Rates: Before the arrival of Griffith's Valuations of the country, other methods of Valuations were used, and one of the most commonly used was the Hearth Rates. It sounds like a simple way of setting the rate; as the name suggests, the rate was set based on the number of fireplaces (or hearths) you had in the house. At the time, bedrooms and kitchens had fireplaces. It was a simple means of evaluating the rate. I suppose a modern-day equivalent would be to evaluate a tax on a house based on the number of bathrooms or televisions in the house! It's no wonder that, at the time, when the taxman or the valuation inspector arrived at an Irish person's house, he was often appalled by the sight of hens and other animals living in the kitchens. The people brought in the animals as a sign of poverty for the inspector, in order to hopefully receive a lower value for the rates to be paid. The Irish parliament made the following declaration in 1662:

> From and after the twenty-ninth day of September, in the year of our Lord God one thousand six hundred and sixty two, every dwelling and other house and edifice that are or hereafter shall be erected within this Kingdom of Ireland … shall be chargeable … and are charged … for every fire hearth, and other place used for firing and stove within every house and edifice as aforesaid, the sum of two shillings, sterling, by the year, to be paid yearly and every year at the feast of the annunciation of the Blessed Virgin St Mary, and the feast St Michael the Archangel, be even and equal portions.

The tax was to be paid by the tenants, not by the landlords. I have unearthed some records for Clonbough and Lissanure around the period of 1665 and 1667.

Griffith's Primary Valuation of Rateable Property in Ireland: This was a valuation carried out between 1848 and 1864 for all the lands in Ireland to establish the level of rates to be paid to each landlord. The Valuations in Tipperary were carried out in 1851.

Bassett's Directory of Tipperary, 1889: This is a manual and directory for manufacturers, merchants, traders, landowners, farmers and others, compiled by George Henry Bassett in 1889. Its database contains over 10,000 records.

Slater's Directory of Ireland: Compiled in 1856, this contains limited information of interest in the context of the current research. Similarly **Pigot's Directory of 1824** is also of little benefit.

The Encumbered Estates of Clonmore, in the Barony of Eliogarty and Ikerrin: Dated 14 July 1853, this does identify the leaseholders' names and lease dates with the Lidwill family.

The Valuation Office of Ireland: Located in Abbey Street, Dublin, the Valuation Office proved to be a great source of information, as it showed all the valuations that span over a period of 120 years and date back from 1856 to 1970. The extracts are summarised. I also have the maps that trace back and track the changes of land ownership over the period for the townlands of Clonbough and Togher. There are a few inconsistencies and gaps but each map and record includes information on the Occupiers; Immediate Lessors; Description of Tenement along with the Rateable Annual Valuation.

Censuses: Although censuses were taken every year from 1821, those from 1861 to 1891 were pulped and destroyed by the British government to save space during the First World War, and those from 1821 to 1851 were largely destroyed in the Four Courts fire of 1922. The 1901 census and the 1911 census are the only surviving full censuses of Ireland open to the public. 1911 census was taken on 2 April 1911.

On the night of the census, the head of the household was responsible for filling out the census form. Another condition and responsibility was to include all people who were present in the house on that night of 2 April 1911. In one or two houses a 'visitor' is recorded as being present and in other cases farm labourers or farm servants are recorded with the other household family members.

Apart from recording the names of the people present in the house on census night, other information was filled in on the census forms, some of which may sound strange today. Along with name, age, sex, relationship to head of the household, religion, occupation, marital status, and county or country of birth, other, more unusual, information was recorded, such as the individual's ability to read or write and ability to speak the Irish language and whether the person was deaf, dumb, blind, idiot, imbecile or lunatic. The 1911 census also asked significant additional questions of married women: the number of years they had been married, the number of children born alive, and the number of children still alive.

Later on, when discussing the individual households 'Between the Crosses', the 1911 census records will be reviewed as applicable. It will also be seen that the townland demarcation lines were different in 1911. Clonbough was divided into Clonbough Lower and Clonbough Upper. The lower part went from the Banjo's to Martin Deegan's. Clonbough Upper went from Doolan's lane to Delhaunty's. There were ten houses in the lower part and seven houses in the upper part. Togher started at Tom Butler's and extended past the Cross of Togher.

The Population Decline of 1841-1851 is described and documented in the wonderful three-book series the *History of Moyne–Templetuohy*.

Further information was gathered from numerous sources of data and records: various civil and religious registers; the List of Freeholders of Tipperary, 1776; Parish of Loughmore West 1827 Register; Tithe Defaulters Listing of 1831; religious census for Templemore and Killivinogue, 1766, and the parish of Loughmore East, 1825 Parish Records and Registers.

KILLAVINOGUE TITHE APPLOTMENTS BOOKS, 1824

The Clonbough townland in Co. Tipperary, North Riding, was located in the civil parish of Killavinogue, in the Barony of Ikerrin, in the Poor Law Union of Roscrea, in the Catholic Diocese of Cashel and Emly, and in the Catholic parish of Templemore. The Tithe Applotments of 1824 for the Civil Parish of Killavinogue can be found in the National Library of Ireland. The Butlers came to Clonboo in 1820 from Loughmore. The details on the records are difficult to read in places, and this is made more difficult by the use of old-time spellings.

Page 17 of the records covers Clonboo and the following entries are recorded there:

Butler, Toby	Cahill, Patrick	Carrick, Earl of
Darmudy, Patrick	Deegan, Dennis	Doyle, David
Dwyer, John	Fahy, James	Kenna, Widow
Kennedy, John	Laffan, Nicholas	Maguire, Mathew
Rourke, John	Rourke, William	Ryan, Richard
Ryan, Timothy	Teely or Feely, Roger	Whelan, William

Page 18 covers Lisanure, and the following entries are recorded there:

Brute, John	Flinn, Timothy	Gantley, John
Gantley, T.	Hanrahan, Martin	Keenahan, Joseph
Whelan, Patrick	Meara, Dennis	

HEARTH RATES

Hearth Money Records for householders in Templetuohy are recorded by Mary Heaphy for the period 1666–1667 for various townlands as follows:

LISSANURE

Morrissey, Thomas (2)	Brophy, Teigh	O'Meagher, Dermot
O'Heany, John	Roe, Phyllis	Ringly, William
Moore, Thos (2)		

CLONBOUGH. 1665

Lunn, Robert (2)	Hannigan, Rd	O'Guinan, Loughlin
Meagher, Thomas	O'Hayden, Phil	Hayden, Nicholas
Hennen, Jan	Scully, Phil	Dooley, Lough
O'Merrigan, Don	Hude, William	McGrath, John
Fogarty, William	Meagher, Don	Hayden, Dan
Bergin, Denis		

GRIFFITH'S VALUATION

Griffith's Primary Valuation of Rateable Property in Ireland is commonly known as Griffith's Valuation. The valuable sidekick to this edition is the Householders Index to Griffith's Valuation. Between 1848 and 1864 all the land of Ireland was surveyed, under the direction of Richard Griffith, for the purpose of establishing the level of rates (local tax) payable by each landholder or leaseholder. Griffith's Valuation lists the majority of land and householders in the country, giving the townland and description of the property (such as land, house, land and house, outhouses, etc.). It also lists the landlord and the annual valuation. Because of the shortage of other records this is a very important census substitute, even though it does not list the age of the landholder or names of family members. Most of the valuations were completed after the years of the Famine and following substantial emigration from Ireland from 1845 to 1851. The valuations in Tipperary were carried out in 1851.

1851 VALUATIONS FOR CLONBOUGH

The 1851 Primary Valuation of Tenements for the Parish of Killavinogue lists the following occupiers, immediate lessors, descriptions of tenements and areas:

CLONBOUGH

Occupier   Mary Corcoran; Immediate Lessor John Butler; House.

Occupier   John Butler; Immediate Lessor Earl of Carrick; House and Lands; 58 Acres and 23 Perches.

Occupier   Patrick Fogarty; Immediate Lessor John Butler; House.

Occupier   Daniel Kavanagh; Immediate Lessor John Butler; House.

Occupier   Mary Doolan; Immediate Lessor John Butler; House.

Occupier   Catherine Dwyer and others; Immediate Lessor John Butler; House.

Occupier   James Maher; Immediate Lessor John Butler; House and Small Garden.

Occupier   Jeremiah Maher; Immediate Lessor Earl of Carrick; House and Lands; 61A, 1R and 26P.

Occupier   Jeremiah Maher; Immediate Lessor Earl of Carrick; Bog; 52A, 2R and 25P.

Occupier   Jeremiah Maher; Immediate Lessor Earl of Carrick; Land.

Occupier   Patrick Cahill; Immediate Lessor Jeremiah Maher; House and Lands.

Occupier   Michael Burke; Immediate Lessor Jeremiah Maher; House.

Occupier   Margaret Steel; Immediate Lessor Jeremiah Maher; House.

Occupier   Michael Lanigan; Immediate Lessor Earl of Carrick; House and Lands; 82A, 3R and 37P.

Occupier   Michael Lanigan; Immediate Lessor Earl of Carrick; Bog; 9A, 2R and 30P.

PARISH OF KILLAVINOGE.

1851

No. and Letters of Ref-rence to Map.		Names. Townlands and Occupiers.	Immediate Lessors.	Description of Tenement.	Area. A. R. P.	Net Annual Value. Land. £ s. d.	Buildings. £ s. d.	Total. £ s. d.
		CLONBUOGH—con.						
—	a	Mary Corcoran	John Butler	House	—	—	0 5 0	0 5 0
7	a	John Butler	Earl of Carrick	House, offices, and land	58 0 23	24 15 0	1 15 0	26 10 0
—	b	Patrick Fogarty	John Butler	House	—	—	0 5 0	0 5 0
—	c	Daniel Kavanagh	John Butler	House	—	—	0 10 0	0 10 0
—	d	Mary Doolan	John Butler	House	—	—	0 5 0	0 5 0
—	e	Cath. Dwyer & others	John Butler	House	—	—	0 5 0	0 5 0
—	f	James Maher	John Butler	House & small garden	—	—	0 5 0	0 5 0
8	A a	Jeremiah Maher	Earl of Carrick	House, offices, and land	61 1 26	27 10 0	1 15 0	29 5 0
—		Jeremiah Maher	Earl of Carrick	Bog	52 2 25	0 5 0	—	0 5 0
—	B { a	Jeremiah Maher	Earl of Carrick	Land	10 1 2	{ 4 5 0	—	4 5 0
		Patrick Cahill	Jeremiah Maher	House and land		2 15 0	0 15 0	3 10 0
—	b	Michael Burke	Jeremiah Maher	House	—	—	0 5 0	0 5 0
—	A b	Margaret Steel	Jeremiah Maher	House	—	—	0 5 0	0 5 0
9		Michael Lanigan	Earl of Carrick	House, offices, and land	82 3 37	45 10 0	2 10 0	48 0 0
—		Michael Lanigan	Earl of Carrick	Bog	0 2 30	0 1 0	—	0 1 0
10		Patrick Clarke	Earl of Carrick	House, offices, and land	22 2 7	14 0 0	1 15 0	15 15 0
11	A a	John Deegan	Earl of Carrick	House, offices, and land	123 0 24	64 0 0	3 15 0	67 15 0
—	n	John Deegan	Earl of Carrick	Land	16 0 34	10 5 0	—	10 5 0
—	A b	Mary Price	John Deegan	House	—	—	0 5 0	0 5 0
—	B a	Nicholas Meehan	John Deegan	House	—	—	0 10 0	0 10 0
				Total,	682 3 21	279 1 0	23 15 0	302 16 0
		CLONMORE. (Ord. Ss. 23 & 29.)						
1		Patrick Landrigan, Joseph Fitzpatrick, Edward Maher, Patrick Brien, Mrs. A. Fitzpatrick, James Delahunt, Joseph Fitzpatrick, Thomas Martin, Reps. Robert Lidwell, Esq.	Reps. Robt. Lidwell, Esq.	Meadow land	17 0 36	15 5 0	—	15 5 0
2		Reps. Robert Lidwell, Esq.	George Goold, Esq.	Meadow land	7 0 5	6 5 0	—	6 5 0
3		Thomas Ryan	Reps. Robert Lidwell, Esq.	Meadow land	6 2 3	5 15 0	—	5 15 0
4	a	Thomas Ryan	Reps. Robt. Lidwell, Esq.	House, offices, & land	83 2 32	{ 25 15 0	1 5 0	27 0 0
	b	John Ryan		House, offices, & land		12 15 0	1 0 0	13 15 0
	c	Judith Ryan		House, offices, & land		12 15 0	1 0 0	13 15 0
5	a	Patrick Brien	Reps. R. Lidwell, Esq.	House and land	109 3 16	{ 6 0 0	0 15 0	6 15 0
		Reps. R. Lidwell, Esq.	George Goold, Esq.	Land		41 0 0	—	41 0 0
6	A	Daniel Murphy	Reps. Robert Lidwell, Esq.	Land	23 0 38	1 15 0	—	1 15 0
—	B	Daniel Murphy	Reps. Robert Lidwell, Esq.	Land	33 1 30	25 15 0	—	25 15 0
—	a	John Coady	Daniel Murphy	House	—	—	0 5 0	0 5 0
—	b	Mary Talbot	Daniel Murphy	House	—	—	0 5 0	0 5 0
—	c	Lawrence Mackey	Daniel Murphy	House and garden	0 0 16	0 2 0	0 8 0	0 10 0
—	d	William Flynn	Daniel Murphy	House	—	—	0 5 0	0 5 0
—	e	James Sullivan	Daniel Murphy	House	—	—	0 10 0	0 10 0
7	a	Daniel Murphy	Reps. Robt. Lidwell, Esq.	House, offices, & land	17 0 26	{ 11 5 0	2 15 0	14 0 0
		Daniel Delahunt		Land		2 5 0	—	2 5 0
—	b	James Carroll	Daniel Murphy	House	—	—	0 5 0	0 5 0
—	c	James Murphy	Daniel Murphy	House	—	—	0 5 0	0 5 0
—	d	James Delahunt	Daniel Delahunt	House	—	—	0 5 0	0 5 0
8	{	Daniel Murphy	Reps. Robt. Lidwell, Esq.	Land	13 0 27	{ 3 10 0	—	3 10 0
		Daniel Delahunt	Esq.	Land		1 5 0	—	1 5 0
9	a	Daniel Delahunt	Reps. Robert Lidwell, Esq.	House and land	4 0 8	2 10 0	0 15 0	3 5 0
—	b	James Carthy	Daniel Delahunt	House	—	—	0 5 0	0 5 0
10	A	Charles Pine	Reps. Robert Lidwell, Esq	House and land	1 3 3	1 5 0	0 15 0	2 0 0
—	B	Charles Pine	Reps. Robert Lidwell, Esq	Land	1 2 3	1 5 0	—	1 5 0
11	a	John Brennan	Reps. Robert Lidwell, Esq	House, office, and land	9 0 2	6 15 0	1 0 0	7 15 0
—	b	Thomas Keeffe	Reps. Robert Lidwell, Esq	House and garden	0 0 37	0 5 0	0 5 0	0 10 0
12		Martin Sullivan	James Martin	House and land	2 2 35	2 5 0	0 15 0	3 0 0

Occupier   Patrick Clarke; Immediate Lessor Earl of Carrick; House and Lands; 22A, 2R and 7P.

Occupier   John Deegan; Immediate Lessor Earl of Carrick; House and Lands; 123A and 23P.

Occupier   John Deegan; Immediate Lessor Earl of Carrick; Land; 10A and 34P.

Occupier   Mary Price; Immediate Lessor John Deegan; House.

Occupier   Nicholas Meehan; Immediate Lessor John Deegan; House.

Author's Note: *From the above valuations, please note that the Mary Doolan on the fifth line was not any relation of my mother's, but part of the Doolan family who lived in Doolan's Garden who owned the field where Tom and Catherine Stamp now live. It was just a funny coincidence that the Doolans owned this land before us and that my mother is a Doolan.*

BASSETT'S DIRECTORY OF TIPPERARY, 1889

Bassett's Directory of Tipperary is a manual and directory for manufacturers, merchants, traders, professional men, landowners, farmers, tourists, anglers and sportsmen compiled by George Henry Bassett in 1889. The database consists of 10,028 records. Almanacs and directories are a most valuable record as there were no censuses carried out. Various people carried out directory records of different counties and areas of the country. Bassett also undertook a directory of Wexford in 1886, three years before Tipperary.

This directory lists the following in Clonbough, Clonmore:

Bergin, Thomas, Farmers Resident
Butler, John, Farmers Resident
Clarke, Patrick, Farmers Resident
Deegan, Daniel, Farmers Resident
Deegan, Martin, Farmers Resident
Lanigan, Martin, Farmers Resident
Maher, Daniel, Farmers Resident
Maher, Jeremiah, Farmers Resident

In Clonmore generally the following are listed:

Byrnes, Delacy, Grocers, Sorrell Hill
Skehan, Jas, Grocers, Dromard
McDonald, Michael, Post Office, Clonmore
Maher, Patrick J., National School, Clonmore
Fitzpatrick, Nora, National School, Clonmore

Bourke, Daniel, Farmers Resident, Clonmore

Byrne, Harry, Farmers Resident, Sorrel Hill

Carroll Timohy, Farmers Resident, Dromard

Connell, Michael, Farmers Resident, Clonmore

Egan, William, Farmers Resident, Graffin

Fitzpatrick, John L., Farmers Resident, Clonmore

Fitzpatrick, Mrs, Farmers Resident, Darcens

Fitzpatrick, Patrick, Farmers Resident, Clonmore

Fogarty, William, Farmers Resident, Killavenogue

Gorman, Martin, Farmers Resident, Cobbs

Guider, James, Farmers Resident, Clonmore

Guider, Mrs, Farmers Resident, Clonmore

Harrington, Mrs, Farmers Resident, Shanakill

Keshan, John, Farmers Resident, Shanakill

Maher, James J., Farmers Resident, Shanakill

Maher, Jno, Farmers Resident, Ballysorrel

Maher, Joseph, Farmers Resident, Shanakill

Maher Michael, Farmers Resident, Clonmore

Martin, James, Farmers Resident, Clonmore

Martin, Michael (Pat), Farmers Resident, Clonmore

Martin, Patrick M., Farmers Resident, Clonmore

Martin, Thomas, Farmers Resident, Clonmore

Murphy, Jno, Farmers Resident, Dareens

Murphy, John, Farmers Resident, Shanakill

Ryan, James, Farmers Resident, Ballysorrel

Ryan, Joseph, Farmers Resident, Shanakill

Ryan, Mrs, Farmers Resident, Ballysorrel

Ryan, Mrs, Farmers Resident, Shanakill

Ryan, Patrick, Farmers Resident, Shanakill

Ryan, Thomas, Farmers Resident, Clonmore

Treacy, Mrs, Farmers Resident, Graffin

1827 SURVEY OF CLONMORE LANDS

This survey, which was done for the payment of rates, takes in all the townlands within Clonmore and includes Clonboo and part of Lissanure. The total area of land in Clonboo was recorded as 243 acres, 3 root and 13 perches, while Lissanure (the section within the parish of Clonmore) was recorded as 108 acres, 11 root and 21 perches. Breakdowns of the Clonboo lands in 1827 are as follows:

OCCUPIER'S NAME	QUANTITY OF LAND			RATE PER ACRE	AMOUNT
	A	R	P	s d	£-s-d
Earl of Carrick	55	1	30	1- 4	3-13-11
David Doyle	3	1	4	1-11	/-6-3
John Kennedy	4	2	16	1-11	/-8-92
Wm Rourke	1	2	0	1-4	/-2-/
Toby Butler	45	1	20	2- 7	5-17-3
Mathew Maguire	1	0	17	3- 4	/-3-8
Widow Kenna	0	1	0	3-4	/-1-16
Patrick Cahill	1	2	0	3-4	/-5-/
Patrick Darmudy	1	0	30	3-4	/-3-11
Wm Whelan	1	0	16	3-4	/-3-8
Nicholas Laffan	30	1	8	3-4	5-1-28
Jim and Richard Ryan	13	3	22	3-4	2-6-32
Denis Deegan	47	3	0	3-4	7-19-26
John Rourke	16	1	0	3-4	2-14-2
Roger Feely	6	2	20	3- 4	1-2-1
TOTAL	**243**	**3**	**13**		**32 -13 - 8**

The Lissanure lands in the Parish of Clonmore included the following:

Pat Whelan 1A, 2R and 22P.

Denis Meara and J. Gantly, 6A, 3R and 8P.

John Gantly, 5A, 1R and 14P.

John Brule[?], 3A, 2R and 26P.

Joseph Keenahan, 57A and 7P.

Joseph Keenahan, 20A, 3R and 7P.

Total Area: 108A and 21P

Total Valuation: £13 8s 2d

The total area of the parish of Clonmore as recorded in 1827 was 3674 acres, 2 root and 31 perches and the rateable valuation for the parish was £425 1s 2d.

Pp 37-39: Extracts from 1827 Survey of Clonmore lands.

Townland	No.	Name	A.	R.	P.			£	s.	d.
Stranakeil		Brought forward	283	1	19			37	1	
	128	Martin Joseph Maher	44	2	30	2	7	5	15	
	9	Edwd. & Danl. Duhan	5	3	18	1	11	"	11	6
	130	Gilbert Donnallan & } ½ John Fermoyle	14	3	6	1	4	"	19	8½
	1	Dennis Lahy & Wid. Tracy	8	2	6	1	11	"	16	4
	2	Danl. & Micht. Breen & W. Delany	19	"	6	1	11	"	16	5½
	3	Thos. John & Wid. Maher	19	"	6	1	11	1	16	5½
	4	John Maher (Orchard)	25	"	"	2	7	3	4	7
	5	Michl. Maher	8	1	13½	1	11	"	15	11
	6	Jmy. Maher	8	1	13½	1	11	"	15	11
	7	James Maher	8	1	13½	1	11	"	15	11
			445	1	11			£55	"	7
Gwalnagona	138	Thomas Langan	1	"	"	1	4	"	1	4
	9	Thos. Butler	4	"	"	1	4	"	7	8
	140	James Tierney	8	"	"	1	11	"	15	4
	1	Patk. Tierney } ½	8	"	"	1	11	"	15	4
	2	Andrew Maher	3	2	"	1	11	"	6	8½
	3	George Roe	287	"	"	1	11	27	10	1
	4	John Shelly	25	"	"	1	4	1	13	4
	5	Danl. Duhan & Co.	14	"	"	"	7	"	8	2
	6	James Darmudy	1	"	"	1	4	"	1	4
	7	Widow Guinane	1	"	"	1	4	"	1	4
	8	Dennis Quinlisk	2	2	"	1	11	"	4	9½
Colliers at the opposite side of the Road	9	{ John Riordan { John Corbett { Wm. Greed { Dennis Tierney	25	"	"	1	4	1	13	4
			380	"	"			£33	18	9
Dromard-Moore	150	George Roe (Loran)	91	2	"	2	7	11	16	4½
	1	Peter Roe	21	"	"	1	4	1	8	"
	2	Patk. Vaughan	2	"	"	2	7	"	5	2
	3	John & W. Long & Michl. Maher	2	2	"	2	7	"	6	5½
			117	"	"			£13	16	

Towns-Lands	Occupiers Names	Quantity of Land			Rate per acre		amount		
		A	R	P	s	d	£	s	
Ballysorrell 185	John Dulahunty	24	2	18	1	11	2	7	
6	John Lahy	16	3	"	2	7	2	3	
7	John Pendergast	4	"	24	1	11	"	7	
8	George Bennett	51	3	15	2	7	6	13	
9	Patᵏ Malone	45	"	"	1	11	4	6	
190	Michˡ Dwyer	7	1	"	1	4		9	
1	Pat. Lahy	5	2	36	2	7	"	14	
2	Connor Maher	6	1	27	1	11	"	12	
3	Dennis Ahern	6	1	27	1	11	"	12	
4	James Russell	8	3	32	2	7	1	3	
5	James Maher	27	7	2	1	11	2	12	
6	Malone (Tappey)	10	"	"	"	7		5	
		214	1	21			£22	8	
Clonboo 7	Earl of Carrick	55	1	30	1	4	3	13	
8	David Doyle	3	1	4	1	11	"	6	
9	John Kennedy	4	2	16	1	11	"	8	
200	Wᵐ Fouske	1	2	"	1	4	"	2	
1	Toby Butler	45	1	20	2	7	5	17	
2	Mathew Maguire	1	"	17	3	4	"	3	
3	Widow Kenna	"	1	"	3	4	"	"	
4	Patᵏ Cahil	1	2	"	3	4	"	5	
5	Patᵏ Darmidy	6	"	30	3	4	"	3	
6	Wᵐ Whelan	1	"	16	3	4	"	3	
7	Nicholas Laffan	30	1	18	3	4	5	1	
8	Jnᵒ & Richᵈ Ryan	13	3	22	3	4	2	6	
9	Dennis Deegan	47	3	"	3	4	7	19	
210	John Rourke	16	1	"	3	4	2	14	
1	Roger Feely	6	2	20	3	4	1	2	
2	John Dwyer	3	2	"	3	4	"	11	
3	James Feely	10	"	20	3	4	1	13	
		243	3	13			£32	13	
Part of Dᵒ Called Lisanure 4	Patᵏ Whelan	1	2	22	2	7	"	4	
5	Dennis Meara & J. Gantley	6	3	8	2	7	"	17	
6	John Gantley	5	1	14	2	7	"	13	

Towns-Lands	Occupiers Names	Quantity of Land			Rate per acre		Amount		
		A	R	P	S	D	£	S	D
Lisanure	Brought forward	26	2	21	3	.	.	3	8
219	John Brute	3	2	26	3	4	"	12	2½
220	Joseph Keenahan	57	"	7	2	7	7	7	4
Do	Do	20	3	7	1	11	1	19	10
		108	"	21			£13	8	2

Wm. N. Falkner }
Thos Bennett } Commissioners

Total Number of acres in the Parish	Quantity			Rate		Amount		
	A	R	P	S	D	£	S	D
	664	3	25	3	4	110	16	.
	1300	"	35	2	7	167	18	11
	1326	1	30	1	11	127	2	2½
	219	1	25	1	4	14	8	1
	163	2	36	"	7	4	15	6
Total number of acres in the Parish of Clonmore	3674	2	37			425	1	0½

Townslands in this Parish		Number of acres			amt of Assessment		
	A R P	A	R	P	£	S	D
Clonmore; House Quarter	89 " 1 "	89	1	"	13	18	7
Do Do	94 " 2 " 1	94	2	1	11	11	7
Do Chapel Quarter	118 " 2 " 20	118	2	20	15	"	11½
Do Derreens, & Malones	156 " 3 " 24	156	3	24	21	17	9
Do Moiners	123 " 1 " 0	123	1	"	15	18	5
Do Cloughile	70 " 0 " 30	70	"	30	9	1	5
Do Charters	67 " " "	67	"	"	7	"	10
	719 " 2 " 35						
Graffin		427	2	3	50	3	8
Buggawn		54	1	6	6	9	11
Stehana		163	2	"	20	19	1½
Shanakil		445	1	11	55	"	7½
Gurtnagona Wm Clive		380	"	"	33	18	9
Dromard Moore		321	2	31	42	15	1½
Glebe		36	"	"	3	9	"
Dromard		354	2	5	30	8	9½
Sorrel-Hill		205	3	5	19	"	2½
Ballysorrell		214	1	21	22	8	9
Clonboo £ 32 " 13 " 8		243	3	13	32	13	8
Lisanure £ 13 " 8 " 2		108	"	21	13	8	2
£ 46 " 1 " 10		3674	2	31	£425	5	2½

of this amt £425.3.4½ there is £400 payable annually to the

RECORDS OF POPULATION DECLINE,

1841-1851

These details are recorded in *History of Moyne–Templetuohy*:

> In 1841, there were 108 people living in Clonboo, with eighteen houses in the townland. In 1851, there were fifty-eight people living there, with eleven houses in the townland occupied. This is a decrease of 47 per cent in people and 39 per cent in house numbers.
>
> In Togher, in 1841, the number of people living there was 181, with thirty-one houses. In 1851 there were 138 people living in the town land, with twenty-five houses occupied. This is a decrease of 24 per cent in people and 20 per cent in houses.
>
> The next townland up the road on the way to Templetuohy, Lissanure, suffered worse. In 1841, there were 216 people living there, with thirty-two houses occupied, and in 1851 the number of people dropped to seventy-seven, with ten houses occupied. This is a decrease of 65 per cent in people and 69 per cent in houses.
>
> The number of baptisms in the parish of Moyne–Templetuohy dropped from 185 in 1841 to 58 in 1851.

These were traumatic times in Ireland, with the failure of the potato crop and the famine of the mid to late 1840s. There were also outbreaks of cholera, other fevers and dysentery in and around 1850. There was a fever hospital set up in Templemore to deal with the volume of people who got sick at the time. My father remembers being told about it as a lasting and bitter memory that was passed down through the generations.

Following on from the Famine times, further surveys of the population were carried out locally at various times. One such survey was carried out by Muintir na Tíre in 1970. Follow-up information is also available in the *History of Moyne–Templetuohy*, such as that which for 1971, 1991 and 1996. In Clonboo in 1971, there were ten people, with three houses occupied. This is the record in the book but it seems hard to accept its accuracy. This 1971 survey must have only included those houses on the Clonboo road which were in the parish of Templetuohy. This number is increased to forty-three people and twelve houses in 1991, and the number of people changes to forty-two with thirteen houses occupied in 1996. This would reflect the entire Clonboo road. The records for 1971 show that in Toher there were thirty-seven people and eight houses. This number changes to forty-five persons and twelve houses in 1991 and further changes to forty persons and ten houses in 1996.

GRAHAM'S ESTATES

Charles S. Graham had the estate of Clonboo. The estate was then vested in the authority of the Land Commission in the 1920s.

The local representatives at the time were J.J. Hassett TD, Barnane, Templemore and Mr Dan Morrissey. Both their help was sought by the tenants in the area at the time and various letters are on file from November 1931. In fact, during pre-Christmas drinks in the house in Lucan in 2008, we were talking about family histories with Fr Denis Carroll and Fr John Hassett. When I read out the following letter, John Hassett confirmed that the TD from Barnane was in fact his grandfather, a Fine Gael TD at the time. He further talked about all the times he spent at his uncle Paddy's house in Lisduff. Of course I knew Paddy and his family well, especially Paddy's son, Pat Joe Hassett, who was in my class in Toher primary school and also went to Templemore CBS during my time. We will come back to this later, so back to the letter.

F.J. O'Connor, Solicitor, from 15 South Frederick Street, Dublin and with an office in Thurles wrote various letters such as this one:

5 November 1931 to John Butler, Clonboo, Clonmore, Templemore

Dear Mr Butler,

I am in receipt of your letter. I had several communications with the Land Commission with regard to this, but nothing has happened. I am now writing asking them to send an Inspector and arrange for a meeting with the tenants so that the matter can be properly disposed of. It would be a pity if the opportunity was allowed pass. However, you may be quite sure I will do all in my power and I will let you know when arrangements are made.

Faithfully Yours,
F.J. O'Connor

A letter to J.J. Hassett TD on 27 November 1931, sets out the tenant's required assistance:

Dear Mr Hassett,

The tenants on the Estate of Charles S. Graham, Co. Tipperary, Lands of Clonboo, Templemore, are anxious to have your assistance in connection with the division of the turbary attached to the Estate. It is necessary to have the matter dealt with now by the Land Commission in which the Estate is vested. I have been in communication with the Land Commission since January 1929, and I enclose the first letters which I received in connection with it. They will be glad if you will take up the matter and see what you can do with the Land Commission.

The names of the tenants are —

John Butler, Clonboo	Martin Butler, Toher
Michael Prendergast, Clonboo	Daniel Lanigan, Clonboo
Michael Quirke, Clonboo	Michael Shelly, Toher
Martin Morrissey, Clonboo	Mrs Guilfoyle, Clonboo

Sincerely Yours,
F.J. O'Connor

DUBLIN OFFICE:
15 SOUTH FREDERICK STREET.

F. J. O'CONNOR, LL.B.,
STATE SOLICITOR.

Thurles,

27th. November, 19 31.

J. J. Hassett Esq. T.D.,

Barnane,

TEMPLEMORE.

Dear Mr.Hassett:-

The tenants on the Estate of Charles S.Graham, Co.Tipperary Lands of Clonboo, Templemore, are anxious to have your assistance i connection with the division of the turbary attached to the Estate. ts necessary to have the matter dealt with now by the Land Commission Estate is vested.   I have been in communication with the Land Commission since January 1929,and I enclose the first letters which I received in connection with it: They will be of assistance to you in identifying the estate.   I will be glad if you will take up the matter and see what you can do with the Land Commission.   The names of the tenants are-

John Butler, Clonboo

Martin Butler, Toher

Michael Prendergast,Clonboo

Daniel Lanigan, Clonboo

Michael Quirke,Clonboo

Michael Shelly,Toher,

Martin Morrissey,Clonboo

Mrs. Guilfoyle.

Sincerely yours,

ENCLS.

THURLES LAND COMMISSION

There are several records of tenants making applications to the commission to have fair rents fixed upon their holdings. Some of these hearings were reported in the *Nenagh Guardian* and the following examples relate to the Clonboo and Toher area in 1893 and 1894.

Nenagh Guardian, 24 January 1894

His Honour took up the hearing of applications to have fair rents fixed upon holdings situated in the union of Thurles.

Charles Savage Graham, landlord; James Greed, tenant. Part of the lands of Clonboo. Mr Morgan appeared for the landlord and Mr Carrigan appeared for the tenant.

In this case, which was adjourned from last sessions, there was a dispute about a reclaimed bog, which the landlord declared the tenant had added to his holdings without permission.

Mr Carrigan – we purchased it and we are paying rent for it. Mr Thomas Keegan, for the landlord, deposed that he had made a survey of the tenant's holding. It measured 28a 3r 8p, and the portion under dispute measured 8a 2r.

His Honour – at the original hearing the area was settled at 86a 1r 8p, and now it is proved to contain an acre more – 87a 1r 8p. The area agreed on at the original hearing clearly included the disputed part; and that being so, he would be inclined to fix a fair rent on the whole area, including the disputed part.

Mr Morgan said he had no objection to allow the disputed eight acres to run into the tenant's holding, provided they would receive rent for it.

Mr Carrigan – That's what we want – to have a fair rent fixed on the whole lot.

The application was allowed to stand till Thursday, when his Honour fixed the rent at £11 10s.

Nenagh Guardian, 19 April 1893

Estate of Charles Savage Graham

Patrick Doolan, tenant

Mr Morgan for the landlord and Mr Carrigan for the tenants on the estate.

Area 51a 3r 18p; rent £23 15s; poor law valuation £20 10s.

Mr Charles Murphy for the landlord, said the area in the original notice was wrong; he scaled the map, and it was 8a 3r 22p more than on the ordnance sheet, on account of a reclaimed bog which was added to the tenant's holding; he only valued this reclaimed bog at 1s an Irish acre.

The tenant said he was in occupation for 32 years; he claimed the buildings as his property; he made about 40 perches of fence; he had to pay about £10 a year for hand feeding for his stock. On account of the flooding there was more than half his farm that he did not graze from

November till May.

Mr James Kelly for the tenant, valued on 32 Irish acres at £15; he said he heard nothing about the reclaimed bog.

Mr Murphy for the landlord, valued at £18 15s 9d; then the reclaimed bog, comprising 8a 3r 32p, at 1s an acre made 8s 8d, making a total valuation of £19 4s 5d.

Daniel Deegan, tenant.
Part of the lands of Clonboo, comprising 93a 9r 32p; rent £56 7s 6d; poor law valuation, about £57 5s.

The buildings were claimed by the tenant who said he drained about 10 or 15 acres; he also made about 155 perches of fence and 58 perches of stone wall; he tilled 12 acres and grazed the rest on which he kept 20 ewes, three horses, ten head of young cattle and four cows; it cost him £21 5s last season for hay.

Mr Kelly for the tenant, valued on 97a 3r statute at a total of £36 13s.

Mr Murphy for the landlord, valued on 93a 1r 38p statute, at a total of £52 1s 5d, he said he would allow him 3s for the drainage.

Martin Deegan, tenant
Part of Clonboo, comprising 88a or 30p; rent £38 12s 6d; poor law valuation, £56 15s.

The tenant proved that the buildings were all erected by himself; he reclaimed about 6 acres and made over 100 yards of fences; he also built about 12 perches of a stone wall; it was half a mile off the public road.

Mr Kelly for tenant, valued on 41a or 33p statute, at a total of £9.

Mr Murphy, for the landlord, valued 88a or 30p at a total of £55 18s 10d.

James Greed, tenant
Part of Clonboo, comprising 36a 1r 8p; rent £14 10s; valuation £14 10s.

The buildings were admitted to be the property of the tenant, who proved the usual fencing and drainage improvements.

Mr Kelly for the tenant, valued on 41a or 33p statute, at a total of £9.

Mr Murphy for the landlord, valued on 36a 1r 8p at £13 7s 3d.

Daniel Maher, tenant
Part of Clonboo, comprising 71a 8r 28p, rent £34; valuation £36 5s.

The buildings were erected by the tenant and 30a had been reclaimed by him.

Mr Kelly for the tenant, valued on 71a 2r 28p at £20 8s.

Mr Murphy for the landlord, valued on 71a 2r 38p at £32 8s 6d. He said he only saw about 5a of reclaimed land.

Patrick Carroll, tenant

Part of lands of Togher, comprising 24a 2r 14p; rent £12; valuation £13 16s.

The tenant proved to having made 800 perches of stone drains. He reclaimed one acre and the buildings were his.

Mr Kelly for the tenant, valued on 22a or 14p as a total of £8 1s 3d.

Mr Murphy for the landlord, at £11 11s 10d, for the drains he would deduct from this 8s.

Martin Lanigan, tenant

Part of Clonboo, comprising 92a 2r 27p; old rent £44; valuation £48

The buildings were the applicant's who made about 40 perches of drains. Over 20a was subject to floods.

Mr Kelly for the tenant, valued at £25 3s, and Mr Murphy for the landlord at £41 9s 6d.

His Honour reserved his judgement in the above cases until he received the report of the court valuer.

Nenagh Guardian, Saturday 24 June 1893

Thurles Land Commission

His Honour Judge Anderson gave judgement on Tuesday in the following applications by tenants to have fair rents fixed on their holdings. Evidence was heard in each of the cases at the last sessions.

Charles S. Graham, landlord:

	FORMER RENT	JUDL. RENT
Patrick Doolan	£23 15s 0d	£19 0s 0d
Daniel Deegan	£56 7s 6d	£49 0s 0d
Martin Deegan	£58 12s 6d	£50 0s 0d
Daniel Maher	£34 0s 0d	£29 0s 0d
Patrick Carroll	£12 0s 0d	£9 10s 0d
Martin Lanigan	£44 0s 0d	£39 0s 0d
Tobias Maher	£24 0s 0d	£19 0s 0d

VALUATIONS OFFICE

The Valuation Office of Ireland, located in the Irish Life Centre in Abbey Street, contains valuations that span over a period of 120 years, from 1856 to 1970. The records found cover the townlands of Clonbough and Togher in the parishes of Clonmore and Templetuohy, in the barony of Ikerrin and in the county of Tipperary. References to maps of the townlands include information on Occupiers, Immediate Lessors, Descriptions of Tenements, and the Rateable Annual Valuations.

Changes in the ownership of the lands have been traced back from 1970 to 1856, but several gaps and inconsistencies appear. However, the information is extremely valuable and very worthwhile. The records are entirely handwritten and changes are written over the original entries, which can make them difficult to read. It also makes it tricky to follow the names.

Starting in 1970, the schedule contains all entries from **1934** to **1970** for Clonbough and Togher. The 120 years of time is broken down into periods of time going back from **1856** to **1863**, then **1864** to **1866**, then **1867** to **1876**, then **1877** to **1883**, then **1884** to **1892**, then **1893** to **1909**, then **1910** to **1933** and from **1934** to **1970**.

CLONBOUGH

Map Ref. 1A; Occupiers Michael Myram, later changed to Katherine Myram; Immediate Lessor, Charles Savage Graham (C.S. Graham); Description of Tenements, House and Lands; Area 1 Acre, 1 Root.

Map Ref. 1B; James Fermoyle; Graham; Land; 4A and 3R.

Map Refs 1C and Pt 8A; Reps of C.S. Graham; Bog; 64A, 2R and 30P, plus 52A, 2R and 25P.

Map Ref. 1D; Edward Guilfoyle; Graham; Land, part Bog; 14A and 3R.

Map Ref. 2A; Mrs Josephine Maher; In Fee; House and Land; 95A, 2R and 38P.

Map Ref. 2B; Peter Carey; Thomas Bergin; Land; 1A, 2R and 20P.

Map Ref. 2C; Patrick Grimes; Tipp NR Co. Board of Health; House and Land; 1A and 20P.

Map Ref. 2D; Joseph Tynan; Tipp NR; House and Land; 2R and 5P.

Map Ref. 2E; Denis Carroll; Tipp NR; House and Land; 2R and 5P.

Map Ref. 2F; Michael Molloy; Tipp NR; House and Land; 1A and 1013.

Map Ref. 3A; Thomas Deegan, later changed to Martin Deegan; Graham; House and Land; 87A, 1R and 28P.

Map Ref. 3B; Thomas J. Deegan, later changed to Martin Deegan; Graham; Land; 88A and 30P.

Map Ref. 4B; Thomas Deegan, later changed to Martin Deegan; Graham; Land; 4A, 3R and 7P.

Map Ref. Part 4B; Thomas Deegan; Graham; Land; 1A, 2R and 23P.

Map Refs Part 4A and 5; Edward Guilfoyle; Graham; House and Land; 19A, 1R and 10P.

Map Ref. 6; Patrick Clarke; In Fee; House and Land; 22A, 2R and 7P.

Map Ref. 7; John Butler; In Fee; House and Land; 55A, 3R and 28P.

Map Refs 8A and B; Josephine Maher; In Fee; 70A, 2R and 8P.

Map Ref. 8C; James Fermoyle; Thurles RD Council; House and Land; lA and 20P.

Map Ref. 9; Timothy Guider; In Fee; House and Land; 92A, 2R and 27P(part bog).

Map Ref. 10A; Reps of Graham; In Fee; Bog; 93A, 3R and 13P.

Map Ref. 10B; Michael Myram; Graham; Land (reclaimed Bog, no value); 1A, 1R and 20P.

Map Ref. 11; Patrick Clarke; Graham; Land; 37A, 2R and 7P.

Map Ref. 12; James Fermoyle; Graham; Land; 2A, 3R and 4P.

Map Ref. 13A; James Greed; Graham; Land; 37A and 8P.

Map Ref. 13D; Revd E. Bourke, PP, later changed to Revd J. Bergin, PP; Graham; Garden; 2R and 29P.

Map Ref. 13E; Parish Priest; Graham; National School House; No area stated other than 'see page 41'.

Map Ref. 14; Sarah Doolan, later changed to Mary Butler; Graham; House and Land; 51A, 1R and 3P.

Map Ref. 15; Margaret Butler; Graham; Land; 56A, 1R and 32P.

TOGHER

Map Ref. 1.2; John Ryan; Graham; House and Land; 24A, 2R and 14P.

Map Ref. 3A; Edward Ryan; Graham; House and Land; 36A.

Map Ref. 3B; Patrick Bergin; Graham; House and Land; 1A and 39P.

Map Ref. 4; James Maher; In Fee; House and Land; 38A, 1R and 8P.

Map Ref. 5A; Patrick Costigan; Graham; House and Land; 15A.

Map Ref. 6; Reps of Graham; In Fee; Bog; 52A, 3R and 33P.

Map Ref. 7; Patrick Costigan; In Fee; House and Lands; 65A and 7P.

Map Refs 8A and B; Michael Loughnane; Graham; House and Land; 4A, 3R and 13P.

Map Ref. 8C; Michael Loughnane; Graham; House and Land; 1A and 10P.

Map Ref. 9; Patrick Walsh, later changed to James Maher; Graham; House and Land; 22A and 1P.

Map Ref. 10A; Margaret Butler; Graham; House and Land; 25A and 2R.

Map Ref. 10B; Jeremiah Maher; Thurles RD Council; House and Land; 1A and 5P.

Map Ref. 12; James Moran; Graham; House and Land; 13A and 18P.

Map Refs 13A and 14; John Ryan; Graham; House and Land; 34A, 3R and 17P.

Map Ref. 15; Daniel Bowe; Graham; House and Land; 13A and 6P.

We now move to the next period, from **1933** to **1910**. The Immediate Lessor will be as above in most cases and were different will be noted below. Also, the Description of the Tenement and the Areas will also be the same unless the land was divided and this will also be noted.

CLONBOUGH

Map Ref. 1A; Mary Myram, later changed to Michael Myram.

Map Ref. 1B; Jeremiah Morrissey, later changed to Martin Morrissey. Note above 1934-1970, changed to James Fermoyle.

Map Ref. 1C and Part 8A; Graham; Bog.

Map Ref. 1D; Patrick Cahill. Note above 1934-1970, changed to Edward Guilfoyle.

Map Ref. 2A; Daniel Deegan, later changed to Thomas Deegan. Original area of 98A, 3R and 38P is changed to 97A, 3R and 18P when Map Ref. 2C is added for Occupier William Grimes, with Immediate Lessor Thurles RD Council, for the area difference of 1A and 20P. Note above 1934-1970, changed to Josephine Maher, but the area in 1934-1970 is 95A, 2R and 38P. The reason for same appears to be that Map Refs 2D, 2E and 2F are added in 1934-1970 for Joseph Tynan, Dennis Carroll and Michael Molloy. The three plots of land were deducted from Deegan's original holding, which changed from Deegan to Maher.

Map Ref. 2B; Mary Meaney, with Immediate Lessor Thomas Bergin. Note above 1934-1970, changed to Peter Carey.

Map Ref. 3A; Daniel Deegan, later changed to Thomas Deegan. Note above 1934-1970, changed to Martin Deegan.

Map Ref. 3B; Martin Deegan.

Map Ref. Part 4B; Daniel Deegan, later changed to Thomas Deegan.

Map Ref. 5; Martin Guilfoyle, later changed to Bridget Guilfoyle. Note above 1934-1970, changed to Edward Guilfoyle.

Map Ref. 6; Patrick Clarke, later changed to Mary Clarke. Note above 1934-1970, changed to Patrick Clarke.

Map Ref. 7; John Butler.

Map Refs 8A and B; Ellen Maher, later changed to John Maher and later changed to Edward Maher. There is a further change when Map Ref. 8C is added, and Occupier is James Fermoyle with Immediate Lessor Thurles RD Council and Area of 1A and 20P. Note the original Occupier above 1934-1970 is changed to Josephine Maher.

Map Ref. 9; Elizabeth Lanigan, later changed to Daniel Lanigan. Note above 1934-1970, changed to Timothy Guider.

Map Ref. 10A; Reps of Graham.

Map Ref. 10B; Michael Myram.

Map Ref. 11; Patrick Clarke, later changed to Mary Clarke. Note above 1934-1970, changed to Patrick Clarke.

Author's Note: *Page 21 missing from Valuation file and Map Refs 12, 13 and 14 are missing. In 1934-1970, the Occupiers are James Fermoyle, James Greed, National School and Sarah Doolan.*

Map Ref. 15; Thomas Butler, later changed to Martin Butler. Note above 1934-1970, changed to Margaret Butler.

TOGHER

Map Ref. 1.2; Patrick Carroll, later changed to James Carroll. Note above 1934-1970, changed to John Ryan.

Map Ref. 3A; Michael Shelly. Note above 1934-1970, changed to Edward Ryan.

Map Ref. 4; Tobias Maher, later changed to James Maher.

Map Ref. 5A; Nicholas Delahunty, later changed to Michael Delahunty. Note above 1934-1970, changed to Patrick Costigan.

Map Ref. 6; Reps of Graham.

Map Ref. 7; Patrick Costigan, later changed to Johanna Costigan. Note above 1934-1970, changed to Patrick Costigan.

Map Refs 8A and B; William Loughnane. Note above 1934-1970, changed to Michael Loughnane.

Map Ref. 9; Patrick Walsh.

Map Ref. 10; Thomas Butler, later changed to Martin Butler. Also changed to 10A when the area is reduced to add 10B and add Occupier Jeremiah Maher with an Area of 1A and 5P, with Immediate Lessor Thurles RD Council. Note above 1934-1970, changed to Margaret Butler at Map Ref. 10A, along with Jeremiah Maher at Map Ref. 10B.

Map Ref. 12; James Moran, later changed to Patrick Moran. Note above 1934-1970, changed to James Moran.

Map Refs 13A and 14; Timothy Ryan, later changed to Margaret Ryan. Note above 1934-1970, changed to John Ryan.

Map Ref. 15; Patrick Fcchily, later changed to Thomas Feehily. Although difficult to read, it appears changed again to James Bowe.

The next time segment is from **1893** to **1909**. The entries have some details missing and tracking forward to other periods is not as transparent as in later periods.

CLONBOUGH

Map Ref. 1, later changed to 10A; Charles Savage Graham; Bog; 124A, 3R and 8P, later reduced to 93A, 3R and 13P.

Map Ref. 10B; Michael Myram; Land/Reclaimed Bog; 1A, 1R and 20P.

Map Ref. 2, changed to 11; Patrick Clarke; 34A, 3R and 32P, later changed to 37A, 2R and 7P.

Map Ref. 3, changed to 12; Martin Morrissey, later changed to Margaret Morrissey; 2A, 3R and 4P.

Map Ref. 4A, changed to 13; James Greed; 28A, 3R and 8P, later increased to 37A and 8P.

Map Ref. 4d; Johanna Fogarty, changed to Pierce Flynn, changed to John Guilfoyle, and then changed to Joseph Downey NST; 2R and 24P.

Map Ref. 5, changed to 14; Patrick Doolan; 45A and 3P, changed to 51A, 1R and 3P.

Map Ref. 6, changed to 15; Thomas Butler; 43A, 3R and 32P, changed to 56A, 1R and 32P.

TOGHER

Map Ref. 1.2; Patrick Carroll; 24A, 2R and 14P.

Map Ref. 3A; Michael Shelly; 37A and 39P.

Map Ref. 4; Tobias Maher; 38A, 1R and 8P.

Map Ref. 5, changed to 5a and 11; Nicholas Delahunty; 15A, 1R and 20P.

Map Ref. 6; Grahams; Bog; 52A, 3R and 33P.

Map Ref. 7; Mary Costigan, changed to Patrick Costigan; 65A and 7P.

Map Ref. 8; William Loughnane; 5A, 3R and 23P.

Map Ref. 9; Patrick Walsh; 22A and 1P.

Map Ref. 10; Thomas Butler; 26A, 2R and 5P.

Map Ref. 12; James Moran; 13A and 18P.

Map Ref. 13a; Timothy Ryan; 34A, 3R and 17P.

Map Ref. 15; Patrick Feehily; 13A and 6P.

The next time segment is from **1884** to **1892**.

CLONBOUGH

Map Ref. 1; Graham; Bog; 124A.

Map Ref. 2; Patrick Clarke; 34A.

Map Ref. 2A; Judith Ryan with Immediate Lessor Patrick Clarke and changed back to Patrick Clarke.

Map Ref. 3; Martin Morrissey; 2A.

Map Ref. 4A; James Greed; 28A.

Map Ref. 5; Patrick Doolan; 45A.

Map Ref. 6; Thomas Butler; 43A.

Map Ref. 4D; Widow McNamee, changed to Timothy Fogarty, changed to Mrs Fogarty; House and Garden; 2R and 29P.

Map Ref. 4E; School House; Board of National Education.

TOGHER

Map Refs 1 and 2; Patrick Carroll; 24A.

Map Refs 3A and 3B; Denis Shelly, changed to Michael Shelly; 37A and 39P.

Map Ref. 4; Tobias Maher; 38A.

Map Refs 5 and 11; Michael Delahunty, changed to Nicholas Delahunty; 14A.

Map Ref. 6; Grahams; Bog; 52A.

Map Ref. 7; Widow Costigan, changed to Mary Costigan; 65A.

Map Ref. 8; William Loughnane; 2A.

Map Ref. 9; Patrick Walsh; 22A.

Map Ref. 10; Thomas Butler; 26A.

Map Ref. 12; James Moran; 13A.

Map Ref. 14; Michael Doolan, changed to Timothy Ryan; 37A.

Map Ref. 15; Edmund Feehily, changed to Patrick Feehily; 13A.

The next time segment is from **1877** to **1883**.

CLONBOUGH

Map Ref. 1; Grahams; Bog.

Map Ref. 2; Patrick Clarke; 34A.

Map Ref. 2a; Judith Ryan; 2R and 16P.

Map Ref. 3; Martin Morrissey; 2A.

Map Ref. 4A; James Greed; 28A.

Map Ref. 5; Patrick Doolan; 45A.

Map Ref. 6; Thomas Butler; 43A.

Map Ref. 4D; Dominick McNamee, changed to Widow McNamee, changed to Timothy Fogarty; 2R and 29P.

Map Ref. 4E; National School.

TOGHER

Map Refs 1 and 2; Patrick Carroll; 24A.

Map Ref. 3a; Denis Shelly; 37A.

Map Ref. 4; John Maher, changed to Tobias Maher; 38A.

Map Refs 5 and 11; Michael Delahunty, changed to Nicholas Delahunty; 14A.

Map Ref. 6; Grahams; Bog.

Map Ref. 7; Patrick Costigan, changed to Widow Costigan; 65A.

Map Ref. 8; Patrick Ryan, changed to William Loughnane; 2A.

Map Ref. 9; Patrick Walsh; 22A.

Map Ref. 10; Thomas Butler; 26A.

Map Ref. 12; James Moran; 13A.

Map Refs 13A and 14; Michael Doolan, changed to Timothy Ryan; 37A.

Map Ref. 15; Edmund Feehily; 13A.

The next time segment is from **1867** to **1876**.

CLONBOUGH

Map Ref. 1; Reps of Hugh Graham; Bog; 124A.

Map Ref. 2; Mary Clarke, changed to Patrick Clarke; 34A.

Map Ref. 2A; Judith Ryan.

Map Ref. 3; Martin Morrissey.

Map Ref. 4A; James Greed; 28A.

Map Ref. 4B; William McKelroy.

Map Ref. 4C; Michael Doolan.

Map Ref. 5; Patrick Doolan; 45A.

Map Ref. 6; Patrick Butler, changed to Thomas Butler.

Map Ref. 4D; Dominick McNamee.

Map Ref. 4E; School House.

TOGHER

Map Refs 1 and 2; Patrick Carroll.

Map Ref. 3A; Denis Shelly.

Map Ref. 3B; Mary Fitzpatrick with Immediate Lessor Denis Shelly.

Map Ref. 4; Jeremiah Maher, changed to Toby Maher.

Map Refs 5 and 11; Michael Delahunty.

Map Ref. 7; Patrick Costigan.

Map Ref. 8; Patrick Ryan; 2A.

Map Ref. 9; Patrick Brennan, changed to Patrick Walsh; 22A.

Map Ref. 10; Patrick Butler, changed to Thomas Butler.

Map Ref. 11; Michael Delahunty.

Map Ref. 12; James Moran.

Map Ref. 13A; Henry Fitzpatrick, changed to Michael Doolan.

Map Ref. 13B; Henry Fitzpatrick.

Map Ref. 13C; Edward Becton.

Map Ref. 15; Edmund Feehily.

The next time segment is from **1864** to **1866**.

CLONBOUGH

Map Ref. 1; Graham; Bog; 88A.

Map Ref. 2A; Thomas Bergin; 95A.

Map Ref. 2B; William Guilfoyle with Immediate Lessor Thomas Bergin.

Map Ref. 3A; Thomas Deegan, changed to John Deegan; 175A.

Map Ref. 3B; Judith Meehan, changed to Patrick Griffin with Immediate Lessor John Deegan; House.

Map Ref. 3C; Edward Long, changed to Catherine Long; House.

Map Ref. 3D; Mary Flynn, changed to Daniel Flynn; House.

Map Refs 4A and 4B; Donnell McNamee, changed to Dominick McNamee with Immediate Lessors Hugh Graham and John Deegan.

Map Ref. 5; Edward Guilfoyle; 5A.

Map Ref. 6; Mary Clarke; 22A.

Map Ref. 7; John Butler; House and Lands; 55A, 3R and 28P.

Map Ref. 8; Jeremiah Maher; House and Land; 61A, 1R and 26P; Lands, 10A, 1R and 2P.

Map Ref. 9; Graham; Bog.

Map Ref. 9A; Patrick Cahill with Immediate Lessor Jeremiah Maher; House.

Map Ref. 9; Mick Lannigan; House and Land; 82A; Bog, 9A.

TOGHER

Map Refs 1 and 2; James Campion and Patrick Doolan, changed to Patrick Carroll.

Map Ref. 3A; Denis Shelly; 37A.

Map Ref. 3B; Mary Fitzpatrick with Immediate Lessor Denis Shelly.

Map Ref. 4; Jeremiah Maher.

Map Ref. 5; Michael Delahunty.

Map Ref. 6; Graham and Patrick Costigan; Bog.

Map Ref. 7; Patrick Costigan.

Map Ref. 8; Patrick Ryan.

Map Ref. 9; Patrick Brennan; 22A.

Map Ref. 10; Joseph Bergin, changed to Patrick Butler.

Map Ref. 11; Michael Delahunty.

Map Ref. 12; James Moran.

Map Refs 13A and 14; Henry Fitzpatrick.

Map Ref. 13B; Henry Fitzpatrick with Immediate Lessor Michael Doolan; House.

Map Ref. 13C; Edward Becton; House.

Map Ref. 15; Edmund Feehily.

The next time segment is from **1856** to **1863**. This is the earliest record of valuations.

CLONBOUGH

Map Ref. 1; Graham; Bog; 131A.

Map Ref. 2; Mary Clarke; 34A.

Map Ref. 2A; Judith Ryan, Immediate Lessor Mary Clarke.

Map Ref. 3; Martin Morrissey.

Map Ref. 4A; James Campion.

Map Ref. 4B; James Doolan, changed to Patrick Doolan.

Map Ref. 4C; Kevin Campion.

Map Ref. 4D; Michael Doolan.

Map Ref. 4E; Michael Maher, changed to William Kirby or Kelby?

Map Ref. 4F; Vacant with Immediate Lessor James Doolan.

Map Ref. 4G; Donnell McNamee with Immediate Lessor James Doolan.

Map Ref. 4H; National School.

Map Ref. 4I; John Baldwin with Immediate Lessor Kevin Campion.

TOGHER

Map Ref. 1; James Campion.

Map Ref. 2; James Doolan, changed to Patrick Doolan.

Map Ref. 3A; Michael Doran.

Map Refs 3B and 3C; Mary Fitzpatrick.

Map Ref. 3D; John Doran

Map Ref. 4; Michael Doran.

Map Ref. 5; Michael Delahunty.

Map Ref. 6; Graham and Patrick Costigan; Bog.

Map Ref. 7; John Bergin, changed to Patrick Costigan.

Map Ref. 8A; Michael Doran, changed to Jeremiah Maher.

Map Ref. 8B; Timothy Bergin, changed to Maher.

Map Ref. 9; Patrick Brennan.

Map Ref. 10; Joseph Bergin.

Map Ref. 11; Michael Delahunty.

Map Ref. 12; James Moran.

Map Ref. 13A; Michael Doolan.

Map Ref. 13B; Thomas Mara, changed to Mary Fitzpatrick.

Map Ref. 13C; Edward Becton.

Map Ref. 14; Michael Dolan.

Map Ref. 15; Edmund Feehily.

Map Ref. 16; Jeremiah Ryan, changed to Patrick Ryan.

Map Ref. 17A; Denis Shelly.

Map Ref. 17B; Mary Fitzpatrick with Immediate Lessor Denis Shelly.

CENSUS, 1901 AND 1911.

The censuses of 1901 and 1911 are in the custody of the National Archives of Ireland. They represent an extremely valuable part of the Irish national heritage. The census returns for 1901 and 1911 are arranged by townland in the rural areas or in urban areas, by street. The 1901 census lists, for every member of each household: name, age, sex, relationship to head of the household, religion, occupation, marital status and county or country of birth. The census also records an individual's ability to read or write and ability to speak the Irish language.

The same information was recorded in the 1911 census, with one significant addition: married women were required to state the number of years they had been married, the number of their children born alive and the number still living.

In the 1901 census, there were 60,462 townlands and 14,000 streets in the country, while in 1911, there were 60,679 townlands and 14,000 streets. The 1901 census was taken on 31 March and the 1911 census was taken on 2 April. The following families are included in the 1901 and 1911 censuses.

TOWNLANDS AND HOUSE NUMBERS AS PER CENSUS OF 1901

KILLAVINOGE

1. Skehan, James
2. Prendergast, John
3. Treacy, Norah
4. Pyne, Catherine
5. Keenan, Luke

CLONBOUGH LOWER

1. Bergin, Thomas
2. Nolan, James
3. Meaney, Mary
4. Butler, John
5. Maher, Daniel
6. Molloy, Patrick
7. Guilfoyle, Kate
8. Lanigan, Elizabeth
9. Clarke, Patrick
10. Deegan, Daniel
11. Grahame, William

CLONBOUGH UPPER

1. Downey, Joseph
2. School
3. Doolan, Patrick
4. Greed, James
5. Morrissey, Margaret
6. Myrens, Michael
7. Morrissey, Jermiah

TOGHER

1. Carroll, Patrick
2. Walshe, Patrick
3. Maher, Tobias
4. Costigan, Mary
5. Delhaunty, Nicholas
6. Feehely, Pat
7. Ryan, Timothy
8. Ringwood, Henry
9. Loughnane, William
10. Shelly, Michael
11. Fitzpatrick, Daniel
12. Moran, James
13. Butler, Thomas

LISSANURE LOWER

1. Cooly, John
2. Darmody, Patrick
3. Kiely, Murty

LISSANURE UPPER

1. Maher, Patrick
2. Bowe, Martin
3. Lawlor, Matthew
4. Carroll, Rody
5. Kennedy, Michael
6. Bowe, James
7. Guider, Timothy
8. Shelly, William

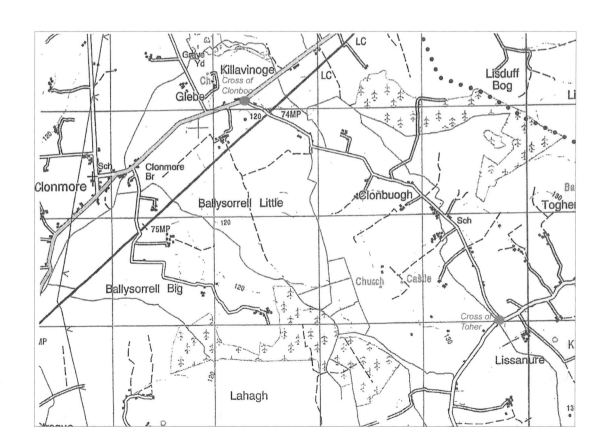

TOWNLANDS AND HOUSE NUMBERS
AS PER CENSUS OF 1911

KILLAVINOGUE	1. Treacy	2. Prendergast
	3. Keenan	4. Skehan
	5. Tuohy	

CLONBOUGH LOWER	1. Grimes	2. Meagher
	3. Meaney	4. Butler
	5. Maher	6. Molloy
	7. Guilfoyle	8. Lanigan
	9. Clarke	10. Deegan

CLONBOUGH UPPER	1. Ryan (school)	2. Greed
	3. Doolan	4. Morrissey
	5. Morrissey	6. Myrens
	7. Delahaunty	

TOGHER	1. Moran	2. Maher, Toby
	3. Walsh	4. Carroll
	5. Delhaunty	6. Costigan
	7. Feehely	8. Ryan
	9. Ringwood	10. Loughnane
	11. Shelly	12. Butler, Tom

| LISSANURE LOWER | 1. Darmody | 2. Kiely |
| | 3. Carey | |

LISSANURE UPPER	1. Lawler	2. Carroll
	3. Kennedy	4. Fitzpatrick
	5. Shelly	6. Kennedy
	7. Guider	8. Bowe
	9. Maher	10. Bowe

CHAPTER 4

THE HOUSES
& THE PEOPLE

The following is a list of all the families who, at various stages in the last 400 to 500 years, lived between, or in the vicinity of, the Cross of Clonboo and the Cross of Toher.

Over 125 familes (or people who had a house), lived along this two-and-a-quarter-mile length of road in that period. There are currently approximately twenty families still living between the crosses. At the time of the 1901 census, there were forty-seven familes living along the road, and although there are name changes, there were also forty-seven familes living there at the time of the 1911 census.

Bergin, Denis	Bergin, Eamonn	Bergin, Michael
Bergin, Thomas	Bourke, Bridget	Bourke, Johnny
Bowe, Daniel	Burke, Michael/Catherine	Butler, John
Butler, Thomas		
Cahill, Patrick	Campion, James/Kevin	Carey, Peter
Caudy, Michael	Carroll, Denis	Carroll, Jim/Johanna
Carroll, Ollie	Clarke, Patrick	Cooly, John
Corcoran, Mary	Cullen, Anastatia	
Darmody, Patrick	Davy, Julia	Deegan, Dan/Martin
Deegan, Phonsie	Deegan, Tomas	Delhaunty, John
Delhaunty, Nicholas	Doolan, James (Garden)	Doolan, Ned
Dooley, Loughlin	Downey, Joseph	Doyle, David
Dwyer, Catherine	Dwyer, John	
Egan, Nano/Daniel		
Fahy, James	Feely, James	Feely, Roger
Fermoyle, James	Fogarty, Patrick	Fogarty, Timothy

Fogarty, William	Flynn, Daniel/Mary	Flynn, Patrick
Gavin, Veronica/Myra	Grady, Kathy	Grahame, William
Greed, James	Greed, Peter	Griffin, Patrick
Grimes, Lar	Grimes, Liam	Grimes, Sophie
Guider, Daniel	Guider, Mick	Guilfoyle, Edward
Hannigan, Richard	Hannen, James	Hayden, Dan
Hayden, Nicholas	Hayes, Peter/Peggy	Hennessy, John
Hude, William		
Kavanagh, Daniel	Kenna, Widow	Kennan, Luke
Kennedy, John	Kelly, Eilish	Kinnane, Ann
Kirby/Kelby, William	Kiely, Murty	
Laffan, Nicholas	Lanigan, Dan	Lanigan, Michael
Lee	Long, Edward/Catherine	Loughnane, Ml/Ann
Maguire, Mathew	Maher, James	Maher, Jermiah
Maher, Michael	Maher, Thady	McCormack, William
McDermott, Nora	McElroy, William	McGrath, John
McNamee, Widow	Meagher, Don	Meagher, Ml/Catherine
Meaney, Michael	Meehan, Nicholas/Judith	Merrigan, Don
Molloy, Mick	Morrissey, Dan	Morrissey, Jeremiah
Moylan, Martin	Myrons, Tommy	
Nolan, Bridget/Maria/Kate	Noonan, John	
O'Guinan, Loughlin	O'Hayden, Phil	O'Meara, Joseph/Kate
Prendergast, Michael	Price, Mary	Pynes, Jim/Catherine
Quirke, Michael		
Rourke, John/Wm	Ryan, Jim/Richard	Ryan, Joe
Ryan, Joe	Ryan, Johanna	Ryan, Judith
Ryan, Martin	Ryan, Patrick	Ryan, Timothy
Scully, Phil	Skehan, James	Stamp, Tom
Steel, Margaret		
Taylor, Dan	Toal, Francis Martin/Josephine/Timothy	Treacy, Nora
Tuohy, James	Tynan, Johnny	
Walsh, Patrick	Whelan, William/Lizzie	

INTRODUCTION

We will start our journey up Clonboo road from the Cross of Clonboo and we will finish at Toher Cross. In recent times, the entire secondary road network was given specific identification reference numbers. The road between the Cross of Clonboo and the Cross of Toher is officially known as L7054. We will meet current, recent and not-so-recent inhabitants, along with some extended family members and some frequent visitors. The visitors continue, but my own memories include visitors like my grandaunt Ann from Kilballyowen, Co. Limerick, who came to visit my grandmother Sarah Doolan for a few days and often stayed for a few months, then casual visitors like Jack Moyney and daily visitors like Ned Looby (the postman).

As I write this introduction, new people, new families are setting up home 'Between the Crosses', and since I started putting these words together a few years ago, other friends and neighbours have left their homes in Clonboo and Toher for their eternal home.

My mother reminded me that in previous generations, the norm was that the son (usually the oldest son) stayed at home on the farm and he would build a new house or live in the existing house with his new bride. This tradition is still in existence and carried on by some, such as Liam Grimes, Tomas Deegan and Donie Bowe. Nowadays it is the daughters who are setting up home in the country with their new husbands. This brings a great variety of new surnames to the townlands, like Stamp, Ryan, Bergin and Carroll.

Recorded in the pages that follow are the families of some fifty households or people who lived 'Between the Crosses', but there are several others who lived there and could not be traced back to current relations or current houses or farms. These people may have sold their houses or farms and moved on, maybe they emigrated during troubled or hungry times, or maybe they just died and the family name became extinct. I am going to mention them here though, and where I found them, in case some reader comes across some connection. Someday, someone from Australia or Hong Kong might come knocking on a door in search of one of these people. It happened when a relation of the Rourkes', who lived where Thady Maher now lives, came looking, back in 1987, from the States.

The Records of Hearth Money Rates dating back to 1666 and 1667, include part of the Clonbough townland and the following people are mentioned. The names recorded for Clonbough were: Rbt Lunn, Rd Hannigan, Loughlin O'Guinan, Thomas Meagher, Phil O'Hayden, Nicholas O'Hayden, Jas. Hannen, Phil Scully, Logh. Dooley, Dan O'Hayden; Don O'Merrigan, Wm Hude, John McGrath, William Fogarty, and Don Meagher. It looks like around 350 years ago, these people lived in Clonbough and today none of these surnames survive. In another 350 years, I wonder will there still be Guiders, Deegans, Mahers, Grimes or Clarkes still living in the area?

Another surname that I came across in my research was brought to my attention by someone looking for a distant relative named Kavanagh who lived in Clonboo. The 1889 Bassett's Directory of Tipperary includes the following names for

Clonbough, some of which are familiar in the context of current or recent inhabitants, but others which are not: Thomas Bergin, John Butler, Patrick Clarke, Daniel Deegan, Martin Deegan, Martin Lanigan, Daniel Maher, and Jeremiah Maher.

The Killavinogue Tithe Applotments of 1824, obtained from the National Library of Ireland, lists the following inhabitants of Clonbough: Toby Butler, Patrick Cahill, Patrick Darmudy, Dennis Deegan, David Doyle, John Dwyer, James Fahy, Widow Kenna, John Kennedy, Nicholas Laffan, Mathew Maguire, John and William Rourke, Richard and Timothy Ryan, Roger Feely or Teely, and William Whelan.

Another source for the people who lived 'Between the Crosses' are the roll books from Toher school. Although some roll books are missing, an invaluable amount of information is still available. Along with details such as ages, there is also information on current residences by way of townland, and also information about previous schools attended, if applicable. This information adds to the growing list of families who lived 'Between the Crosses' in the townlands of Clonboo, Toher and Lissanure.

As noted earlier, we will visit about fifty different families as we make our journey up along the road, but in combining the various sources of information, some one hundred and twenty-five different families have been found to have at some stage lived 'Between the Crosses'.

Let us start our journey up the road, from the Cross of Clonboo…

TRACEY/RYAN

The Traceys lived in the first house up from the Cross of Clonboo, on the left-hand side. Nora Treacy lived there; she was a widow aged fifty at the time of the 1911 census, and had two daughters, Ellen, aged eighteen, and Mary, aged seventeen. Joe Ryan then lived there when he married the eldest daughter, Ellen Treacy. The other daughter, Mary (Molly) married Tommy Boland and they lived down past Loran Creamery. Tommy and Molly Boland had two children, Tommy and Nora, while Joe and Ellen Ryan had three children, Josie, Nora and Lar. Josie Ryan married Martin Scully and they lived in Knock, near Roscrea, where they reared a large family. Lar never married. Nora Ryan married Richie Fanning.

There are farm buildings on the site of the house now. My own memories of the area were Richie Fanning and his wife Nora feeding cattle, as we would see them on our way home from school after being dropped off at the Cross of Clonboo by Lucy Bergin. Lucy drove the bus, that yellow school bus, and she had a tough enough job, bringing a full busload of country teenagers five or six miles every day. Fair dues to her; she always seemed to control the situation well. We were on the second run from Templemore. The first run in the morning and in the evening was from Templetuohy through Strogue/Castleiney and the second run went to Clonmore, through Dromard onto Lisduff and Errill. Eamonn Campion ('Smiler' –

an appropriate name because he always had a sunny disposition) was the last pupil off the bus in Clonmeen. I met him recently at Sr Eileen Clarke's funeral and he hasn't changed a bit. We waited at Tighe Mhuire at the junction of McDonagh Terrace and Mary Street in Templemore. We would be waiting at the 'Divers' archway or in Jim Cahill's shop if it was raining. We would play handball at the 'Nuns' wall beside Tighe Mhuire. It was a good wall for handball; a natural arena with the footpath on the opposite side of the road acting as the dead ball line. Although several people played handball there, I remember Eamonn Cody, Mick Ryan (of the Hill), Martin Bourke and Pa Delaney as prominent players. There are apartments built there now, with windows and doors punctuating the wall, so no handball, anymore! We had nearly an hour there every evening and to be honest we didn't always study or play handball, but that is maybe for a separate book!

Richie Fanning came from Carlow and after he married Nora they lived opposite Tommy Deegan's on the main road from Templemore to Rathdowney, in a lovely house which I later found out was an old RIC Barracks. Before the Fannings, the Floods lived there. Six of the Flood children attended school in Toher. Nora Flood started school in Toher in 1916, and the following year, Christopher, Mary Anne and Bridget started school. Maggie started in 1920 and Christina started in 1922. The house and grounds were always tastefully kept and still are. Richie and Nora Fanning had three daughters: Eileen, Mary and Theresa. As I said above, I remember Richie and Nora foddering cattle, but I never saw the three girls foddering. For those reading (including my own children), you won't find the word 'foddering' in the dictionary, just ask an older person from the country! Getting back to the non-foddering girls. By the way, I checked with Mary, she didn't mind that description! We met at a recent function in Clonmore, my brother Pat's fundraiser for his second visit to Niall Mellon's Home-Building Project in South Africa. Mary was there with her husband Michael, along with Johnny Delaney and his wife Noreen Shanahan from Drom. My grandaunt Maggie Farrell, who lived in Drom beside her brother Jim Farrell, often talked about the two Shanahan girls. I knew Mary going to school and Noreen ended up in Dromard.

Back to the Fannings (as you can see I will diversify off in tangents now and again!). Mary Fanning is living at home and is married to Michael Brennan from Loughmore. They have two sons, Richard and Martin. Eileen is married to Michael Costigan and is living in Clonakenny. Teresa is married to Pat Kennedy, they live in Templederry and have two children, Maria and Philip.

OUTSIDE THE CROSSES

Author's Note: *Although this section is about the people who lived between the crosses, there are related comments about people who need to be included. After all, it is not their fault that they weren't born or grew up in the right place! It will happen during the book, so please bear with me if I wander from time to time.*

RAILWAY BRIDGE

A story is told at home about a relation of mine, a trainee Christian Brother called Denis Butler, who was (we think) born 24 February 1850. Denis heard the sad news that his mother had passed away and after pleading with his superiors to be allowed home for the funeral, he was denied. His superiors then sent him to Dublin on the train on the day of the funeral. As the train passed by the railway bridge in Clonboo, it slowed down to a crawl. The young fella could see across the fields to his home place and could see all the ponies and traps around the house and the crowd gathering for the funeral. He stayed on the train but always suspected that his superiors had put him to a severe test of his faith and obedience. A cruel and heartless test in my opinion.

The railway bridge, like all such structures, has its own identification number and the Clonboo bridge is OBC 199.

The Dublin to Cork railway line was built around 150 years ago. The bridges would have been built around the same time. A job was done on the bridge around the late 1990s or early 2000s, when the stonework and the walls got a new look. Work was also done to the underside over the rail tracks. My father told me that the original proposed route of the railway line was to be further up the Clonboo road, but was changed to its current location to prevent going through the bog and so avoid the extra cost of doing so.

The railway line was called 'The Great Southern and Western Railway', as recorded on the valuation maps. In 1846, there were hopes that the extension of the Dublin to Cork railway line through North Tipperary would be a source of good local employment. In September, lands were acquired in Templemore. Action on the extension of the railway line was soon under way. On 6 October 1846, the laying of the first stone of the Templemore section took place at Greenwood, about a quarter of a mile from the town.

Along the railway line, in Dromard and other areas, there were several crossings over the line where houses and farms were located at the other side of the tracks. The railway lines ran between the houses and the road. There are still crossings, but CIE (Iarnród Éireann) in some cases and the people themselves in other instances, have made alternative routes into their homes to avoid having to cross over the rail lines.

The man responsible for the building of most, if not all, of Ireland's railways, was a man called William Dargan. He was called 'the Father of Irish Railways' and he was from our neighbouring county of Laois, or as it was known then as the 'Queen's county'. By the way, Offaly was known as the 'King's County'. Tipperary is known as the 'Premier County'

William Dargan was one of Laois's most famous sons. He was born on 28 February 1799, near Killeshin. He worked for some time as an apprentice to the pioneering Scottish engineer Thomas Telford and helped to construct the London to Holyhead road across the mountains of north Wales. This was the main route from London to Dublin and Dargan was determined that the Irish portion of the road should be the equal of the British one. He returned to Ireland, set up his own contracting company and built the Howth to Dublin road, thus completing the London to Dublin link. At that time, Howth was the terminus for boats from Holyhead.

In 1831, Dargan won the contract to build Ireland's first railway line from the new port of Dún Laoghaire to Dublin, again finishing off the highway to London. The success of this project, which he completed in one year despite having to overcome huge engineering difficulties, led to many more railway contracts. Dargan ended up building most of Ireland's railways, some 800 miles in total.

So Dargan built or carried out the contract for the current railway line that crosses 'our road' under the Clonboo railway bridge. Of course this is not technically correct, as the railway bridge is actually located in the townland of Killavinogue (the townland changes at the 'Banjo's'). As I travel by train on the Dublin–Cork railway line, I always try to look out the window of the train to recognise the houses, fields and places that I remember or should recognise. It is always difficult, because the train goes so fast passing these familiar places. I try to picture what the houses look like from the road, as you drive past them in a car; the train gives you a totally different view, mostly of the backs of the houses. Also as you pass under bridges your view changes from one side to the other and totally change your orientation and what you think you are looking out for.

As well as building the railways, William Dargan opened up the port of Belfast by dredging out a new shipping channel and using the waste material to create the artificial Queen's Island that Harland & Wolff now occupies. This was where the *Titanic* was built and it is now being developed as a new commercial, cultural and residential part of Belfast City. Dargan also developed the seaside resort of Bray, along similar lines to Brighton, and built many miles of canal, including the Ulster Canal. In 1866, he was badly injured falling from his horse and, unable to maintain control of his many enterprises, he died in 1867, bankrupt and broken. He is buried in Glasnevin Cemetery.

The new cable bridge supporting the Luas line at Taney Cross, Dundrum has been named the William Dargan Bridge in honour of the 'Father of Irish Railways'.

NOONAN

John Noonan built a house for his family between the railway bridge and Penders. John lives there with Catherine Carroll (a daughter of Bobby Carroll, who is a nephew of Neddy Guilfoyle). They have three children: the first son Denis, presumably named after his grandfather Denis Noonan, a daughter, Carol, and son Jack, born in November 2009.

John was one of the gang going to school and also a staunch GAA man. He is still an enthusiastic supporter and a great follower of Clonmore, J.K. Brackens, Tipperary and Limerick. His father, Denis, was also a great Gael, having worn the blue jersey and gold sash of Clonmore, as well as becoming actively involved in the club at official level and as a selector. Denis came from one of Tipperary's scenic gems, the Glen of Aherlow, where the lush valley of the River Aherlow runs between the Galty Mountains and the wooded ridge of Slievenamuck. Bounded by the villages of Galbally and Bansha, the glen was historically an important pass between Limerick and Tipperary and a notorious hideout for outlaws. Denis Noonan died in 1985. Martin Bourke summed up the man in his great book published in 1988, *The GAA History of Clonmore, Killea and Templemore*:

> On 13 September the Clonmore club suffered a severe blow with the news that Denis Noonan had died after a short illness. He was a man of many interests and talents but his greatest must have been his total dedication to the GAA, both as a player and official. Having played most of his club hurling and football in his native West Tipperary (Aherlow) and taken a keen interest in the running of the club and division, it was inevitable he was going to play a big part in the Clonmore club once he moved to here in 1964.

Denis was on the team that won the Mid Junior final in 1970 after a gap of thirty-eight years. That team had a strong spine, with Tom Ryan playing at full-back, Johnny Bourke at centre-back, John Egan and Mick 'Curley' Maher at centre-field, and the forwards led by Pat Egan and Paddy Egan. Seamus Quinn was captain on the day. Although I was only seven years old, I do remember that time, as it brought overwhelming joy to the parish with bonfires burning at the crossroads around the village. Of course in those days the centre of night-time activity was in Byrne's pub, about half a mile from the village, opposite Tommy Deegan's field in Sorrell Hill.

Denis was also a game-shooting enthusiast. During the shooting season of November and December, you would always see Denis and his eldest son Pat, along with Johnny and Philly Bourke, out shooting pheasants. They would shoot up in Maher's and down in the bog. On their way home, a cock pheasant would be left in to my mother. A beautiful and richly colourful bird, the cock pheasant also had a tasty wild flavour, although the meat was scarce and you always had to watch out for the shotgun pellets. My grandmother Sarah Doolan had a stuffed cock pheasant up in her house, in the parlour. It is a crime to shoot a hen (female) pheasant, and by that I mean it is against the law.

John Noonan's love of Limerick hurling followed close behind his love of Tipperary, as his mother Maureen was from Galbally, Co. Limerick. I think Garyspillane was the local club team.

I met John Noonan recently and I have to clarify that his house is actually not Clonboo at all; in fact it is in the townland of Killavinogue. There is a small stream on the railway side of the Banjo's house that separates the two townlands. This also means that Greed's, Prendergast's and Johnny Bourke's houses are all in the townland of Killavinoge.

PRENDERGAST

Mick Prendergast (Mick Penders) lived in a house opposite Peter Greed's, on the left-hand side coming up the road from Clonboo Cross. There is no house there now.

Mick's parents were John (b.1833) and Eileen (b.1841). Mick had two sisters, Mary and Ellen (Nelly). Mick was born in 1872, Mary was born in 1876, and Nelly was born in 1880. Nelly married Jack Keane who was the postman in Clonmore and she moved to Dromard to live at Keane's. I remember their son Gerry Keane well, driving a Honda 50 motorbike around, in and out to town (Templemore). When the 1911 Census was taken Mick Prendergast recorded that his two cousins James Phelan and Lizzie Phelan were in the house that night. James is noted to be a farmer, aged fifteen and Lizzie is noted to be a scholar, aged eight.

Going back, for a moment, to Gerry Keane going in and out of 'town'. Templetuohy was known as 'the village', although Clonmore was also a village and closer. But, up our road, if you said you were going to, or had been in the village, everybody would know that you meant Templetuohy. If you were 'in the town', you had been in Templemore.

Mick's other sister Mary never married and she eventually moved to Keane's also and lived there with her sister Nelly and Nelly's husband.

GREED

A gifted craftsman … Sweet Afton cigarettes … quiet spoken – these are my memories of Peter Greed, who lived in the first cottage on the right-hand side as you turned up from Clonboo Cross.

Peter was a carpenter of the Master Joiner type, who took great pride in his work. He worked for a wide range of people and nearly always worked on his own. There are not too many, if any, carpenters of this quality around today. Peter did not have the benefit of current power tools or computer-aided programmes that can cut out profiles and shapes within tolerances of fractions of millimetres.

Peter had a cousin who lived in Toher up Doolan's lane by the name of Jimmy Greed. Peter did a lot of work in our house. We took off the roof of the house in 1975/1976, a job we started a few days before Christmas 1975. We had a thatched roof, the type of which is still used in some rural areas of Ireland. In most cases nowadays, the thatched cottages are found in west of Ireland, where they are tourist attractions and reflections of times gone by. Some of the tourist 'thatched cottages' are actually slated or tiled roofs, with thatch fitted on battens over the slates. However, at home the thatched roof was the genuine article. I remember the roof being thatched on a few occasions, and the timber scallops that were used to knot and tie down the straw thatch. In the latter years of thatching, river reeds were used instead of straw as they lasted longer. But in 1975 we decided to remove the thatched roof, lower the ceiling in the kitchen, and create a new inside porch. I remember the high ceiling sloped to the profile of the kitchen. It was some day, the day the thatch was taken off. I only barely remember it – I was twelve years old – but I remember loads of old thatch being taken away in tractors and trailers.

Peter Greed put on the new roof, which needed purpose-cut timbers as square walls were a rare thing. The new ceiling provided an attic space but also cut out the space above the banister of the stairs leading up into the loft bedroom. By putting in the lower ceiling and forming a new porch, the heating of the house was easier. As I remember, we also moved the range to the outside of the chimney breast at this time. Martin Sweeney from Templemore did all the plastering – no easy job, I can assure you.

The loft was the warmest room in the house, as the heat from the range rose straight up. The top of the stairs which led to the loft had a very handy landing from which to watch television below in the kitchen, or to just watch what was going on below. If you kept very quiet nobody would even know you were there. It was a great place to wait for Santa on Christmas Eve, but most times you would be hunted in to bed or you would fall asleep. One time I caught my head between the banisters (i.e. the verticals); it was easy to get your head in but on the way back out, the ears got in the way!

Depending who was 'coordeeking', it was often more entertaining than the television. After all there was only one channel, RTÉ (note, RTÉ singular) and it was only on from late afternoon until eleven or twelve at night. Oh, and by the way, the picture was black and white. It's hard to believe the progress and advances in the whole way of life, especially in technology, that have developed over the past twenty-five years or so. The way of life as described by my grandmother Sarah Doolan from when she was growing up appeared primitive to me, in the same way as my own children will not recognise the way we grew up. God knows how their children will live and the advances in technology that are yet to be discovered. (That's if we haven't self-destructed in the meantime!) It is said and it has been proven over the years, with graduates coming out of college, that the studies they undergo during those college years will be redundant in terms of the technology they will have to work with during their working years.

They used to say that the first mention of a TV in the Bible was when Our Lord was seen in the 'Bush'. A 'Bush' was the main make of TV back then, along with the old-style gramophone electric radio transistors. The days of the neighbours gathering around a radio to hear Michael O'Hehir commentating on hurling matches seem to be from a distant time in the dark ages. This gathering happened because not everyone had a radio. Today, in the modern house, there are TVs along with all sorts of electronic gadgets in every room. The kids have radios on their watches and portable DVD players.

I was out looking at a redevelopment construction site in Beaumont a few years ago, which included a Sister of Mercy nursing home. We were been shown through the nursing home by the Matron, a Clare woman married to a Tipp man as it so happens, when she brought us in to the room where Michael O'Hehir died. It was the only en suite bathroom that they had and he was their most important guest for the number of months he stayed there. She said it was the biggest funeral ever to leave the nursing home. He was indeed a legend in broadcasting and in sport generally, especially in GAA and horse-racing circles.

Getting back to the Greeds … Peter Greed died on 18 April 1982, aged sixty-two years and is buried in Killavinogue Cemetery, in past Noonan's house.

Peter's father was Tom Greed, who married Mary Bergin from Dromard, an aunt of Danny Bergin and grandaunt to Liam, Eilish and Donal. Mary Greed (*née* Bergin) died on 5 December 1961, aged seventy-four years. Tom and Mary had seven sons and two daughters: Jimmy, Paddy (locally known as 'Ransom'), Jack, Tom, Bill, Mick, Peter, Kitty and Mary.

Jimmy lived in Clonboo. He never married but had a strong relationship with Kit Fitzpatrick. Jimmy died on 27 March 1975, aged fifty-nine years.

Paddy ('Ransom') married Mary. He died on 6 September 1972, aged fifty-six years. Paddy was a carpenter and lived in Lacey Avenue, Templemore, and he had six children: Biddy, Mary (lived in Hillcrest, Lucan and died on 16 February 1999, aged forty-four years), Geraldine, Hannah, Paddy and Thomas.

Jack (RIP, d.1966) married Maureen Wolf and moved to Askeaton, Co. Limerick. They had six children: Thomas, Tony, Teresa, Ann, Mary and Katherine.

Tom married Norah. He died on 21 May 1989, aged sixty-four years. Tom worked in Dovea before starting his own building firm in the 1950s. He and Norah lived in Bank Street, Templemore, and then moved to the Roscrea Road in 1960. They had eight sons and five daughters: Tom, Johnny (RIP), Fergal, Joe, Jim (RIP), Liam, Donie and Noel (RIP), Carmel, Norah, Bernie, Trish and Maureen (RIP). I knew some of the boys as they went to school in Templemore. Jim was in my class, Liam was a bit younger than me, and Joe, who is a bit older than me, married Carmel Kirwan from Clonmore.

Bill (William), (RIP), married in Birmingham and he and his wife had three daughters: Bridget, Ellen and Mary.

Peter (RIP) lived in Clonboo, or more officially he lived in the townland of Killavinogue. Peter is mentioned above and was the only Greed that I remember living there.

Kitty (Catherine), moved to London where she married John O'Shea. She died on 14 October 1990, aged seventy-one years. They had four children: John, Mick, Margaret (RIP) and Mary. Mary and Mick are twins.

Mick (RIP) did not marry and spent most of his life in hospital.

Mary worked in Dublin and had two children, Paul, who moved to West Harrow, Middlesex and died on 21 May 1994, aged fifty-three years, and Lilly, who married Larry Daly and lives in Cork. Mary died on 29 September 1969 aged fifty-nine years.

KEENAN

Luke Keenan originally lived in the same house, but I only remember Peter Greed living there. This house was built for Luke and his wife Judy. They had a daughter called Winnie. In 1911, when the census was recorded, Luke was seventy-two years old and a widower. The form also records that his 'grand-daughter' Winifred, aged fifteen years, was in the house that night, along with three visitors: Michael Loughnane, his wife Margaret and their three-year-old son, Michael. Keenan is the spelling used for the surname in the census forms but Kenehan is also used in other records.

By all accounts, Luke was a bit of a poet. The *History of Moyne–Templetuohy* features one such poem, aptly named. The poet is celebrating getting his new house with the acre and it goes as follows:

Luke's Cottage

Farewell to the skraws and scallops,
Farewell to the soot drops and rain,
Farewell to the smoke and the cobwebs
That frequently moythered my brain.

Those filthy vile plagues are all over
And forever again I disown,
I fancy myself now in clover
Since I got a new house of my own.

Many is the journey I travelled
From Killavanoge to Roscrea,
In pursuit of a cottage and acre
And hear what the Guardians might say.

At last they agreed and consented,
Full justice to me they have shown,
They gave me a plot and a cottage
And now I can call it my own.

By plans, schemes and specifications
The Labourers Act was composed,
To better our sad situation
And pleasure and comfort disclose.

I wish all the poor men of the nation,
From Cork to the County Tyrone,
Were possessed of a cottage and acre
They freely might call it their own.

Hurrah for our brave Irish members
Who struggled by night and by day,
The labourers cause to defend it
Their actions we'll nobly display.

Brave Tanner with courage unshaken
Through Ireland his actions are known,
He secured the poor man in an acre
And a slashing fine house of his own.

By Luke Kenehan, Clonboo

DEEGAN

Tommy Deegan bought the house and the small plot of land around it in later years. The house was bounded on two sides by Tommy Deegan's land. His son Phonsie lived there for a few years and did a lovely job modernising the house and extending same. Peter and all the tradesmen who were born and lived there would be proud of the current dwelling. Phonsie married Siobhan Burke from Dareens in 2005 (see later in Deegans) and in 2008, moved to a new house that he built in Sorrellhill, near the home place. They have two children, Sarah and Thomas.

BOURKE

Johnny Bourke could be classified as a blow-in, but Johnny and Siobhan have been in Clonboo since the early 1980s. Johnny built their house himself and every time I go home he seems to be at some 'new project', especially in the garden or outside somewhere. It is one of the side effects of time off, as a secondary school teacher. Johnny has a good eye as a tradesman in his own right and has done a great job on the house. His house is next door to where Peter Greed lived, so maybe some of Peter's skill rubbed off on Johnny. Siobhan is a qualified nurse and they have four children: Mairead, John, Joanne and Maeve.

Johnny, the eldest of seven sons, built the house on a portion of his mother's field. His mother was a great woman and I fondly remember her. Her husband John died when the boys were young. There are common connections back in the Borroleigh area. John Bourke was a native of Knockakelly, Borrisoleigh, while his wife Peg's mother was a Shea from Garranagrena. My grandmother Sarah Doolan (*née* Farrell) was born and grew up in Garranagrena, Borrisoleigh. Peg's uncle Ned Shea and my grandmother, as they say in Tipperary, were always 'great', meaning they were good friends. John and Peg Bourke lived in Dromard, about a mile away from Johnny's house. Peg died on 22 June 2004 aged eighty-three years. Siobhan's mother Johanna Delaney Meehan died on 17 October 2005.

THE FAMILY OF JOHN AND MARGARET (PEG) BOURKE

Johnny Bourke married Siobhan Meehan, children Mairead, John, Joanne and Maeve
Tommy Bourke married Bernie, children John, Paul, Mairead and Bernadette
Philly Bourke married Catherine Boyle, children Cathal, Cliodhna and Sean
Paddy Bourke married Theresa Lee, children Marguerite, Robert, Padraig, Shane, Ailise, Niall and Katie
Seamus Bourke married Kathleen Cody, children Sinead, Shonagh, Eoin and Ciara
Martin Bourke
Joe Bourke married Veronica Kirwan (RIP), children Ericka, Erin and Joseph

All of these men come from a staunch GAA family. They were great servants to hurling in the parish of Clonmore, later part of J.K. Brackens, and with Seamus, Paddy and Martin wearing the county colours for Tipperary with distinction.

I used to go to Bourke's in Dromard for my summer holiday, all that distance (a bit over a mile) for a week or so. Jack Ryan from Errill (brother of Mary Nolan) used to stay there too. We were always good friends with the Bourkes and still are. Paddy used to come over to Clonboo a lot before he got married; he nearly always played cards around Christmas and slept up in the 'loft'. Seamus shared the same political outlook as the boss man and would also be over to analyse the results around election time. Johnny was always a regular visitor and still is.

GRIMES

Billy 'The Banjo' Grimes and his mother Sis lived on the turn on the other side of the road from Johnny Bourke's house. It was a dangerous bend for a while, until the County Council 'cut off the turn'. This is the term used for the council buying a bit of land at each side of the turn and forming a new triangle piece of land when both ditches are cut out, so that car drivers can see going around the bend in the road.

I often remember going in to see Sis Grimes on my way home from school in Templemore to deliver some message that she would have asked me to bring her. It is only fair to say that others would also be bringing her messages, especially Joe Bourke and also Mickey Clarke and Tom Clarke. She was a lovely woman and we always had a good chat about The Banjo.

My children always refer to the turn in the road as 'the Banjo's turn'. He was a great character and is probably deserving of a book in his own right. My memories are of a Honda 50, an entertainer, a handyman, a man that loved a drink, a great mouth-organ player, a man with great catchphrases, and one often mentioned in conversations. He competed in Flea Ceoils all over Ireland and was highly regarded and respected wherever he played.

There are several, but 'Ah, ok, I'll have a go' was a well-used part of his vocabulary.

Anybody you meet within a large area surrounding Clonboo will know The Banjo and will have a story to tell about the same Billy Grimes.

He had a brother Tommy who lived in Templemore and died on 24 February 2009. Sis (Sophia Rooney, from Garryduff) Grimes died a good few years ago, around 1980, and Billy died on 10 February 2003, aged seventy-two years. Both are buried in Templemore Cemetery.

The house was sold in recent years and the new owners, the Bourkes, have done it up and extended it. It was a small cottage with an upstairs loft and a small plot of land around it.

The earlier generation, Will (b. 1853) and Catherine (b. 1859), were grandparents to both the Banjo and Billy Grimes of Clonboo. Will and Catherine Grimes had ten children – eight sons and two daughters: Dick, Mary, Bill, Jack, Jim, Kate, Paddy, Joe, Tom and Lar. Dick, Bill and Jack were all stonemasons.

Paddy married Sophie and they had four boys: Tommy, Pat, Billy (Banjo), and Mick. Paddy died in the early 1960s, perhaps '62/'63. Will's son Lar was Billy Grimes of Clonboo's father (see later).

Johnny Bourke, who lives across the road from the Banjo's, sent a very good appreciation of the Banjo to the *Tipperary Star* and it is recalled here with the author's permission:

Banjo Grimes

Every once in a while a person comes into our midst who leaves a lasting impression on all who knew him. Such a person was William Grimes, affectionately known as 'the Banjo'. The story goes that while he was building a wall someone noticed that the blocks in the centre of the wall were about an inch away from the builders' line used to keep the wall straight. Bill solved the problem immediately. He pulled the string to the centre block and continued his work. I don't know if the person plastering the wall noticed anything but the wall is still standing.

Another story that you might appreciate occurred while he was in England. A cement block fell on his foot and he had to be taken to the doctor. He decided to wash the injured foot before presenting himself for examination. The doctor examined the foot and couldn't decide if it was swollen, so he decided as a comparison, he should have a look at the other foot but upon seeing the other foot, the doctor asked Billy if the two feet were at all even related! Billy hadn't bothered to wash the other foot at all.

Billy died on Monday 10 February [2003]. Great gloom and sadness descended on the parish of Clonmore, when news began to filter through of his death. Although he was in failing health for some time his passing was a great shock to all his many friends.

To say that Billy was different was an understatement. He was indeed a unique individual who brought colour, good humour and laughter everywhere he went. Indeed some of his sayings will still echo in the houses of Clonboo a hundred years from now and the stories that surrounded him throughout his life will always be heard in the locality. Who would ever forget his reply to the doctor who told him that age, wear and tear was causing him problems with his knee? 'That is strange,' said Bill, 'the other knee is the same age and it is perfect.' Or his reply to the Garda who stopped him while driving 'under the influence' many years ago. The Garda had been trying to overtake Bill for some time and eventually succeeded and stopped him. He began to inform Bill that he was drunk, driving in an erratic way and that the Morris Minor was making a great of movement across the road! 'That's great,' replied Bill, 'I thought myself the steering was going.'

Bill did a great deal of work around Errill and Rathdowney. Indeed you could say that Errill was his second home and there was not a person in that area that he did not know. He was involved in the building of Clonmore Hall and the Church in Errill.

The stories could go on and on. But there was another side to Bill Grimes. He was a very intelligent man who could talk about many a topic. He was very good at tracing events that had occurred in the locality, with all its people in years gone by. He loved music and all associated with the music scene. He won a few plaques and medals, rattling out tunes on the old mouth organ at the various Fleadh Cheoils down the years. Wrestling was also of interest to him and although he did not have the physique to tackle some of these big fellas himself, he always enjoyed the bouts on the television.

He loved nature and the countryside and spent many hours looking at nature programmes on TV. He always expressed a desire to visit the Blasket Islands and said that the Glen of Aherlow was the finest place he had visited. He had a great love for his home place and would have been devastated had he been forced to spend his last days elsewhere.

Alas, all is over now. The little Cabin, as he called his home, is again quiet and still. The mice he failed to catch before his passing, still run across the floor. No more will he hear again the sound of barking dogs or the crowing rooster breaking the early morning silence. Bill has gone to a great life where his knee will never pain him again. One can see him surrounded by his many friends who have gone before him, listening to his many stories and great sayings. And if there is music there I'm sure Bill will blast out a few tunes himself.

It was great to have known Banjo. Thanks Bill for the laughter and all the wonderful memories. May you rest in peace.

Johnny Bourke

TYNAN

The last family who lived in this house and the only family I ever remember living there were Tynans, but they only moved in there in and around 1958-1960. The first family to live there were Phil Mockler and his wife, in the 1930s. The second family to live there was that of Joe Ryan. They later moved to Toher and had four children: Fergal, Johnny, Margaret and Mary. I remember Johnny and Mary going to school in Toher. Fergal and Margaret are a small bit older and I know the house, in a short lane beside Loughnane's on the left-hand side. We used to pass it going to Kyle or Rathdowney. I think that house was built around 1929, when my own grandmother Sarah Doolan came to live in Clonboo.

The Tynans lived near the Grimeses, on the same side of the road, right next to Carrols/Taylors in an adjoining house. Johnny and Bridget had seven children: Mary, Breda, Margaret, Statia, Catherine, and twins John and Tom. That was a big family when I was growing up and nowadays it would be almost unheard of, as we all live to the average of 2.6 children per family unit – whatever that means! Bridget came from Killea and there were twelve children in her family: Billy (RIP), Stephen (RIP), Kathleen, Nancy, Winnie, Mary (RIP), Bridget (RIP), Peggy (RIP), Theresa, Agnes, Tommy and Mick.

Johnny lived in Lisduff in his early years, at the Terrace, before moving to Clonboo. His father and mother lived there, Tom and Mary Jo. There were five children in the family: Maire, Tom, Johnny, Statia and Kitty. Both Kitty and Johnny have passed away. Statia died in 2010. She was married to a Maher and lived in Roscrea. Johnny worked in Lisduff quarry (which will be mentioned later) and I remember him well, cycling up the road after a day's work. I think he used to cycle with Richie Fanning who drove a lorry in the quarry and lived opposite Tommy Deegan's, near the cross of Clonboo. When he came home he was busy again.

I remember a story about Johnny trying to put one or two of the children to bed one night. There were lots of single travellers who went around the rural parts of Ireland all year round. They would come into an area, do a bit of work with a farmer, sleep in the hay barn, get a bit of food and a few bob, and after a while move on without ever overstaying their welcome or over stretching the generosity of the local people. By their nature, these men were older looking than their years and often the worse for wear, depending on the weather and the previous night's accommodation. One such man was Jack Moyney. There was an element of fear in children's eyes at the prospect of meeting one of these lads, especially at night-time on the road, but there was never any reason to be fearful.

Johnny Tynan was having fierce trouble in getting one or two of the kids to come in and go to bed one night so when all else failed he went out into the yard and said, 'If ye don't come in I will give ye to Jack Moyney.' As soon as he said it a voice spoke up, 'You can keep your feckin' children, I have no use for them either.' It was Jack Moyney who happened to be passing on the road at that exact same time!

Johnny had to give up work after some health trouble. In later years he moved to Celbridge to live with his daughter Catherine, and he died on 11 December 2004, aged seventy-three. Catherine married Bernard Regan on 17 June 2005.

Bridget Tynan was a redhead and sometimes showed her temper, but in a nice way. I always got on well with her and often called in to visit her and Johnny. It's a thing that never happens nowadays, children calling in to see or visit older people and families. I suppose the times have changed and now there are so many news reports of missing children and terrible things happening to children. You can't blame parents for being so mindful and protective of their kids. Bridget died on 17 November 1999, aged sixty-four years.

Of all the children, I think only the twin boys had red hair, and they are as gentle as lambs. All the children are moved away from Clonboo, to various places including Dublin, Celbridge, Kilkenny, Roscommon, Borrisoleigh, etc. Mary lives in Clonmel. Breda married Tom Gleeson on 8 January 1985. They live in Kilkenny and they have eight children: Michelle, Amanda, David, Shane, Luke, Lorna, Ben and Martha. Margaret married Tommy Mulligan on 18 August 1990. They live in Roscommon and have one daughter, Shauna. Statia married Johnny Treacy on 30 March 1985 and they live in Borrisoleigh. They have five children: John, Martin, Emma, Jamie and Christopher. John Tynan married Hazel Wallace on 4 June 2004. Tom married Mary Campion on 29 January 1999. They live in Kilkenny and have two children, Jory and Oisin.

Ger Maher from County Limerick and Ann Carroll (a daughter of Bobby Carroll), along with their two daughters Katie and Louise have lived there for the past few years. Sadly Ger passed away in 2010.

CARROLL/TAYLOR

Peggy Carroll lived next door, adjoining Tynans. She married Dan Taylor in her middle years and then the house became known as Taylors'. Dan came from Castleiney, a neighbouring townland of the famed Loughmore/Castleiney parish, probably one of the greatest GAA parish clubs for their devotion to the game in the county and their relative size. There have been more successful clubs and more famous clubs that produced more county players, but I don't think there has ever been such a true and consistent club at all levels in football and hurling. In Clonmore we regard Loughmore/Castleiney as our greatest rivals. Over the years, there were many bitter struggles and it is fair to say Clonmore always raised their game against Loughmore over and above their ability. But at the back of it all, there is always great admiration and respect on both sides.

So anyway, Dan was accepted into the parish and my strongest memories of Dan were his gentle disposition and his ever-faithful dog, which went everywhere with him. He always had a small Jack Russell for bits of hunting but mainly for company. I also remember Carroll's for budgies; hearing them chirping away when you would go in the door. I don't know how that poor dog slept in front of the fire with all the noise those birds used to make, but they were always beautiful colours, greens and yellows in particular.

Originally Denis and Liz Carroll (Liz originally from Clonakenny) lived there. Denis was from Moyglass/Fethard. They had four boys and four girls. I remember Din Carroll; he died on 12 April 1973, aged eighty years. He died a few months before my own grandmother Catherine Butler who died in July 1973. Liz Carroll died on 23 September 1981, aged ninety-one years. Denis and Liz had four boys and four girls. The boys were Bill, Pat, Jack and Mick, and the girls were Peggy, Una, Mary and Josie.

Bill married Josephine Taylor. He died on 18 September 2000. Pat married Mary Callaghan from Dunkerrin. Jack married Mary Maher from Clonmore. Mick married Kitty Lee.

Peggy married Dan Taylor from Castleiney. Una married Jimmy Heaney. May died in her twenties in 1950. Josie died when she was only eight months old.

Jack Carroll died in 2004. He was a good friend of the family and a good friend of my father's. He loved playing cards. There are some number of great card players in Heaven today, as most people around home say.

Dan Taylor died on 10 March 1988, aged sixty years. Peg Taylor died on 2 May 2009, in her mid-eighties. She was the last of the Carrolls, that generation are all dead now, but the next generation are spreading their wings, although not in Clonboo.

SKEHAN

Opposite Tynan's and Carroll's, in ruins (or ruins almost gone), lived Skehans, James and his wife, Mary. James was born in 1834 and Mary was born in 1848. They were married in 1876 and did not have any children. Their niece Myra Gavin (b. 1902) also lived there; she went to Toher school and was later the teacher in Toher National School, from around 1923 to 1940. There was also a Veronica Gavin who started school in Toher in 1917 from Clonboo. She must have been a sister of Myra's.

The house was recorded as being in the townland of Killavinogue, which I thought had finished at the Banjo's. Grimes's is the first house in Clonbough Lower, but obviously Killavinogue continues along the other side of the road up to at least the lane onto Deegan's bog. When Skehans' house went up for sale, Pat Laffin bought it and the field behind it. Pat Laffin was married to Julia Bourke, a sister of John Bourke's and that's how Bourke's got to be the owners of that field and Johnny Bourke built his house there.

LANE INTO TOMMY DEEGAN'S BOG

Will McCormack lived up this lane, a good bit up. He did not access the house from the Clonboo side. We used this route going to cut turf in our own bog, but Will used to go through Tommy Deegan's main house at Sorrellhill off the main road. Will's mother was Mary (b. 1834). In the 1911 census it was recorded that William McCormack was sixty-six years of age that year and that he lived there with his sister Catherine McCormack, who was sixty-eight years of age. The McCormacks were both single and their address was Ballysorrell Little, Killavinoge.

The house is long gone, but Will died around the 1930s. At the time of his death Luke Keenan was living with him. The story goes that Luke, being the younger man, did the business end of the work, such as going for messages, collecting the weekly pension on a Thursday, etc. Will Cormack died on a Thursday, time of the day unknown, but the story goes that Luke found him dead in the bed, but collected the pension before telling anyone. When the Gardaí came later in the day, they asked Luke some questions about Will Cormack: name; address; age; married or single? To the last question Luke answered, 'neither'. When asked to explain, Luke said, 'Will never looked at a woman in his life.'

Pynes also lived up this lane, not as far in as Will Cormack. Catherine (b.1836) was the mother, and the children were Jim (b.1874) and Catherine (b.1879). The lane into Tommy Deegan's bog used to be known as Pynes's Lane, and still goes by that identification.

DOOLAN'S GARDEN

There was a house on a small plot of land to the left of the lane into Deegan's bog, but on the road side, about seventy-five or eighty years ago, known as Doolan's Garden.

In the Valuation Office of Ireland schedule dating back from 1856, there is mention of Doolans:

1856 to 1863, James Doolan with a change to Patrick Doolan.
1867 to 1876, Michael Doolan and Patrick Doolan, with a holding of forty-five acres.

STAMP

On the same site, or beside Doolan's Garden, is a new house built by Tom and Catherine Stamp. Tom, a devout Dublin GAA supporter, married Catherine Butler and they have three children: Eamonn, Joseph and Aine. Tom decentralised (a word in common usage nowadays to describe a move from Dublin to the countryside) and Catherine moved down the road from the home place, a quarter of a mile or less, to a new house built in 2003. Tom works as a solicitor and Catherine works in the civil service. Tom has settled into the country way of life well. He has to leave the light on, as it gets very dark when the lights are turned off in the nearest built-up area – Fitzpatrick's pub in Clonmore village. Tom is a passionate supporter of Dublin GAA and travels in all weather to watch and support his beloved Dubs. His sons are beginning to show signs of different county allegiances, which must be a compliment to their mother. Once they support a county and show an interest in the native sports, Tom will never have a problem having a quiet pint in Clonmore.

TUOHY

James and Margaret Tuohy lived in Killavinogue with their four daughters. I couldn't find any later proof of them staying around the area. I'm not exactly sure where the house was located, other than it was above Shehan's and not up as far as Maher's. James was born in 1857; his wife Margaret was born in 1877. At the time of the of the 1911 census, the four girls living in the house were: Catherine, aged fifteen; Margaret, aged thirteen; Mary, aged eleven, and Elizabeth, aged nine.

MEAGHER

Michael and Catherine Meagher lived somewhere between Banjo Grimes's and Meaney's. They were living in Clonboo when the 1911 census was taken. They may have just lived for a short while in Thady Maher's parents' house, or they may have lived in a house that my father vaguely remembers was around the Crooked Stile area. Michael Meagher was born in Co. Tipperary in 1866 and his wife Catherine was born in Co. Limerick in 1869. We also know that Michael was a farmer and Catherine was a National School teacher. She retired as Principal of the girls' school in Clonmore in 1912. She was only fifty then, so maybe they moved from the area at that time.

MAHER

Thady Maher and his wife Kathleen (*née* Carey) live in a house built in December 1990 on the left-hand side of the road. They have two children, Sadie and John.

Behind this new house was Thady's parents' house, which was built in the early 1800s by O'Rourkes, who were land agents for some of the landlords in the area. The O'Rourkes were very involved in the effort to get a school built in Toher to replace the existing hedge school. This new school was built in the 1830s.

Back in 1996, Thady Maher's mother received a letter from a Mr Innis O'Rourke III of Glen Cove, New York, USA. The letter was written on 24 November 1996. He said that he and his wife visited Clonboo in 1987 and called to the house of Johnny Butler, who told them that their ancestors lived in the house then owned by Mahers. That was back in the 1850s, and the landowner at the time was The Earl of Carrick. They were enquiring about any information of graves of their ancestors in the area.

The next owner was Tommy Bergin, a retired priest, who sold on to Tom Deegan, who was an uncle to Mary Clarke (*née* Gleeson), sometime before 1920. Denis Carroll lived there for a while; he rented it while his own house was being built nearby. Pierse Hayes and his wife also rented the house for a while. They had two children who went to school in Toher: Billy and Peggy.

Tom Deegan sold the house and farm to John Maher in 1943 (Nov./Dec.). There is a reference in the excellent three-volume book *History of Moyne–Templetuohy, A Story of a Tipperary Parish*, about the sale of Clonboo House with a farm of approximately ninety acres and some outhouses for £2,200, having failed to sell at public auction. The lands were described as being of prime dairying and fattening quality with an appropriate amount of tillage, and the two-storey house having been recently refurbished. The sale was reported to have been on 27 November/4 December 1943.

John Maher's parents were Dan and Ellen Maher. Dan died on 29 January 1903, aged fifty-seven years, while his wife Ellen died on 9 November 1919, aged fifty-three years. They had five children: John, Ned, Bridget, Mary Kate, and a baby that died at seven months old. Mary Kate died on 15 April 1903, aged seven years. Ned died in the late 1930s (28 May 1938) and Bridget never married. They lived in behind us, further up the lane. Bridget lived in this house while John went to Loughmore. He came back to Clonboo at the first opportunity, when he bought the house and land from Tom Deegan in 1943. Bridgie Maher, who lived up the lane, inside us, died on 17 October 1954. At the time of the 1911 census, Ellen was a widow and head of the family, aged fifty. Living there at that time were her daughter Bridget, aged twenty-three, her son John, aged twenty-one, and her son Edward, aged twenty.

The make-up of the land and the dividing of the farm into two parts is later discussed, but in essence there were, overall, seventy-five Irish acres. The front part (our house) got thirty-six acres and the inside part (Maher's) got thirty-nine Irish acres on account of it being off the road.

John Maher was married to Josephine Ryan from Drom and they had five children: Danny, Thady, Eileen, Joan and Eamonn. They came to Clonboo in February 1944. Josephine died on 29 April 1994, and John Maher died on 4 September 1945. I often called to Mrs Maher for apples and to see new lambs, and I always called her Mrs Maher. Johanna Ryan, Mrs Maher's mother (Thady's grandmother) from Drom, died on 18 May 1954.

As I mentioned, Thady married Kathleen Carey from Ballysorrel and they have two children, John and Sadie. They lived in Ballysorrel after they got married, before coming to live in Clonboo. Thady's a solid card player, and, along with John, is part of the card game on Christmas night at home.

Sadie married Eamonn Bergin, and they live up the road past Neddy Guilfoyle's, on the same side of the road as Guider's. They have five children: Jack, Edward, Martin Sarah and Kate.

Danny is living in the home place. Eamonn died on 2 August 1973. Eileen became a nun; she died on 22 October 2002, aged sixty-four, and is buried outside Kilkenny. She was a great organ player and often played for the choir at Mass in Clonmore.

Joan married Tommy Carroll from Ballybrista, Templemore (in the parish of Loughmore) and they have six children: Denis, Eamonn, John, Josephine, Aileen and Mairead.

CROOKED STILE

There used be a stile, or stone-like wedge gap, in the ditch at the turn in the road down from our entrance where people could get through but animals could not. It was used for a shortcut down to Maher's across the field. Our field on the left-hand side used to always be known as the Crooked Stile field. In those days all fields had to have names so that when the young lads were being sent to get cattle or sheep, or to thin turnips or turn hay, they would be able to follow instructions. Also, if you were bringing in cows and saw a ewe or a cow sick, you could say to your father that there was a ewe caught in a wire fence in the Wellfield, or one of Dan Guider's suckler cows in the Three Corner field, or you could tell your mother there was lovely mushrooms or wild blackberries in the quarryfield, etc. Nowadays, with all the ditches gone, all the names are worthless and anyway the young lads wouldn't do the jobs unless they had a quad bike equipped with an MP3 player. The automatic 'hurley in hand' for beheading thistles has been replaced by designer gadgets and four-wheeled engine-powered skateboards.

A hurley or two were always left outside the front door of any house where there were a few young lads, always ready and handy for a quick game in the yard or a bit of belting the ball against the barn wall. Any time you left the house to go down the fields for cows or cattle, the hurley was in hand, like part of your clothes, like putting on your shoes.

NOLAN

There was a house down at the Crooked Stile before 1930 but no remains are evident today. The Nolans lived there: James (born 1823), an army pensioner and his wife Mary (born 1831). James was born in Laois while Mary was a Tipp woman. I don't have any record of Nolan children living there. It may well be that the Nolans moved here when they retired.

MEANEY

Meaneys lived at the end of our lane on other side of the road. I think Mick was the father's name. He had six children: Mary (b.1851), Kitty (b.1853), Mag, Sarah, Mick (b.1856) and Tom. They are all dead now, RIP. Kitty died in 1933, while Mary was the last of the family to die, in 1943. Mag and Sarah went to America and never came home. Mick and Tom worked locally.

When the girls were in the States, they used to send letters home along with a few bob every month or so. John Butler, my grandfather would read the letters for Mary as she could not read or write. The postman would come down the road (not a very regular occurrence in those days as there was no junk mail) to deliver the letter to Mary. A few minutes would pass, as the letter and its contents were removed, and then Mary would come across the road for my grandfather to read the letter. The usual news would come from America until one day the postman came, delivered the letter, and after a few minutes had passed there was still no sign of Mary. Later that day, Mary was over doing a few jobs and my grandfather said, 'Did you not get the letter from America this morning?' Mary replied, 'Yeah, themselves and their feckin letters!' There was no money in the letter that month!

When the last of the Meaneys died, the Carey family of Templequain, Errill got the house and two acres as next of kin. One of the Carey daughters, Mary Ann and her husband, Michael Caudy lived there until 1947. They had a family of four at the time: Eddie, Margaret, Stephen and Peadar. They went to Toher school. In 1947, they went to live in Gurteen, Castleiney. They had other children there, but their names are unknown.

After 1947, Johnny Hennessy, his wife Kathleen and son John lived there for a number of years. They rented the house from the Careys. Peter Carey is named as the owner in the Valuations Office records. The Hennesseys stayed there until the early 1950s, when they moved to live in Lisdaleen, Templetuohy, where they had twins, Adelade and Margaret. Adelade married a Leahy.

Thady Maher bought the house and the couple of acres around the late 1950s or early 1960s and he cleared off the ditches to open it all into the fields around, which he owned. That clearing of the ditches may not have been done for a few years after Thady bought it, as I vaguely remember some remnants of ditches or ruins in that field. I was born in December 1962, so I'm not sure if that's correct.

I have the original copies of the bills for Mary Meaney's funeral in 1942. My grandfather must have taken care of the arrangements. The date of the invoice is 20 January 1942, from Thomas Davey, Hardware, Timber and Seed Stores; Family Grocer, Wine, Spirit and Tobacco Merchant. There is also a note at the top left-hand corner that says 'Agent for Mooney's Manures'. It also proclaims that the shop contains Guinness XX Stout, Jameson's Old Malt and Bass Pale Ale and that postal establishment-motor hearses and all funeral requisites are supplied.

There is a caveat on the docket which reads, 'all my seeds are selected with the greatest care; but I give no warranty with them, either express or implied; neither do I guarantee any of them, nor will I be responsible for the Crop' That is a fairly good exclusion clause, which would impress the current generation of legal 'wigs' and test their ability to get a drafting job in Thomas Davey's establishment.

The docket simply reads, in ink handwriting, the following:

To Undertaking of the late Mary Meaney,
Including Coffin, Hearse and Habit £12-17-6
1 Bottle of Whiskey £1-0-0

1 Firkin of Stout £2-11-6
Tea 1/- Sugar 1/-2-0
Bread 1/6-1-6

£16-12-6

January 20th '43 By Cash
With Thanks

Two one-penny stamps were stuck at the bottom to make it a legal document.

Agent for Mooney's Manures.
HARDWARE, TIMBER AND SEED STORES.

Templemore, _January 20th_ 19_42_

M__r. John Butler Clonboo__

BOUGHT OF THOMAS DAVEY

Family Grocer

WINE, SPIRIT AND TOBACCO MERCHANT

GUINNESS'S XX STOUT, JAMESON'S OLD MALT and BASS'S PALE ALE

Posting Establishment—Motor Hearses and all Funeral Requisites supplied

All my Seeds are selected with the greatest care; but I give no warranty with them, either express or implied; neither do I guarantee any of them, nor will I be responsible for the Crop.
GUYS

To Undertaking
of the late Mary Meaney
Including coffin Hearse
                    Habit £ 12-17-6
1 Bottle Whiskey   1-0-0
1 Firkin Stout   2-11-6
Tea 1/- Sugar 1/-   2-0
      Bread 1/6   £   1-6
                  £ 16·12-6
Jany 20th '43 By Cash £ 16-12-6

With Thanks

BUTLER

Our own house is next on the road, and we will pick up more details in Chapter 8, where all the Butlers get a mention!

My mother and father live there now and are in good health, thank God. It was of course a busier house years ago, and still is on the days the grandchildren come around. These days Eamonn, Joe, Aine, Kiera and Zoe keep the old folks on their toes and they wouldn't like it any other way. The three older grandchildren, Aoife, Sean and Sarah also make occasional visits. Myself and Sarah make the odd run on a Sunday afternoon, and myself and Sean always call for dinner en route to Thurles for a match. Sean likes a good country dinner on a Sunday! Johnny likes to go 'early' to matches in Thurles (Matt says that Johnny likes to see the men painting the white lines on the pitch), whereas the younger lads like to call to the County Bar, Jim Kennedy's or Bowe's before the match, to savour the atmosphere and join in the banter. As a result, the dinner is always early on a Sunday in Clonboo. You recall *D'Unbelievables* when Pat Shortt and John Kenny are talking at the back of the church … John says to Pat, 'We had the dinner at eight o'clock this morn' so that we could have a right good run at the day.' Anyway, I have no problem with an early dinner and was often glad to have it as my breakfast after a Saturday night down in the village, in Fitzpatrick's.

While I live in Lucan, the rest of the current generation live around the home place in Tipp. I am the oldest, then came Ned, then Catherine, followed by Pat and Matt. Catherine got married to Tom Stamp and they live about a quarter of a mile down the road, with their three children: Eamonn, Joe and Aine. In 2008, with the construction industry in severe decline, Pat decided to return to education at Mary Immaculate Teaching College and at the same time moved back to live in the home place in Clonboo. Matt married Niamh Buckley and they live in Templetuohy with their two daughters, Kiera and Zoe. Matt and Niamh received planning permission for a new house, which they intend building near the Crooked Stile. My brother Ned died tragically on 11 August 1987 at the young age of nineteen. It was a devastating time for our family and is still a desperately sad memory that will always remain. We will never forget Ned and the fine young man he was. He was a hard-working and diligent farmer, who perfected his trade while attending Agricultural College in Multyfarnham, Co. Westmeath. He was very well liked and had a very wide circle of friends. I will never forget the day I heard the news that Ned had died. I was down thinning turnips in Skehan's with my father, when Mick Ryan from the Hill came into the field with the sad news. My father went up home to tell my mother, while I walked up home alone, trying to take in the whole shock of it all. Ned enjoyed life; he loved everything about the land and the farming business. He attended every 'field evening' that was held or organised anywhere in the surrounding area, near or far. He won several trophies for stock judging. He knew and enjoyed his work; farming was his life at work and leisure time. We miss him but he is never too far away.

A lot of my own memories of growing up are recorded in Chapter 6.

FERMOYLE

Jimmy Fermoyle originally lived near Guider's, before moving to a house next door to us on the right-hand side. His father, also named James (b.1870) worked for a number of years in Dan Deegan's.

Jimmy married Molly Morrissey and they had three children: Jimmy, Molly and Margaret. Jimmy married Mary Grimes and they had two daughters, Esther and Helen. Esther married Gerry Carroll and moved to Two-Mile Borris where they have two children of their own, Michelle and Diarmaid. Helen married Martin Ryan from Ballycahill, and they have a son called Paul. They live in the same house, but it is a very different house today, as extensive work has been carried out. Martin did nearly all the work himself and it is a great credit to his patience and commitment to the task, which became a labour of love, as far as I could tell. He might disagree and say it was a right pain in the rear end. I'm sure it would have been easier to knock it but it was good to keep the general outline of the original house for posterity.

Molly married Pat Hanrahan and they had three children: Johnny, Jim and Mary. Johnny and Jim did not marry, but Mary married Oliver Brown.

The other sister married a man named Casserley who was a soldier in the Irish army, stationed in Templemore during the war. They had two children, Raymond and Margaret.

Being our closest neighbours, Fermoyle's would have been the house that I visited most as a young boy. I went on lots of trips with Jimmy Fermoyle, on the ass and cart, down the bog lane to Morrissey's to feed a few cattle. I would have spent time on the bog but it was worth it for the great cup of tea that Mary would make. I liked a good strong cup of tea and still do. Mary's tea was always guaranteed to be strong. Jimmy had a few acres of hay every year and this would usually be trammed (traymed). It's amazing that on someone else's farm you worked harder and enjoyed the work more than at home. My mother says the same about eating, that a child would eat something in a stranger's house that would only be thrown out if she made it at home.

There was a gap in the ditch at Fermoyle's, so I didn't even have to go out on the road to get there as I cut across the field. The story goes that when I was young (very young), I gave Esther and Helen a cat which they became very fond of and the cat was so well treated that it stayed at Fermoyle's. As happens, people have disagreements and we occasionally had differences of opinion. My mother and father always knew when there was a falling out, because from our kitchen table they could see me coming through the hole in the hedge with the cat under my arms. In the event of a row I would take back the cat. But I always gave it back when a suitable cooling-off time had passed, like an hour or two. I had good times at Fermoyle's and when I went down home to Tipp my own son Sean used to often go out to

Fermoyle's (Ryan's now) to spend some time with Paul Ryan.

Jimmy Fermoyle died on 21 October 1982, aged seventy years. Mary Fermoyle passed away on 31 March 2002 at the age of sixty-nine years. When Ann visited Clonboo in the 1980s, she stayed at Fermoyle's and Mary was very good to her. I often think of Mary when I leave the tea bag in the cup of boiling water a bit longer than normal and end up having a strong cup of tea!

MOLLOY

Mick Molloy lived right at the end of the bog lane on the other side of the road from Grimes. Mick (b.1882) never married and lived there himself. He had two or three sisters, one of the sisters was Margaret (b.1881). One of the sisters married Danny Morrissey, while one married a Carroll from Firke, and the other Sylvester Campion from Rathdowney. Mick Molloy's parents were Patrick (b.1831) and Mary (b.1841) Molloy.

GRIMES

In 1948, Lar Grimes and his wife Nell Kiely came to live in Clonboo. Grimes's house was originally built in 1935 for Mick Molloy. Lar's father was Will Grimes, who had eight sons and two daughters: Paddy, Lar, Bill, Tom, Jim, Joe, Jack, Dick, Mary and Kate. I remember Lar Grimes and his wife Nell, a lovely woman. Lar and Nell had five children: Eileen, Jimmy, Larry, Billy and Mary.

Eileen was the youngest and she got married and moved to Ballinrobe, Co. Mayo, when she married Peter Gormely and had four girls: Siobhan, Carmel, Mairead and Sheila. They are all married. Siobhan married Kevin Murphy, Carmel married Kevin Feeney, Mairead married Alan Rogers and Sheila married Andy Walshe.

Jimmy died on 15 March 1959 at the young age of seventeen years.

Larry married Kitty and they lived in the Park in Templemore, where they had two children, Lar and Mary Ellen. Lar married Samantha Shanahan and Mary Ellen married Brendan Collins and they live near Drom on the road to Borrisoleigh.

Mary married Jimmy Fermoyle and lived about 100 yards down the road.

Billy married Maureen Sullivan from Barna, Dunkerrin and they stayed in the home house and had four children: Liam, Sean, Maura and Laurence. Liam got married a few years ago and built a fine house beside the home place. Maura married Gordon Conroy and moved to Portlaoise, where they have two children, Joanne and Liam. Sean and Laurence have built new houses for themselves in Cobbs, on the way into Templemore. Billy's love of music has passed down to the children. Sean and Lar are both accomplished musicians and singers and we have had many good days and nights at weddings and other social occasions where they have played.

LIAM GRIMES

Billy and Maureen's eldest son, Liam married Michelle Carroll from Coolderry, near Birr, Co. Offaly on 8 September 2001 and they live next door to the home place in a new house. I only found out in recent times that Michelle comes from the same parish as Tom Parlon, who is the current Chief Executive of the Construction Industry Federation. It was Tom who told me that he knew the Carroll family. It is funny how the world moves around, as Tom would have been better known at home in Tipp in his role as a past President of the IFA (Irish Farmers' Association), then I got to know him in his job as a Progressive Democrats TD for Offaly and in his government post of junior minister with responsibility for the Office of Public Works, and now he is Director General of the Construction Industry Federation, which heads up an industry in which I am involved.

DOWN THE BOG LANE

There were three houses down the bog lane: Myrons's, Morrissey's and Delahunty's.

MYRONS (MYRENS)

There were four children in the family: Tommy, Mick, Jimmy and Mary. The father was Michael (b.1843) and the mother's name was Mary (b.1858). Mick (b.1893) worked on our farm for a number of years and died in the late 1950s. Tommy (b.1895) married Kathy Grady (originally from Littleton) and moved to Clonmore. My memory of Tommy Myrons is undoubtedly Sweet Afton cigarettes – I don't think I ever saw him without them. He lived beside Billy Guider on the left-hand side of the road, near Ballysorrel Lane.

MORRISSEY

Jer Morrissey (b.1846) and his wife Mary (b.1850) lived almost at the end of the bog lane, at the entrance to the bog. I was often down around the house, but that was twenty years after anyone lived there. Jer and Mary had two sons, Martin (b.1876) and Paddy (b.1881). Jimmy Fermoyle's mother was a first cousin of Martin and Paddy.

Martin and Paddy died within days of each other in the 1950s. There were also two daughters, Ellen (b.1878) and Mary (b.1880). I often went foddering cattle on an ass and cart with Jimmy Fermoyle down to Morrissey's, as Jimmy got the place after the brothers died.

DELAHUNTY

John Delahunty and his wife Mary also lived down the Bog Lane. John (b.1885) was a gardener, and his wife Mary was born in 1881. There is no record of any children.

CLONBOO BOG

We never cut turf in Clonboo Bog but I did some time down there with the Bourkes, Neddy Guilfoyle, Jimmy Fermoyle and Billy Grimes. As a young fella you were often sent to give a day to someone in the bog – bottled thae (not tea) wrapped in a cloth – the air so pure you'd eat anything that was put in front of you. I loved catchin' turf, but I was never allowed cut turf and I hated barrowing turf, especially during wet summers when you would have to push wet turf ages to get dry ground. I suppose futtin' turf was no joke either.

Various 'rights' were allotted to farms, lands and households over the years. Examples of such rights were rights of way, rights of pasture and grazing, rights of entry and rights of turbary. These rights were collectively known as 'appurtenant rights'. Initially, the Land Commission had no power to issue such rights, but various Acts have subsequently been passed to confer such powers to the Commission. The Land Acts of 1931 and 1965, along with various amendments and Practice Directions, including the latest in 1998, have formalised these powers.

People got plots of turf as a result of turbary rights that were given with land and farms. The right to take turf for fuel in a house was a right of turbary. This right was very valuable and related to the dwelling house on the land and not to the land in general. There were various disputes about the exact definition of the right. The turbary right, in some cases, related to the quantity of turf that could be removed, while other turbary rights referred to the removal of bog mould for use as manure only.

These rights were written on the folio of the land, as opposed to the right written on the folio of the dwelling house. Enforcement was always difficult in relation to what use you were making of the turf you removed and which house the turf was delivered to. That is why various families worked in the bog on different people's plots of turf. The help given in cutting turf was rewarded by cutting some turf for yourself.

We did not cut turf in Clonboo bog but had turbary rights in the bog behind Maher's house, where many a gallon of thae was drank and several buckets of sweat lost. We went into the bog by car through Skehan's field, in past where Jim Pynes and Will Cormack lived, although there weren't even ruins there at that time. When we walked to the bog we went through Thady Maher's fields, up the lane from our own house in Clonboo.

We had an ass at home for a few years. I drove the tractor around the farm when I was about fifteen years old. Before I was allowed drive the tractor, I would drive the ass and cart. He was a lazy ass and you would have to give him a few belts to get him moving. He always had a long, sad face and I could not but feel sorry for him. If I was taking him to the bog to work, I would have to beat the lard out of him to get him there and you would have thought that he'd never make it home. But as soon as you turned him for home he would gallop all the way. He was the greatest faker of all time. 'You would have to beat an ass to get him to go to the bog but he would gallop home!'

Author's Note: *All council houses built got one acre of land. The house was always built tight to the corner of the plot, so that the owner could get maximum use of the piece of land to sow vegetables and graze a cow. In later years, the plot size was reduced to half an acre, such as at Tynan's and Carroll's.*

GUILFOYLE

Martin Guilfoyle married Brigid Delaney from Barna, Templetuohy. His mother was Kate Guilfoyle (b.1824). Martin was born in 1861 and he had a sister, Mary who was born 1859. Mary was deaf. Martin and his wife Brigid had two children, Neddy and Catherine. Brigid's sister Mary also came to live there with them and she died around 1963/64. Brigid herself died in 1954.

Neddy was seventeen when his father died and Neddy himself died on 17 July 2004. He was born in October 1913 but had never married. He was a great age of ninety when he passed away, and only spent a short time in hospital. Another card player in heaven! He used to always come down on Christmas night and was likely to get cross if the cards were not coming too good for him. I think some of the others, especially Paddy Bourke, liked to rise him to add a bit of excitement to the game. All the card players that came on Christmas night had their own ways and their own sayings. Toby Maher used to curse his luck or his hand of cards if there was a 'red four' dealt to him. Dan Maher was capable of playing the cards in unusual ways or doing unorthodox things, just to cause confusion or start an argument. All part of the craic!

Catherine married Bob Carroll and moved to the Derries, Errill, where they had five children: Bobby, Martin, Jack, Sadie and Patricia. Robert (Bob) Carroll died on 25 July 1978, aged eighty-four years.

There were always lovely apples in Guilfoyle's orchard, the only problem being the orchard was at the other side of the yard. You had to cross the yard to get in and they always had a dog or two. I'm not saying anything more about it, but where there is a will there is a way. Nowadays, it's hard to get children to eat fruit from a bowl in front of them. If they had to take their lives in their hands to get an apple maybe they would appreciate it more. Simple pleasures of life … how innocent …

yet a good lesson in the experiences of life.

Neddy was a great man for a bag of Emerald sweets and always had a supply of red lemonade. That reminds me of another character that came around the area, Frank Rooney. Frank had the travelling shop, a Volkswagon van, a bit like a Hiace van, with groceries and household commodities. Frank called to Neddy and I think Sis Grimes (I'm not sure about anyone else on the road). If you needed anything, your mother could send you up to get it from 'Rooney'. I never knew him as Frank. Apart from Rooney calling, Neddy often travelled by pushbike to Clonmore for messages or sometimes to the town. Like Peggy Taylor, I well remember Neddy walking his bicycle up the steep hill at the railway bridge. Again like Peggy, he would freewheel down at the other side. In those days there was no help with gear changes on the bicycles, and if anything, the sheer size and weight of the bike's frame made it hard enough to even walk beside it and push up the hill.

An appreciation of Neddy was printed in the *Tipperary Star* on 10 September 2004:

On Friday 11 July, the death occurred at St Joseph's Hospital, Nenagh, of Edward Guilfoyle, Clonboo, Templetuohy. Although at an advanced age his passing brought great sadness to all his many friends in the locality. Neddy was born in 1913 and he had one sister, Catherine, who married Bob Carroll, of the Derries, Errill. He lived his long life in his native Clonboo and only spent a few days in hospital before his passing. It was wonderful that his nieces, nephews and good friend Mary Nolan were able to look after him so well in later years when his health started to fail and that he was able to live at home. And home was so important to Neddy. He loved farming and was still involved in cattle rearing up to recent times. His trip to the mart was always something that he looked forward to, but he had a special love for the bog, and spent many summers there saving the turf. Indeed there are many stories associating Neddy with the bog, but we will not dwell on them here. Suffice to say that his neighbours could recall many of these episodes with at least a little smile. Neddy had a fond love of hurling matches and in his younger days would have travelled, often by train, to the different games. He also played the game of cards. It is unlikely that he would have been able to hold his own with some of the top card sharks, but he liked the game. His colleagues might not always agree with the way he played his hand but Neddy was usually right – at least he thought so. However, time changes everything, and another house in Clonboo has become silent. No more smokes rises from the chimney to tell his neighbours that Neddy was alive and ok. His little garden plot where he grew his many fine vegetables over the years is overgrown with weeds and nettles. The bog he loved so well is now in purple bloom.

Neddy's ninety-two years on this earth has come to an end, but his spirit will forever dwell among the little fields of his native Clonboo.

May he rest in peace.

BERGIN

Eamonn Bergin married Sadie Maher from Clonboo (Thady and Kathleen's daughter) on 23 August 1996, and they built a new house a number of years ago. Eamonn moved from Camlin, a neighbouring parish, while Sadie only moved up the road, albeit having spent her younger years in Ballysorrel. They have five children: Jack, Edward, Martin, Sarah and Kate. The Bergin children are regular visitors to our house in Clonboo where they spend a lot of time with my mother. They just call her 'B'. They always got on well with the folks at home and continue that friendship.

GUIDER

Nowadays Dan Guider and his wife Joan live where originally Danny Lanigan and his wife Ellen Ryan (Dromard) lived. Ellen was an aunt of Denis Ryan of The Hill. Danny Lanigan (b.1871) had two brothers, Mick (b.1867) and Martin (b.1878), and with a sister Mary (b.1876) who married a Clarke from Lisdaleen. Mick died in 1956 and Martin died in early 1951, both in their eighties. Danny died on 1 December 1950, and his wife Ellen died on 8 March 1961. Lizzie Maher worked in Lanigan's for a number of years. She later married Din Carroll and moved down the road to where Peggy and Dan Taylor were the last residents.

Danny and Ellen had a daughter, Elizabeth (Bab) who married Tim Guider from Castleiney on 15 February 1949. Bab and Tim lived in Clonboo and had six children: Danny, John, Mary, Pauline, Tim (RIP) and Kathleen. Tim died on 16 January 1970 and his wife Bab died on 12 December 1990.

I only barely remember Tim Guider but I remember Bab well; she was a good friend to our family and a regular caller. She also visited my grandmother Sarah Doolan and as I used to be up there a fair bit, I would often meet her there. There was one thing about Bab: she knew well that I liked beans and every time I went up to Guider's, she would always make beans for me. (Actually my own son Sean is partial to a few beans, now that I think of it.) Bab was a devil for talking and in those days you had to rely on the gas cooker to heat the beans. Nowadays the microwave can produce beans heated to exact temperatures, in those days, if you took one eye off the saucepan and stopped stirring, the beans would be stuck to the bottom of the saucepan and burnt. I never told her, but there is nothing worse than burned beans. It didn't turn me off beans, but after a while I kept an eye on the beans myself when they were being heated.

Dan and John stayed in Clonboo farming and the girls left home. Mary is living in Templemore and working in healthcare. Pauline married Liam Ryan and moved to the Silvermines and they have two boys and three girls: Denis, William, Geraldine, Bernie and Maria. Kathleen married Seamus Ryan and they have one girl, Ailish and they live in Cappawhite, west Tipperary. Dan married Joan Boyle from Barnane and they have five children: Brendan, Catherine, Timmy, Paul and Daniel. Brendan is keeping the Clonboo flag flying on the hurling field, and plays for J.K. Brackens. Dan and Joan's son Timmy married Norma Kelleher from Macroom on 26 July 2008 and they have one daughter, Naoise.

Hurling used to be played in Clarke's yard, but when the numbers got a bit big, or it got too dangerous (although, to be honest, it was always too dangerous), we would move out into Guider's field. I remember hurling there. There was a well in the middle of the field.

MORRISSEY

Danny Morrissey lived down the lane opposite Guiders' gate. He married Maggie Molloy (refer to Molloy's who lived next to Grimes). Danny had a brother, Martin, who lived in Gortderrybeg (or Loran area). Danny's sister Mary (b. 1881), married Jim Fermoyle, and they were Jimmy Fermoyle's parents. Another sister married Ger Maher and lived up the road in Toher in the house in which that Mick Bergin now lives. There were approximately two acres of land with the house and Jimmy Fermoyle farmed this when the Morrissey's were all gone. The mother, Margaret, was a widow at the time of the 1901 census. She was born in 1856. The house is no longer there and Clarkes now own the land.

CLARKE

The children, Breda, Mickey, Anne and Tom are my generation. Patrick and Mary are my parent's generation. The Clarkes were always close friends to the Butlers. I have great memories, along with a few scars and marks, of hurling in Clarke's yard. It was a perfect setting, being large enough to have up to eight or ten playing, and having an enclosed pitch surrounded by the house on one side and by outhouses and walls on the other sides. It also had the yard gate at one end and a barn door of the same size directly opposite at the other end.

Patrick used to stand in the porch and give comments and instructions. Sometimes he would stand in goal, depending on the numbers playing. It was hard going and often ended in rows and fights, but a lot of 'sweat and blood' was left in that yard. There were no mobile phones then, in fact at the start there were no phones at all, until we became Templetuohy 28 and Clarkes were Templetuohy 31, as far as I can recall. All we needed was to listen; we'd hear the roars and know a match was on in Clarke's yard. We'd be on the bike and up the road.

The Cantwells played there, Ryans of the Hill, Mahers of Toher, Guiders and many more 'visiting clans'. Actually, from the matches in the yard we set up a hurling league where there would have been up to thirty playing. It was widened to include the Bourkes, Shellys, Ryans of Toher, Loughnanes, Deegans and Everards. There was no hurling in Toher school and Clonmore parish then hadn't enough to make an underage team, unlike nowadays.

Patrick Clarke died on 30 December 1986. I remember it well, as both families were always close and he died on my birthday. Yet another great card player in Heaven! Patrick was part of the original card game held in our house every year on Christmas night, the others being Neddy Guilfoyle, Dan Maher, Thady Maher, Paddy Bourke, Toby Maher, Jack Carroll, Mary Cody and, in later years, Jim Fitzpatrick, Jim Maher, John Maher and ourselves.

Mick Clarke, Patrick's father, married Bridgie Ryan from Curriganeen. They had three children: Patrick, Eileen and Mary. Both girls became nuns. Mary (Sister M. Patricia) died on 14 July 2005 in the Holy Faith Convent in Glasnevin. Eileen died on 14 March 2009, also in the convent. Eileen entered the convent in 1948, and at that stage her sister Mary was already there. Between both, they gave over 120 years of service to the Sisters of Holy Faith Order.

Patrick married Mary Gleeson and they had three boys and two girls: Mickey, Tom, Patrick, Breda and Anne. Patrick died in February 1966, at three months old. Tom married Breda and they live in Dualla. They have five children: Tom, Meadhbh, Padraic, David and Muireann. Tom is the Principal in Charleville secondary school; he was a fine hurler in his day and he was a good friend of mine growing up in Clonboo.

Anne Clarke married Ollie Carroll from Rock Forest, Knock, and after a number of years living in the neighbouring parish, they moved back to Clonboo and built a new house just up past their own house opposite the school. They have three children: Anne-Marie, Stephen and Emma.

Mickey lives at home and Breda lives in Templemore.

The earlier generation of Clarkes were also Patrick and Mary. Patrick died in April 1910, aged seventy-two years, and his wife Mary was born in 1850 and died in October 1917, aged sixty-eight years. Two of their children died at young ages: Thomas, in September 1906, aged twenty-six years, and Winfred, in December 1905, aged twenty years. Their other son, Patrick (b.1876) married a Lannigan and lived in Lisdaleen. She was a sister of Danny Lannigan (see Lannigan, next door to Clarke's, later Guider's). There were three girls: Maggie (b.1884), Catherine (b.1886) and the last, whose name is unknown. One married a Guider from Killenagh, one married an Egan and the other married a Madden. There was also a Jim Clarke (b.1887) and he was the father of Toby Clarke from Borrisoleigh. Jack O'Donnell worked there on the farm for a number of years. Mary Clarke tells me that Pat lived in Dublin, Mary went to Co. Cork, Eileen lived in Co. Clare, and Seamus went to London – all of them creating their own family trees among the wider world.

At the time of the 1901 census, the following entries were recorded as being in the Clarke house on 31 March 1901: Patrick, father, aged sixty-two; Mary, mother, aged fifty-two; Patrick, son, aged twenty-seven; Thomas, son, aged twenty-two; Katie, daughter, aged nineteen; Winfred, daughter, aged eighteen; Michael, son, aged fifteen; Maggie Ryan, niece, aged four, and Thomas Henderson, nephew, aged eighteen.

GREEDS

James Greed married Johanna Doolan and they had one son and four daughters. They lived about three quarters of the way down a lane beside the school, up past Clarke's on the left-hand side. The Doolans lived further down the lane. As they lived up past the stream and on the left-hand side of the road, they lived in the parish of Templetuohy rather than the parish of Clonmore. James Greed (b. 1879) had a brother Tom who was Peter's father (see previous entry, Peter Greed). James also had another brother, Joseph (b. 1887) and two sisters, Maggie (b. 1883) and Mary (b. 1889). James's wife, Johanna (b. 1878) was a sister of Ned Doolan's. James died on 3 April 1927 and his wife Johanna died on 15 December 1964. They had four girls and one boy: Lizzie, Josie, Mary, Brigid and Jimmy. Lizzie married Paddy Meade and they lived in Dareens, Clonmore, where they had four boys: Jim, Tom, Joe and Pat Joe. Jim and Joe are twins. Paddy Meade died on 3 December 1982 aged seventy-seven years, while Lizzie died on 18 April 2002 at the age of eighty-five years.

The others – Josie, Mary, Brigid and Jimmy – never married. Josie worked all her life in England and died there on 30 November 1999. Jimmy died on 27 March 1975, Mary on 14 February 1991, and Brigid died on 5 November 1994.

Paddy and Lizzie Meade's children now have their own children. Tom is in the home place in Dareens. Pat Joe is married to Margaret and they have three children: Padraig, Yvonne and Lisa. He built a house at the home place and runs the farm with Tom. Joe is married to Catherine Lahart from Johnstown. They have a boy and a girl and they live in Clonmel. Jim is married to Anne Breen and they have six children, five boys and one girl. They live in Longorchard, Templetuohy. Jim has Jimmy Greed's place in Toher, the original Greed home place.

The Greeds and the Doolans gave the land free of charge for Toher school to be built.

DOOLAN

Sarah Farrell came to Clonboo/Toher in 1929. She married Ned Doolan and they had one daughter, Mary who was born 20 June 1941. Ned Doolan died on 16 December 1942, aged seventy-one years. When he died, his only child Mary was only one and a half years old. Sarah Doolan lived until she was ninety-three years old, and died on 6 February 1990.

Sarah came from a large family in Borrisoleigh, which included Paddy, Phil, Jim, Edmond, Rick, Mick, Annie, Mary, Christina, Katie and Johanna. We will come back to this generation later.

The Doolans lived in a long lane beside the school. Jimmy Greed lived in the same lane. Peg Fogarty, one of the teachers, was from Two-Mile Borris and she stayed with my grandmother for a number of years. She cycled from her home on a Sunday evening, went to Doolan's, taught in the school all week and then cycled home to Two-Mile Borris on a Friday evening. The cycle journey was at least twelve or fourteen miles.

Doolan's was a great place to go, with lots of things to do. The lane into the house was narrow and had its fair share of potholes. If there were cattle in or around the hay-barn field, then the gate had to be kept closed all the time. It was a right nuisance having to get out to open the gate, then drive through, then get out again to close the gate.

But I remember loads of things about Nanna Doolan's, from the massive lilac tree at the right-hand side of the yard on the way down, to the fields, to the great selection of fruit trees at the back of the house. There were two apple trees: one ordinary apples and the other cooking apples. The cooking apples were for making tarts and the ordinary apples were for eating. They were massive trees, and the back window of the kitchen was dark because the tree took all the light. There were also red-berry and blackcurrant trees; the blackcurrants were lovely. After a while you would get tired of topping and tailing the blackcurrants, so you would eat the lot – tails and all. Nanna Doolan was a great woman for making apple jelly and potato cakes. The jelly was made from her own apples, while the potato cakes had a lovely taste and flavour. Home ingredients freshly made and cooked over the open fire – magic. There are two other sweeter tastes that I recall from my childhood. The taste of a boiled egg chopped in a mug with a lump of butter, and the heel of the loaf of bread broken into pieces and put into a mug with a spoonful of sugar and boiling milk poured over it. That was a night time treat called 'googgie'. Down the fields there were loads of nut trees and you would bring loads home and get out a nice-sized stone for cracking the hazelnuts. There was always a small hole or indentation in the wall capping where the nut would nicely sit before cracking it. As they say, 'sweet as a nut'.

The house itself had a main living room and kitchen combined with a parlour and a bedroom downstairs and there was a loft room upstairs. There was a big open fire, and I mean *big* and *open*, in that the chimney spanned nearly the width of the room and narrowed to a chimney size as it rose. The fire was on the floor, and there was some suction up that chimney. The large cast-iron 'crane' structure or fire grate swung from one side, with a double horizontal frame providing several options and uses. From these flat bars and adjustable fixing points you could hang pots, kettles, saucepans, etc., to cook whatever you wanted to cook.

Two other things about the open fire. The open flames gave instant heat to cold hands on a winter day. The flames also helped to make the nicest toast you could ever imagine. All you had to do was simply cut a slice off the loaf (before sliced bread was commonly available) and with a fork stuck to one end, hold the slice near the open flames. At the appropriate time and to your individual taste, you could switch over the fork to hold the other side of the slice and wait for it to toast. Perfect every time. But you had to watch out for it getting burned as it took less that a minute to toast the bread over a flamed fire.

The other thing I remember about the fire in Doolans was the use of a goose's wing to clean up the ashes and dirt around the fire. The goose wing was a practical item to use and a great example of how the older generation never believed in wasting anything. Every house had fowl around the farmyard and there were always a few geese, along with ducks, hens, and the odd turkey. Apart from the food when the fowl was killed, hens, ducks, and geese also provided a regular supply of eggs. If you ever had a duck egg, you would know that one egg would do you. The goose wing was a strong limb of the bird and you would always find one or two near the fire in Doolans.

When using the fire crane, the cooking time depended on how close the particular utensil was to the fire below. Also, if you made a cup of tea, you could put the teapot down on the floor beside the fire to let the tea 'draw'. There was always something on the fire cooking food or boiling water, because there was no point in wasting the fire. The fire would be lit everyday winter and summer. There was some mountain of ashes at the other side of the yard wall. You could burn anything in the fire provided you could get it in the door of the house! I often remember large lumps of timber lying across the kitchen floor with one end on fire in the hearth and the other end being used as a seat by someone reading the paper or in conversation.

In those days there was no waste. The rainwater that fell on the roofs was caught in a barrel at the end of shoots and used to wash hair and clothes. The rainwater was always so soft compared to the spring water, which was a hard limestone that always clogged up kettles and pipes. The rainwater was also given to cattle or sheep.

There was a great tranquility in Doolan's house and I fondly remember spending many hours there talking and often just sitting there with my grandmother Sarah. To me she was special and I think I was special to her too. I suppose that happens with the first grandchild, but it needs to be reciprocated. I used to call in there a lot after school and during the weekends, but I only remember staying a few times. I had a bicycle, of course, but the walk only took about fifteen or twenty minutes.

Thinking back to those times when the fire was always on, at night my grandmother used to cover the last of the cinders with ashes so that you could not see any red cinders. I used to do it too. You would think that this would smother the last bit of heat in the red cinders, but in fact it kind of sealed them so that in the morning, seven or eight hours later, you could shake up the ashes and there, sure enough, would be the lovely red cinders, ready to start a new fire. If you forgot to cover the cinders, or if they were too weak or poor in the first place, then the fire would be dead in the morning. In such a situation there were a few options to start a fire. One was with the assistance of a firelighter, but this was the easy way and in the countryside you cannot always depend on having a firelighter. Other options always included small pieces of turf called 'kieronns' (although I'm not sure of spelling). These were finger-size pieces of turf that broke off the larger sods of turf and were always found at the bottom of the pile of turf in the shed. Another ingredient to start a fire was 'kindle', or small pieces of dry timber, so light it nearly looked like straw. This would nearly instantly light itself, but it would burn off quickly unless you had enough of it and you would also need slightly larger bits of timber sticks with it. So a combination of the thin sticks of timber and small pieces of turf did the business. Another thing we did was to use newspaper; we tore up sheets and twisted them hard to compact them into rigid spirals of six or eight-inch barrels. Now it was not a case of piling these items all together and hoping that the fire would light. The key was to put them all together in a wigwam shape, in the correct order, with the main fire material such as sods of turf, lumps of timber or the toughest one of all, coal, placed in the right spot. The ultimate idea was to get the light stuff, the small pieces of turf, the timber kindling or the twisted paper, to burn long enough and be placed in the right location to eventually set fire to the big pieces of fire-wood. If you failed it was a big disappointment, and nobody ever liked to admit to not being able to light the fire. Some tough fires to light would be the ones on a wet days or when you only had coal.

Sarah Doolan died on 6 February 1990, and on 24 March a tribute article appeared in the *Tipperary Star* by someone who simply signed themselves as 'A Constant Visitor'. The article spoke volumes of the woman and reflected the views of a great many people. It went as follows:

Just a month ago Mrs Sarah Doolan chose to leave us for a better place, having spent ninety years plus amongst us. A member of the Farrell family, born at Garrangrena, Borrisoleigh, she later moved to Kilvilcorris, Drom. Both place names were often nostalgically mentioned by Sarah. She married Ned Doolan, Clonboo and adapted readily to residing in the Clonmore–Templetuohy locality. Being widowed and left with a very young daughter did not daunt this tenacious lady. She carried on her farming work in spite of adversity. Regardless of this difficult task Sarah took a keen interest in every aspect of life – current affairs, nature, heritage, the media, etc., late election results or sporting fixtures being relayed from abroad often holding her interest until the early hours. Sarah's home was open house for a multitude of relatives and friends. Her outgoing hospitable nature and genuine concern for everyone's welfare endeared her to all with whom she came in contact. Her culinary expertise was no mean effort. The cakes, chutneys, jellies, jams, etc., which her skilled hands produced were just scrumptious. In her declining years she was lovingly cared for by her family. In the last few weeks friends and neighbours vied for the privilege of sharing their time to be of assistance. No surprise you would say – fitting as a reciprocal of the care Sarah lavished on everyone. As she lay in her coffin, the smile of contentment on her face was indicative of the happy and prayerful environment which surrounded her in her last days. Memories of a great woman will evoke not a few prayers from many whose privilege it was to have known her.

RYANS/DOWNEYS

There was a house attached to or part of the original schoolhouse. The school was always known as Toher School but at the turn of the 1900s the address was Clonbough Upper, and the school was House No.1 in Clonbough Upper, as per the 1911 Census. Johanna Ryan and her brother James lived there. Johanna (b.1887 and d.9 November 1973 at the age of eighty-seven) was the National School Teacher and her brother James (b.1885) worked as a Solicitor's Clerk. Johanna Ryan later became Mrs O'Meara and was a grandmother to Batt O'Meara, who taught me Maths when I attended secondary school in Templemore CBS. Batt also coached us when we played underage hurling and football. Johanna Ryan was the Principal of Toher School between 1909 and 1950. In 1923, Toher became a two-teacher school when Myra Gavin joined as an assistant. Before Ryans, James and Katie Downey lived in the house. James was the school teacher between 1897 and 1909. James was born in 1874 and Katie was born in 1876.

TOHER SCHOOL

Toher school is located at the end of Doolan's lane, on the left-hand side as you travel up the road, approximately halfway between Clarke's and Deegan's. It closed in 1998.

I have given the school its own section due to the various sources of information and its significance on our road. We were very fortunate to have the school within a safe walking distance of our house. In my estimation, well over 1,200 children and adults attended Toher school during its almost sixty-year existence.

In the following pages, I have recalled some of my own school-day memories, along with some selected classes.

SCHOOL DAYS

We lived less than half a mile from Toher school and our school day finished at three o'clock every day. Most people walked to and from school. There was none of this lark about getting dropped to school by your Mammy or Daddy – only for the first few days of baby infants did that ever happen. Of course, some children had bicycles, like the Mahers of Toher, and I think John Bergin, but apart from that we all walked. Now, in fairness, the Hassetts and Ryans of the Hill got dropped off and picked up because they lived in Lisduff and Dromard respectively, over a mile and a half away. I would say Hassetts and Campions who also lived in Lisduff were over two miles from Toher school.

Going at a walking pace of three or four miles per hour, the less than half-mile journey should not take more than seven or eight minutes from Toher school to home. Myself and Pat Joe Hassett typically took a bit longer to get home. Pat Joe was usually picked up by his father, Paddy, or by one of his older brothers, but they would meet him on the road instead of having than Pat Joe waiting for them at the school. We would walk on, until we would meet his lift.

Pat Joe Hassett was in my class in Toher school for the latter part of my primary school years. It's not intended to be confusing or sound strange, but it was usual in Toher school to have different classmates over the different years. In those days, pupils were often kept back for a year, as decided by the teachers. Children were allowed to start school at ages under four, and there were no strict rules or guidelines at the time. It was often about keeping the attendance numbers up at a certain level. When I started I was three years and eight months. Actually, I went in for a few days at the end of the previous school term, in the old school, at the ripe old age of three years and six months. My friends during the early classes from infants to second class included: Maura Bergin, Breada Tynan, Kathleen Maher and Tom Clarke. When I finished primary school, my classmates were: Pat Joe Hassett, Ann Clarke, Maura Bergin, Breeda Maher, Donie Bowe and Ann Ryan.

It was traumatic enough going from a class sometimes as small as four to a class of six, but I adapted without any major long-term damage … Only joking! – sure it was great to get so much attention from the teacher, it was almost one to one private tuition. Sarah, my youngest daughter, started school in September 2005 and there were twenty-six in her class. At the time she started, I recalled that at one stage I remember there were only twenty-eight in the whole school in Toher!

On our long walks home from school, myself and Pat Joe Hassett, along with others, would solve the worries and troubles of the day. One day, my father overheard us discussing the benefit of winning the Hospital Sweepstakes (which was a precursor to the Lotto, with the funds going to Irish Hospitals' Foundation). My father was inside the hedge and recalls the conversation, which was summarised by Pat Joe and myself agreeing that if we won the Sweepstakes, we would buy Walsh's in Templemore. Walsh's in Templemore was the contemporary equivalent to Smyth's Toys or Toys 'R' Us.

Every so often, the County Council opened small shore-hole gaps in ditches along the road into people's fields. These gaps were designed to allow surface water to drain off the road when it rained heavily, or over a prolonged period, thus avoiding flooding on the road. The gaps or gulley holes were at both sides of the road and usually at fairly regular intervals, maybe about eighteen or twenty feet. We used to play a game with a football, kicking it from one side of the road to the other, trying to roll it into the gullies. It was a bit like crazy golf with a football, but it made for a long and slow journey home from school. So, the less than half-mile walk home, often took between a half and three-quarters of an hour. Sometimes the walk was shorter if Pat Joe was picked for a lift or if we met his father to collect him, or if we forgot to bring the ball!

Left: Toher old school.
Right: Toher new school.

There was always a football in the school – usually always a bust football. The pitch we used for the matches was small so it was a good thing that the ball was burst, as you could not kick it that far. There was no hurling allowed in the school, due to possible injuries I suppose, and the fact that the two teachers were female and may have had a lesser interest. We had problems with numbers of boys to play matches but the girls of Clonboo, Toher, Lissanure, Dromard and Longorchard were well able to admirably defend the female gender among all-comers from the male species on the football field. My son Sean would be horrified to hear we played football with girls but we had to make up a team for the greater good of the sport! Of course sometimes the girls wouldn't play; they had no problem letting us down at short notice and going off to play Tag, or Hide and Go Seek, or Willy Willy Wag Tail, or Hopscotch, or Call-Over, or Simon Says. We boys didn't like those games, of course, but we had to play them sometimes so that the girls would play a match some other day. As I said, the things we had to do for the good of keeping the game of football alive!

TOHER SCHOOL ROLL BOOKS (SELECTED CLASSES)

We will go through the roll book in more detail later, but I just want to pick out a couple of years when I was attending Toher school and list the classes at that time.

In 1970, when I was in my fourth year at school and in second class, the other pupils and classes were as follows:

Infants: Statia Tynan, Seamus Fogarty, Michael Moylan, Ned Butler, Patricia Loughnane, Noreen Bergin, Margaret Tynan, Kathleen Loughnane, Catherine Ryan, Liam Fogarty and Seamus Maher.

First Class: Tom Bergin, Geraldine Driscoll and John Bergin.

Second Class: Ann Ryan, Kathleen Maher, Breda Tynan, Jack Butler and Tom Clarke.

Third Class: Kathleen Guider, Maire Bergin, Mary Tynan, Margaret Loughnane, Ann Clarke, Breeda Maher, Donie Bowe, P.J. Hassett and Maire Ni Calaithe[?].

Fourth Class: Tom Guider, Johnny Ryan, Ger Moran, Sile Maher, Sally Moylan and Kathleen Driscoll.

Fifth Class: John Guider, Billy Lougnane, Michael Clarke, Mick Ryan, Maura Bowe, Michael Loughlin and Mary Moylan.

Sixth Class: Michael Maher, Michael Loughnane, Jimmy Bergin, Breda Clarke and Eileen Bowe.

Seventh Class: Tom Ryan, Brid Loughnane, Helen Fermoyle, Margaret Ryan, Breeda Hassett, Pauline Guider and Jane Bergin.

A total of fifty-three pupils attended the school that year and we were taught by Mrs Bergin and Mrs Fogarty.

In 1974, the four new classes, two infant classes along with the first and second class, were as follows:

Infants: Miriam Deegan, Catherine Butler, Mark Campion, Liam Grimes, Sean Hayes, Seamus Ryan, Anna Statia Fogarty and Tim Bergin.

First Class: Tomas Deegan, Tommy Hayes, Seamus Hassett, Mary Ryan and Veronica Campion.

Second Class: Seamus Fogarty, Mickey Moylan, Ned Butler, Maire Fogarty and Statia Tynan.

HEDGE SCHOOLS

The Penal Laws introduced in the late 1600s limited Catholics' rights to land and they also forbid Catholics to attend school. This forced the creation of 'hedge schools', where Catholic children were taught in secret by teachers who travelled the country and were paid by parents. Travelling teachers were often paid with crops and food, instead of money. According to the Penal code, which came into effect in the first decade of the twentieth century, no Catholic could teach anywhere in the country, and Catholics who were sent abroad for their education lost all rights to property and ran the risk of being outlawed in respect of all civil rights. Teaching could be a hazardous occupation for Catholics, as the penalties for those indicted could be as severe as transportation into penal servitude to one of the British colonies in America or elsewhere. As householders who harboured schoolmasters were also liable to prosecution, schools were conducted out of doors in many districts in the opening decades of the nineteenth century, when–

ever the weather permitted. Many of the schoolmasters moved around from place to place, living upon the hospitality of the people and conducting their schools on the sheltered and sunny side of a hedge or bank. In 1823, Daniel O'Connell founded the Catholic Association to drive the movement for Catholic rights. The membership was a shilling a year or a penny a month, which became known as the 'Catholic Rent'. With Catholic Emancipation achieved by Daniel O'Connell in 1831, a new education system was introduced, that finally gave Catholics a route to a formal education with an established national primary school system.

There were a large number of hedge schools around the country, and there was one in Togher, in the same location as the school we all went to. I am informed that the O'Rourkes, who were land agents for some of the landlords in the area, were responsible to a large extent for getting the school built in 1839. The O'Rourkes lived in the house currently owned by Thady Maher.

The old school was located were the playing pitch later was, at the end of the school property at Deegan's end. When the new school was built and opened in 1966, the old school was knocked.

I only just remember going to school for the few days before the summer holidays in the old school, in June 1966, where we wrote on slates using chalk (although I don't think we used slate in the new school). I was only three and a half years old in June 1966, and I did not officially start school until I was four years old. Toher always had problems in keeping the attendance numbers high enough to justify and maintain their two teachers. The school roll book records my formal education as starting in January 1967.

Whatever about the use of chalk and slate, we did use ink from an inkwell in the school form. There was a little ceramic ink holder in the top right corner of your desk. The ink holder was about the size of an egg cup. The big thing that you had to have, of course, was blotting paper, which was essential to soak up the constant mess of ink that ran too freely. We were always a mess and our hands and fingers were always covered with ink. Thank God for the invention of the biro. Those multicoloured biros were deadly, in blue, black, red and green. You were lucky to have one of those.

The year 1950 was a notable one for Toher school, as it marked the retirement of Mrs Johanna O'Meara (*née* Ryan), who had started teaching in the school in 1909. Toher was a two-teacher school from 1923, with almost fifty children attending, but in September 1952, with only around thirty children on the roll, it reverted to single-teacher status again.

From 1952 until 1955 Margaret Bourke, who married Ned Fogarty, was the teacher, and in 1956 she was replaced by Alice Kennedy, who married Tom Bergin, and she continued as teacher until 1995. In 1966, Toher became a two-teacher school again, and Margaret Fogarty, who had spent eleven years teaching in Kylemakill school in the interim, returned to Toher to join Mrs Bergin.

The national school in Toher was described in the Templetuohy parish records of 1961 as a very old building that was little above the standard of a shed, falling well below the sanitary and general health requirements of a national school. In March 1966, a new school was built on the site of the old building and officially opened a couple of months later with the celebration of Mass. Alice Bergin was the Principal at the time.

When Mrs Fogarty retired in 1995 she was not replaced, and when Mrs Bergin retired in 1997, Miss Ryan was appointed in her place. Miss Ryan was in turn replaced by Mary Butler, who took charge of the school in January 1998. The school closed on 26 June 1998. There were only six children in the school when it closed: John Paul Costigan, Elaine Clarke, David Costigan, Joanne Moylan, Mary Moran and Teresa Hartigan.

Various photos of pupils in Toher school tell their own stories of past and current generations, including those families that have remained in the area and those families that have left or whose name has sadly died out.

In 1846, Dominic McNamee was the Master of Toher school, which had an average attendance of thirty-five children. A photo of Toher national school from 1926 has the two teachers, Mrs O'Meara and Miss Gavin surrounded by thirty-six pupils. Most of the names have been mentioned elsewhere. Miss Gavin, Myra, was a niece to the Skehan's who lived down opposite Carrolls in Bourke's field.

Jimmy Bowe, Jimmy Guider, Josie Darmody, Nelly Loughnane, Mary Ann Fitzpatrick, Ciss Maher, Katie Shelly, Stephanie Guider, Kit O'Meara, Brigie Maher, Kitty Loughnane, Nora Darmody, Nellie Ryan, Bill Carroll, Martin Clark, Ciss Fermoyle, Maggie Kennedy, Ciss Guilfoyle, Mary Ann Darmody, Katie Maher, Mary Costigan, Bridgie Darmody, Patrick Costigan, Tom Moran, Neddy Guilfoyle, Connie Costigan, Jackie Shelly, Martin Long Fitzpatrick, Joe O'Meara, Mick Shelly, Joe Ryan, John O'Meara, Jim O'Meara, John Maher, Danny Bowe and Bill Shelly.

Another photo of the school taken in the early 1960s shows thirty-one pupils, some of whom still live in the area with their own families.

Carmel Ryan, Mary Guider, Mary Hanrahan, Kathleen Costigan, Mary Loughnane, Theresa Costigan, Martin Moylan, Paddy Moran, Johnny Hanrahan, Joe Moylan, Sean Moran, John Guider, Seamus Moran, Esther Fermoyle, Breda Loughnane, Pauline Guider, Eileen Loughnane, Helen Fermoyle, Martha Driscoll, Rita Moore, Arm Loughnane, Jim Maher, Gerry Moylan, Michael Maher, Jim Hanrahan, J.J. Ryan, John Loughnane, Fergal Ryan, Jack Carroll, Breda Clarke and Tom Moran.

CARROLL

Ollie Carroll married Anne Clarke and moved to Clonboo after a number of years living in Clonakenny. They built a new house on Clarke's land opposite Toher school. It was unlucky that the school closed, as their three children would never have been late for school, living across the road. Anne was in my class during the last few years in Toher school and was in the same year in secondary school, although I went to the Brothers (CBS) while she went to the Nuns (Sisters of Mercy). She was a good ally and social advisor during my secondary school years!

DEEGAN

The Deegans came from the Islands, Loughmore, around the 1820s. It is not called the Islands any more. Roughly described, they lived on an extension to Lisheen lane, which was also close to the end of another lane called Clogheraily More. This other lane, Clogeraily More, is where my family, the Butlers, came from, our own family. Both families lived in Clogheraily.

There were two brothers, **Dan** and **Martin**. The farm was divided in two between the brothers; Martin lived in the inside farm and Dan lived in the outside farm in Clonboo. Martin bought Sorrillhill House and farm from Dudley Byrne for a figure reported to be around £850 pounds, which is where Tommy Deegan now lives.

Dan was born in 1851 and died around 1929. He married Nano Meade from Templetuohy, who was born in 1851 and died in 1935. They had five children: Tom (b.1887), John (b.1886), Hannah or Hanoria (b.1890), Molly or Mary (b.1892) and Babe or Ellen (b.1888). Jimmy Fermoyle's father (also named James) worked in Deegan's for a number of years.

Tom, never married and farmed where Martin Deegan's farm is now.

John married a Costigan and had an only son, John, a solicitor. John senior lived in England. His father bought Bergin's in Clonboo for John to come home to but he died in England. His son John, the solicitor, was only two years old when his father died. The house was then resold and John Maher, Thady's father, bought it at the end of 1943, in November or December.

Hannah married Tom Gleeson from Rathnavogue and they had four daughters and one son: Mary, Ciss, Jack, Josie and Statia. Mary married Patrick Clarke, Josie married Tony Cantwell (Moyne) and Statia married a Campion from Errill. Ciss and Jack never married. Mary Clarke is mentioned separately earlier with the Clarkes. She was just 12 months old when her younger sister Ciss was born. Mary was brought to Clonboo, to Deegan's, in a pony and trap, not to stay there but to be company for her granny, as her aunt Molly was soon to be married. But that aunt didn't make the move for another three years or more, so Mary remained. As Mary herself told me, 'for better or worse, the rest is history'. I think history will clearly show that Clonboo has been a better place because Mary Clarke stayed. So, as they say, she never went home, having being reared in Clonboo, and she then married Patrick Clarke.

Molly married Dick Cummins from Camblin, Roscrea and they had one son, Dick, and three daughters: Maureen, Eileen and Peggy. Dick Cummins died on 29 March 2009.

Babe married John Whelan from Fernville, Rathdowney, and they had no family.

The **second brother** of the original family, **Martin** married Anne. They had eleven children: Martin, Phonsie, Dan, Tom, John, Mick, Ciss, Mary, Annie, Josephine and Joseph. The 1911 census records that Martin and Anne had a larger number of children and that some of the childrenn died in infancy. At the time of the 1911 census the youngest of the family was Josephine, at eight months old, and the oldest was Annie, at twenty-three years.

Martin (b.1892) married Maeve Bannon from Ballycahill and they lived in Shanageary House, Rathdowney, which his father bought in the late '40s. They had four children: Maeve, Noleen, Hughie and Ann. Martin sold the farm and bought a shop in Templemore, which is currently known as Doherty's Hardware. He sold the shop and moved to England, where he reared his family. Maeve married and had two boys. Noleen married and had one girl and one boy. Hughie married and had one boy. Ann married Michael Shields from Durrow and had ten children. The three girls live in England while Hughie lives in Newry.

Phonsie (b.1898) became a priest and ministered in Australia.

Dan (b.1893) married Agnes Scott from Knockfinn, Rathdowney and lived in Shanbally House, Cullahill, Rathdowney, which his father bought for him in the '40s. They had three children: Martin, Josephine and Donal. Martin became a priest and ministered in England. Josephine became a Presentation Nun. Donal runs the farm and is married to Margaret Bergin from Garrin, Borris-in-Ossory. They have ten children: Dan, Martin, Liam, Fintan, Joe, John, Paul, Agnes, Ann-Marie and Brid.

Tom (b.1902) married Mary Flanagan from Moycarkey and they had eight children: Martin Tommy, Paddy, Maura, Nancy, Stephanie, Eileen and Patricia. We will come back to Tom's family later.

John (b.1890) went to America and died there at a young age.

Mick (b.1899) emigrated to Australia and married Mary Fitzgerald. They had two children, Nancy and Kevin.

Ciss married Patrick Costigan of Toher and they had eight children: Connie, Martin, Pat Joe, Josephine, Annie, Mary, Kathleen and Teresa. Connie married Eileen Cooke from Ballycahill and they live in Toher. They have nine children: Caitriona, Padraig, Helen, Martin, Conor, Ann Marie, Thomas, John Paul and David. Connie and Eileen's daughter Catriona is married to Michael Cleary, former Tipperary hurler and All-Ireland medal winner. Martin married Mary Maher from Borrisoleigh and they now live in Harristown, Rathdowney.

Ciss's son Pat Joe married Frances Adams from Dublin and is living in the USA. They have four children: Alison, Patrick, Carin and Brian. Josephine married Johnny Everard and lives in Templetuohy. They had eight children: Brendan, Mary, Pierce, Conor, Sean, Diarmuid, Enda and Andrew, who died in infancy.

Annie, another daughter, died young. Mary married Ned Dempsey from Dublin. They have four children: three girls and one boy. Teresa is married to Cyril Byrne from Wexford. They live in Dublin and have four boys. Kathleen married John Egan of Dareens, Clonmore, a strong GAA man and proud wearer of the centre field jersey for his parish. They have five children: Siobhan, Katherine, Lorraine, Pat and Lorcan. Katherine is married to Paul O'Brien from Clonmore and they have one child, Larry.

Mary (Molly) (b.1906) married Willie Cullen of Cloone, Templemore and had three children: Pat, Timmy and Ann. Pat married Patricia Moynihan from Athlone and they have four children: Elaine, Louise, Jonathan and Timmy. Elaine is married and living in Tullamore, Louise is married and living in England, Jonathan is married to Mary Ryan from Ballyduff. Timmy married Delia Mullaney from Moyne and they have four children: Mary, Willie, Michael and Elizabeth. Mary is married to James Carroll from Errill and they have four children.

Ann is married to Michael Ryan from Drom and they have four children: William, Denis, Ann Marie and Elizabeth. Denis is married to an Irish girl and living in America.

Annie (b.1888) became a St John of God Nun. Her name in the convent was Sister Felix and she lived in the convent in Wexford.

Going back to Tom Deegan. **Tom** (b.1902) had eight children: Martin, Tommy, Paddy, Stephanie, Maura, Nancy Eileen and Patricia. Tom died on 15 June 1980, aged seventy-seven years. Tom Deegan bought Clonboo (outside farm) in 1961 for £9,000 and this is where Martin (Jnr) lived and farmed until his death on 5 March 2006. Paddy farms in Clonboo Upper (inside farm) and Tommy (Jnr) farms in Sorrilhill House, where they were all born.

Martin married Alice Kennedy from Moyne and they have four children: Tomas, Miriam, Marty and Aidan. Tomas married Ann Gunnell (from Roscrea) and they have a son and a daughter, Grainne and Cormac. They live just up the road from the home place. Miriam is married to Kevin Everard and they have three girls: Niamh, Eimear and Caoimhe. Marty is married to Sinead O'Connell from Leitrim and they have two children, Jack and Andrew. Aiden, who is the youngest, married Carmel McDonald in December 2008. Carmel is a daughter of Michael and Mary McDonald. I remember Mary McDonald, *née* Kiely, who was the local health nurse who called and attended to patients of the area who were housebound. Having the same Loughmore roots, we were always close to the Deegans.

Paddy married Ann Madden from Clonmore and they have three children: Mervyn, Lorraine and Anita. Mervyn got married in the States, Lorraine married Paddy Clarke from Templemore and Anita married a Galway man in 2009. Paddy was a regular caller to our house in Clonboo as he stopped in on his way back and forth from Castleiney.

Tommy married Margaret Ryan from Drom (sister of Dennis Ryan MCC) and they have six children: Paul, Ailish, Phonsie, Thomas, Mary and Denis. Paul is married to Mary Teresa Butler. They live outside Gorey and have three children: Muireann, Orla and Stephanie. Ailish married Kieran Barron from Donegal and they have two children, Ronan and Conor. Phonsie married Siobhan Burke from Killea and used to live Between the Crosses in Peter Greed's original house. They now live in a new house in Sorrillhill near the home place and they have two children, Sarah and

Thomas. Siobhan is a daughter of Peter and Josephine (*née* Fitzpatrick) Burke. The other children, Tomas and twins Denis and Mary, are still in their youth.

Maura married John Delaney from Dunkerrin, but John has passed away (RIP). They have six children: Mary, Stephanie, Aileen, Michael, Thomas and Declan. Mary is married to Michael Reidy from America and they live there. They have four children: Elizabeth, Nora, John and William. Stephanie is married to Declan Prendergast from Durrow and they have three children: Roisin, Cathal and Aoife. Thomas is married to Nicola O'Brien from Athlone and they have two children, Emma and Lucy. Michael, Declan and Aileen are not married yet.

Nancy married Rody Tierney from Templetuohy and they are now living in the Midlands. They have four children: Jim, Michelle, Keith and Roderick. Jim is married to a German girl and they have three girls. Roderick is married to Grainne Timlin from Athlone. Michelle and Keith are not married yet.

Patricia married Jim Fogarty from Moyne. They have three children: John, Thomas and David. John is married to Jackie from Boherlahan and they have two children. David and Thomas are not yet married.

Stephanie (RIP) and Eileen both joined the Brigidine Order of nuns in the 1960s.

CLONBOUGH CASTLE

In Paddy Deegan's field there are two ruins, one a church and the other a tower house. Small churches associated with tower houses and their gentry residents date back to the latter part of the fifteenth century. The church was dedicated to St Anne and is sited some 250 yards west of O'Meagher tower house.

The chapel is estimated to date from the sixteenth century and measures 9.35m by 4.15m internally (approx. 28ft by 12ft). Only the ruins remain of the chapel, which was in the medieval parish of Killavinogue, the earlier parish church of which is sited in the townland of Glebe. The tower house was once in the ownership of the Ikerrin branch of the Butlers. In 1654, Pierce Butler, Lord Ikerrin, was the owner. He held the townland of Clonboo, which formed one denomination with Dromard, which was the only section of the parish of Killavinogue he held. The tower house was probably occupied by his chief tenant, whose name is not known, and the church built nearby was probably a family sponsored chapel for the 'ease' of the locals.

Fr James Everard referred to the chapel as a former 'chapel of ease', as it was a local rather than a parish church. Fr Everard was parish priest in the area around the 1750s. At this time, as a matter of interest, the Pope was Benedict XIV.

Originally, Templetuohy, Moyne and Killavinogue were administered in the same parish. This was the case up until 1758, when Killavinogue, the civil parish now represented by Clonmore, was detached from Moyne/Templetuohy and joined with Templemore. Clonmore became a distinct parish from 1800 to 1815

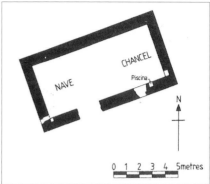

St Anne's church, Clonboo, 'Chapel of Ease'.

and then joined again to Templemore.

The term 'chapel' was generally used by the Catholic clergy and people in the eighteenth century for their places of worship, and it was the term also used by the authorities for those places. The authorities did not countenance the use of the word 'church' for any place of worship except the buildings being used by the Established Church. The term 'Mass house' appears to have been an earlier term used in the latter part of the seventeenth century for the crude shelters and cabins used to provide protection from the elements for the priests, the servers and the people as the Mass was being celebrated.

GRAHAME

The Grahame family lived somewhere around Deegans, but I'm not sure where the house was located and when the family moved out of the area. There was a big family and they may have lived further up Deegans Lane. The 1901 census recorded William and his wife Kate, aged forty-six and forty respectively, and their nine children: Richard, aged eighteen; Mary, aged sixteen; William, aged twelve; John, aged ten; James, aged eight; Kate, aged eight; Patrick, aged six, Joseph, aged four, and Thomas, aged one. The parents, William and Kate, along with the two eldest children, Richard and Mary, were all born in Laois.

BOWE

The Darmodys lived where Donie Bowe now lives. There were four girls and two boys in the family. I have the following information on the children: Patrick, Dan, Joanna (b.1875), Brigid and Lizzie. Patrick (b.1877) and his wife Norah (b.1883) lived there along with Patrick's sister Lizzie (b.1882). Another sister was Mary-Ann (b.1880). An uncle, James (b.1846) also lived there.

Mary-Ann Darmody married Larry Fitzpatrick and went to live in Clonmore, where they had two boys, Paul and Noel. Mary-Ann died on 7 August 1975, aged fifty-nine years. Bridgie married a sergeant from Cork and Josie never married. Nora never married and died at a young age. Dan married Josie McGrath from Clonmeen, while Paddy went to America in the late '50s and I think he married.

The farm and house were sold and bought by Danny Bowe. Danny married Ann (Nan) Fitzpatrick from Ballybrophy and they had three children: Eileen, Maura and Donal. Donie was in my class in Toher school and was an accomplished singer. He has continued to compete in Scór and other competitions all over the country. In 2004 he won an All-Ireland title in sean-nós singing. Donie is married to Sandra and they live in the home place, where they have two daughters, Daniella and Leona. Danny Bowe died in May 1991 at the age of seventy-two, while his wife Nan died in January 2000 aged seventy-nine.

Darmody's lane (currently Bowe's lane) requires a short mention. Originally the entrance to Darmody's farm was through a lane up past Moylan's, near the Cross of Toher, where you had to go in the short lane and then travel around the headland of a field to get to the house. (The headland of a field is the outer-most perimeter track of a field near the ditch, if you know what I mean.) In any man's language it was a long way to get from the public road to the house. Over the years the Darmodys used to take shortcuts through Deegan's from the road nearly opposite Tom Butler's. The Deegans never minded, and never minded either when the Darmodys started to bring cattle and other animals from the road through this route. After another while, deliveries with cars and lorries were made through this route, and stones were put down to stop the grass being cut up. And so a formal lane was formed. The Darmodys maintained the lane and used it all the time. Ditches grew at each side and the current lane was formed by the establishment of rights of way and by usage over a number of years, but the land was owned originally by the Deegans.

COOLY

The Cooly family lived somewhere between Darmodys and Bergins. The parents were John and Margaret, who were born in County Kilkenny in 1841 and 1842 respectively. Their four children were born in Tipperary: Thomas (b.1871), James (b.1873), Anne (b.1881), and Joseph (b.1885).

LANE AT SCHOOL SIDE OF TOM BUTLER'S

There were three houses in this lane, all are now gone:

Paddy Walsh had one house. He married Johanna and had a son, Patrick and a daughter, Katie. Jimmy Maher of Toher now owns this land. Paddy was born in 1822 and his wife Johanna was born in 1836. Their son Patrick was born in 1871 and Katie was born in 1873.

Jim Carroll and his brother **Michael** also lived in this lane. This land was originally bought by Ryans of Toher and later by Jimmy Maher. Jim was born in 1880 and Michael was born in 1882. I think Jim got married, but no further information was available. An article from the *Tipperary Star* of 11 February 1939 records the outcome of a court case about turf rights involving James Carroll. At the court case in Templemore in January 1939, the question of the rights to banks of turf arose when two brothers sued James Carroll, Toher, Templetuohy, for ten pounds each for the trover and conversion of turf. One of the brothers Martin Butler and the defendant had been farmers on the Graham estate and had banks of turf set to them, but when the estate had been taken over by the Land Commission neither party had paid annuities. The Justice said that neither party, strictly speaking, had any rights as they were not paying anymore. He did not want to put on a heavy fine but felt that he had to impose one to stop such a thing. He gave a decree for £1 and £3 13s expenses.

Just some further information on the Carrolls. The parents were Patrick and Katie Carroll. They had a large family of five sons and three daughters: James, Michael, John, Bridget, Katie, Richard, Johanna and Patrick.

The Delhauntys lived in the last house on the lane. The father and mother were Nicholas (b.1837) and Ellen (b.1841). There were four boys and one girl in the family: Michael (b.1879), Jack (b.1881), Paddy (b.1883), Jim (b.1885) and Kate (b.1884). None of them got married, as far as I know. Paddy went to America. They had seven acres of land and they lived off this farm and its proceeds. Nowadays, it is nearly impossible for one family to live off seventy acres. Costigans of Toher now own this land.

BUTLER (OF TOHER)

Thomas (b.1839) married Bridget Gorman (b.1845). The 1911 census records that they had twelve children, of which ten were still living at the time of the census. The census records the parents, Thomas, aged seventy-two, and Bridget, aged sixty-six, along with three of the children who were in the house that night. They were: Bridget, aged thirty-nine, Martin, aged thirty-eight and Denis, aged thirty-one. From Toher roll book I could establish that Thomas was seventeen years old in 1902; Edward was nineteen years old in 1902; Mary was six years old in 1874, and Ellen was six years old in 1887. The other children were Patrick (b.1870), John (b.1874), William (b.1876), Thomas (b.1878), James (b.1885) and Thomas (b.1887).

Martin Butler married Margaret (Greta) Ryan. Martin's sister Bridget died in April 1965. Ned (Edward) married one of the Cose Byrnes in Clonmore and lived in Rathdowney.

Martin and Greta had six children: Brid, Angela, Carmel, Tom, Eddie and Michael. Brid married Sean Lawlor, lives in Templemore and had two sons, Declan and Brian. Declan is a leading light in J.K. Bracken's Golf Society. I met him recently at Conor Fitzpatrick's Captain's Day at Gowran Golf Club. Angela moved to America and married Thomas O'Kelly from Kilmallock, Co. Limerick. Carmel married Dan Campion from Moyne and they have nine children: John, Martin, Kevin, Catherine, Rita, Angela, Dermot, Fintan and Monica. Dan Campion would be a cousin of my mother's through the O'Maras of Moyne (I don't know how many times removed as a cousin). Tom stayed in the home place and married Rene Russell and they have three girls: Margaret, Mary and Paula. Margaret and Mary are married. Margaret married Colin Murphy from Dublin. They live in Thurles and have three children: Conor, Niall and Hannah. Mary married Pat Grey from Kells, Co. Meath. They live in Oldcastle, Co. Meath and have two sons, Ben and Rory. Rene's mother Mary (Mai) Russell died on 1 June 2004, aged eighty-four years. Eddie and Michael, the two other boys, went to the States and married there. Eddie married Ann Hennessy from Ballyduff, Co. Kerry and they have two sons, Kevin and Eric. Michael married Mary Regan from Castlerea, Co. Roscommon and they have three boys: Martin, P.J. and Michael.

Greta Butler died in November 1993, while her husband Martin died in May 1952, over forty years earlier. My grandmother Sarah Doolan and Greta were good friends, and Greta used to come down to Doolans a few times a week. The two of them would be a regular fixture, sitting beside the open fire, when I would call in on the way home from school or if I was sent up for a message by my mother. They were second cousins, and great company for each other.

DEEGAN

Tomas Deegan is living between Bowe's lane and Mick Bergin's in a new house built in recent years. Tomas is Martin and Alice's oldest son. He is married to Ann Gunnell from Roscrea and they have two children, Grainne and Cormac.

BERGINS

Mick Bergin from Lismorrougha, Errill, married Josephine Moore from Killoran, Moyne. They came to live in Togher in September 1967, and they had four children: Jimmy, Teresa, Jayne and John.

Before Bergins lived there, Ger Maher lived there. He married Bridgie Morrissey, a sister of Mrs Fermoyle's, and they had three children. Toby died young in his twenties, around the 1930s. Ciss (Margaret) married Philly Gleeson of Dromard and the other daughter, Bridgie never married.

When the mother died, the father Ger and daughter Bridgie moved to Gleeson's in Dromard. They sold the house in Toher to Mick Guider of Clonmore. Mick and his brothers Jack and Tom were cousins of the Clarkes. After a number of years, Mick Guider sold the house to Mick Bergin.

The Bergin children all married. Jimmy married Helen Gibson from Cloughjordan. They live in Lissanure, Templetuohy and they have three children: Damian, Emma and Jason. Theresa married Pat Hartigan from Templemore and they had five children: Jacinta, Patrick, Lorraine, Therese and Katie-Anne. Jacinta married Dietiviar from South Africa, and they live in Germany. Patrick and his partner, Evelyn Langan from Donegal, live in Roscommon. Lorraine is single. Therese and her partner Jonathan Hogan, from Castleiney, live in Lissanure, where they have two children, Ruth-Ava and Olivia. Katie-Anne, the youngest, is in school. Jayne married Rody Cawley from Nenagh. My father claims to have introduced them to each other at a political function many years ago, but they may have a different version of the story. They have two children, Yvonne and Sara-Jayne, and they live in Templemore. John married Edel Bourke from Drom. They live in Dublin and they have four children: Diane, Michelle, David and Brian. John was slightly younger than me; he was the same age as Tom Clarke. He was a tenacious hurler and wore the blue and gold of Tipperary in a number of grades, including on the All-Ireland winning minor team of 1982. He was living in the parish of Clonmore but played hurling for Templetuohy, as did his brother Jimmy. They were both part of the mini hurling leagues that were played over thirty years ago in the locality. It was handy that they played for 'Touhy, because we could bring a few of the Bourke's from Dromard.

KIELY

The original Kiely family were Murty (b.1841) and his wife Maggie (b.1843). They had two daughters and two sons: Maggie (b.1883), Mary (b.1885), Murty (b.1888) and James (b.1893).

The Kielys lived right beside Mick Bergin, on the same side of the road. This house, at the turn of the 1900s, is recorded as being located in the townland of Lissanure Lower. Murty Kiely was married to Mary Grady from Littleton. Mary's sister Kathy married Tom Myrons. Murty and Mary had seven children: James, Paddy, Neddy (Edward), Mairead, Theresa, Maura and Sadie. The family moved up the road and lived just on the Templetuohy side of the cross of Toher. I remember Jimmy cycling up and down the road. Like Peg Carroll and Neddy Guilfoyle, he often got off the bicycle and walked it up the hill at the Railway Bridge.

Sadie married Frankie Fogarty in Templequain near Errill. Frankie is a nephew of Mrs Carey. Refer back to Meaneys who lived across the road at the end of our house and you will see that the Careys owned that house after Meaneys were gone, along with approximately two acres of land. In the late '50s or early '60s, they sold the two acres and the ruins of the house to Thady Maher. Thady owned the field around it and he cleared the ditches and let it all into the one field. The rest of the Kiely family went to England, as far as I know. The house beside Mick Bergin's is no longer there.

MOYLAN

Originally, Tim Guider (b. 1826) and his wife Johanna (b. 1831) lived where Mickey Moylan now lives. Tim and Johanna had four children: Margaret (b. 1863), John, (b. 1867), Johanna (b. 1869), and Timothy (b. 1871). At the time of the 1901 census, a nephew Patrick Toal (b. 1898) and a niece Ellen Toal (b. 1899) were in the Guider house. The Toal children went to school in Toher so they must have lived in Guiders.

The second son, Tim married Sarah Bergin from Bawn, Courraghneen, Roscrea and they had two daughters, Josie and Mary. Sarah's brother Tommy Bergin came to live with them and died in the early 1960s.

Josie, the older daughter, married Martin Moylan from Camlin, Roscrea. Mary married Charles Fitzpatrick and they had seven children.

Josie and Martin Moylan lived in the home place, and they had ten children: John, Tim, Martin, Joe, Gerard, Con, Mary, Veronica, Sarah and Michael. Josie Moylan was a great character; I remember her well. She died on 12 July 1979, aged fifty-nine years, and her husband Martin died on 21 June 1980, at the age of seventy.

John and his partner Mary Anne, originally from Australia, live in London. Tim married Marie Liston from Moyne and they have four children: Robert, Lance, Siobhan and Fiona. They live in Sydney, Australia. Martin married Maria Tsypisos from Australia and they have three children: Jeremy, Joanna and Caitriona. They too live in Sydney, Australia. Joe married Mary Donnelly from Australia and they have five children: Sean, Brendan, Kathlyn, Marita and Claire. They live in Melbourne, Australia. Gerard married Margaret Joyce from Clonmore and they have three children: Niamh, Wayne and Lisa-Marie. They live in Thurles. Con married Bridget Crimmins from England and they have four children: Finbarr, Conor, Bridget and Tara. They live in Melbourne, Australia. Mary married Kieran Flannery from Birr and they have three children: Sinead, Raymond and Fiona. They live in Clareen, Birr. Veronica died in infancy. Sarah married George Spencer from Roscrea and they have four children: Martina, Tracy, Clodagh and Michelle. They live in Roscrea. Michael married Estelle Rafter from Birr and they have two children, Joanne and Edelle. They live in the home place in Lissanure.

SHELLY'S FIELD

There are a few fields of land up around the Cross of Toher and opposite Moylan's which are owned by Ryans of the Hill, Dromard, Clonmore. There was no house on the land. The land was owned by Michael Shelly, who was married and had one daughter, Bridie. Bridie married Dennis Ryan of the Hill. She is a good friend of the family at home in Clonboo and a regular visitor. Denis Ryan died on 31 May 1996, aged seventy-three years. All the Ryans, Tom, Mick, Ann and Catherine, went to school in Toher. Ann was in my class and is married to Eamonn Cody in Ballysorrell, Clonmore. They have three children: James, Denis and Edward. I recently met Catherine, who married a Killarney man, John O'Dea. They live in Two-Mile House, just outside Naas, and they have three children: Shelly Anne, Jack and Michael. Mick is married to Audrey Murphy. They live in Dromard and they have three children: Denise, Donnacha and Anthony. Tom married Marie Kennedy and they have four children: Denis, Maura, Aidan and Brid. Tom Ryan tragically died on 1 March 2001 at the age of forty-three years.

SPIRIT'S BUSH

There is a Spirit's Bush up around Darmody's lane. Well, we were always told that growing up, but it might have been made up to frighten us. I'm not sure if it is still there, but there is no way I would have cut it down!

PATRICK FLYNN (AND WAKES)

From the previous list of Clonbough entries, most of the people have been tracked back to their home place, but there are a number that remain unaccounted for in relation to their place of residence.

One such resident was Patrick Flynn, who we think lived up past where Deegans live, near where Bowes or Darmodys lived. He lived there on his own and had no known relatives from the area or from any of the nearby parishes.

When Patrick Flynn died, the story goes that he was laid out and the wake started in the house on the first night that he died. A wake was, and still is, an important part of country life. When a person died, the clock in the house was usually stopped to show the time of death, and restarted when the funeral was over or when the corpse left the house. Wakes were a big occasion, with loads of drink and refreshments provided. With no known relatives, all the local neighbours put money together and bought stout, whiskey and some snuff. A huge gathering at a wake would be talked about for a long time, as a good wake was a reflection on the dead person's popularity and a good farewell to a loved one. The wake also helped close relatives and friends through their grief.

The term 'as plentiful as snuff at a wake' is commonly used nowadays to describe an abundance of something or other. Near the door of the wake house each visiting mourner took a pinch of snuff or a pipe of tobacco. Before sniffing or lighting up, the mourner said a prayer for the dead person and offered condolences. A family member always stayed in the room with the corpse and someone always stayed up during the night with the dead body.

The laypeople kept the corpse and said the prayers and rosaries during the wake. When the corpse arrived at the church, then the clergy took over the proceedings, including the funeral Mass and the burial. The problem with Patrick Flynn's wake was that with no immediate relative, the wake went on from one night to another with no plans to take the body to the church. Late one night, when the wake was in full swing, the parish priest arrived at the house to find out what was going on. He asked, 'Have ye any notion of sending this man to the chapel?' and he received a reply from one of the so-called mourners, 'Oh, God no, sure the boys from Galmoy were over last night to see if they could have him for a few nights!'

NEDDY LOOBY

Neddy Looby was our postman when I was growing up. At first he had a pushbike but most of the time I remember him having a Honda 50 motorbike. A postman's job wasn't easy in those days, although there was no junk mail to deliver. Getting post on a daily basis was not a common occurrence, although some deliveries were regular, such as demand notices for rates and letters from America. Like all rural postmen, Neddy Looby was one of the main sources of news and goings-on in the locality. As well as delivering post, he also collected letters to be posted and took them back to the post office. For some people who lived on their own, Neddy Looby was often the only person they met on a particular day. Of course a lot of houses were in off the main road, and along with vicious dogs, bad roads, and opening and closing gates, the glamour side of the postman's job was hard to identify at times.

The time it took Neddy Looby to deliver the post varied greatly, depending on the volume of post and the stoppages and delays. He often got off the bike to stand in goals if we were having a match in the yard and he would stop for cups of tea, to collect cabbage plants, to pass on messages, etc. Of course Ned had several ways of shortcutting the deliveries, which would not be strictly following procedures, such as meeting someone along the road or giving the post to a child on the way home from school.

Christmas time was always great crack. We would be at home from school and Neddy Looby would often have to bring a driver, as very few houses would let him pass without offering a festive drink. He had post for almost all the houses at that time of year because of Christmas cards. There were probably thirty or forty houses on his run, so work that out in terms of alcohol consumed!

Neddy Looby was born on Easter Monday 1916, a famous day. He was appointed postman in 1956 and retired from the job in 1982. He came from one of the oldest families in Templetuohy and married Christine Leahy from Clonmore in 1943. They had five children. His great love, without any doubt, was the fiddle. He was an accomplished fiddle player and won competitions all over the country. He was as they say, 'a character'. Sadly, Neddy Looby died in January 2009.

The telephone exchange was based in the post office in Templetuohy. To make a local phone call you had to wind up the phone to get Mrs Griffen or Mary Fogarty, the postmistresses, who had to connect you manually. Our number at home was Templetuohy 28. If you needed to get a connection to a number further away, the exchange in Templetuohy would have to contact a bigger exchange in Thurles or Portlaoise. Mrs Griffen was a great source of information. If you rang to get connected to Clarke's or Toby Maher's, you wouldn't even need the number. As well as that, Mrs Griffen would be likely to tell you that Toby was gone to Thurles, because he was on earlier looking for the time of a funeral going from Moyne to the Cathedral. The exchange, although slow, provided an invaluable service and kept all the community in touch with each other. It is fair to say that that was a part of life that is badly missing from modern built-up areas. People who lived in houses hundreds of yards and miles apart were closer together than people nowadays who live literally on top of each other. Ask anyone living in an apartment block today and they would find it hard to tell you four or five of their neighbours' names – in fact they mightn't have ever met them! The exchange in Templetuohy continued to be manually operated until 1984.

LIME KILNS

There were six lime kilns in the Clonboo area, while there were sixteen in Lissanure and a further ten in the Toher townland. Lime was the principal manure which farmers in the region used to apply to their land, combined with farmland manure generated on their own farms, and turf mould, which they brought from the bog. Landlords built lime kilns for the production of lime for their own lands around the late 1800s. The spreading of lime contributed to the increased productivity of good land and to the reclamation of poorer and marshy land. As other types of artificial manures became available, the use of lime kilns gradually stopped.

DEVIL'S BIT/RIVER SUIR

The Devil's Bit takes up a good lump of the horizon from the Clonboo townland. Its story is simple (and true!). The mountain is part of Slieve Bloom range of mountains and stands 1,577 feet in height.

The story goes that long ago the Devil was passing over Ireland when he dropped in to have something to eat. He took a large mouthful out of the mountain. Some say he broke a tooth taking the bite, and others say he did not like the taste so he spat it out. The lump that he spat out landed in Cashel and the locals, at the time, built a castle upon the piece of rock. This place is known today as the Rock of Cashel, a famous national landmark and, as my Cashel friends keep telling me, it forms part of the emblem on the Tipperary GAA jersey. This historical site houses an imposing Cathedral and round tower encompassing some 2,000 years of history. It was once an important ecclesiastical centre and home to the Kings of Munster.

Not all of the rock was spat out in a clean spit, so to speak. Parts landed or dribbled out of the Devil's mouth as he travelled away from Templemore. If travelling in the car to Nenagh, you can see bits of the rock in fields and along the side of the road around Drom, Borrisoleigh, Barnane, etc. … well that's what we were told by our parents!

The Devil's Bit is also known in Irish as Bearnan Eile. Despite not being a relatively high mountain, it offers fine views of the surrounding countryside. It is possible to see nine counties from its summit: Tipperary, Offaly, Laois, Kilkenny, Waterford, Cork, Limerick, Clare and Galway.

The tower on the approach to the summit is known as Carden's Folly. The Cardens were an Anglo-Irish aristocratic family who owned much of the land in the area in the eighteenth and nineteenth centuries. A folly was a name given to a structure which was built for ornamental or ostentatious rather than practical purposes. The ruins of Carden's castle are on the lower slopes of the mountain. The illuminated Christ the King Cross was dedicated by Archbishop Jermiah Kinnane and erected on the 'Rock' in 1954 to commemorate the Catholic celebration of Marian Year. The ancient custom of climbing the Rock continues to this day. On Rock Sunday, which is celebrated annually on the Sunday closest to the feast of St James on 25 July, young and old take on the challenge of climbing it. Mass is then celebrated at an altar located close to the holy well at the base of the rock. A statue of the Virgin Mary was erected there in 1988.

The River Suir rises on the slopes of Devil's Bit mountain and flows down by Templemore. It passes south through the county and forms a lush land-rich pastoral stretch of land known as the 'Golden Vale'. The river, according to legend began to flow on the night that King Conn of the Hundred Battles was born. It flows in a southerly direction through the towns of Templemore, Thurles, Cahir and Ardfinnan. After Ardfinnan it flows in an easterly direction through the towns of Clonmel and Carrick-on-Suir, and through Waterford City, before it enters the sea at Waterford Harbour near Dunmore East. The Suir meets the the Rivers Nore and Barrow at Cheekpoint, and the three rivers are known as the 'Three Sisters'.

LISDUFF QUARRY

Another very visible landmark on the horizon at the end of our lane is Lisduff Quarry. It was primarily used by CIE for the stone under and around the railway sleepers on the railway tracks. There was a huge conveyor built high over the road from the quarry to the railway line. A train would come along with empty dump-truck carriages. The digger machines would load up the hopper at the quarry side and the conveyor would transfer the stone up the belts, over the road and into the carriages. Off it would go. We often went down to see the carriages being loaded, as the noise of the stone travelling over the road on the conveyor up high, and the noise and dust rising when the stones fell into the carriages, generated a bit of excitement for young minds. We used to try and recreate a similar exercise in our own yard with smaller gravel piles and using bean tins or plastic cups that were used to measure sheep dip.

The quarry in Lisduff was very labour intensive from the 1930s up to the 1960s, and there could have been fifty or sixty men working there at any one time. A small village was built for some of the workers and their families. The houses were built from metal sheeting and were located between the quarry and the main road. There were two rows of houses; about ten or twelve families lived there. Johnny Tynan lived there before he moved to Clonboo. The group of houses was known as the 'Terrace'. I barely remember them. They were there in the '60s but they are all gone a long time now.

Before the automated conveyor belt and other machinery were installed, the stone and gravel was transferred across the road in buckets on a rope. This exercise was always worth seeing. Most of the workers came from the surrounding areas and they would all come to work on bicycles. Distances of up to ten miles on old-fashioned bicycles on bad roads was tough going in the morning, and worse in the evening during the summer and winter after a hard manual day's work.

Pat Joe Hassett lived just beside the quarry. He was in my class in Toher and I thought he had it all, living there. Of course when they were blasting in the quarry, he really had it made!

We used to walk the train tracks, especially when I was on my holidays in Bourke's. The train tracks were right behind their house. It may appear highly dangerous, but at the time trains didn't run as often or as regularly as they do nowadays. The stones used around the train tracks were ideally sized for use as ammunition. The ESB put their poles up along the track lines because the timber poles could be transported by the train wagons. However, after the ESB erected the poles, they would take a while before the wires were tied on. It was an industrial demarcation thing that the guys who put the poles up could not but the wires on to them.

It's a bit like the guy who was going along the grass verge outside a Bed & Breakfast in Roscommon digging holes equal distances apart. An American tourist was watching the man, going along digging the holes, all morning. By lunchtime he had twenty-five or thirty neat holes, which went on for a couple of hundred yards.

The American, on returning to the Bed & Breakfast to collect a coat, was impressed by the progress made, but when he returned later in the afternoon the man was busily filling all the holes. The American wondered what the man was doing and thought of the waste of time and energy, so he asked the man what he was doing. The man explained that the guy that was supposed to put the trees into the holes was out sick that day!

Going back to the ESB poles, the absence of wire meant that those shiny white ceramic isolators at the tops of the poles had no real use. The ESB never used all of the isolators in any event, we told ourselves. We had ready-made ammunition all around us, so we got great target practice, clipping lumps out of the ceramic pieces on top of the poles. It was an ideal setting and stood to us in years to come for various sports – bowling, clay pigeon shooting, darts, skittles, etc.

There was also a train station in Lisduff, but I don't remember it myself as it closed down in 1962 (I was born in December 1962). It started operating in and around 1894. Johnny Bourke, in his article for the *Rathdowney Review* of 2005, mentioned that Lord Castletown was responsible for its location, as he wanted to get people to the game-shooting expeditions that he regularly held in Lisduff. The station was a great facility for the local people and a very valuable asset to the community and to farmers. There was a store located near the station around which rotated the local activities of the area. Local shops collected their supplies from this store, which had stock delivered by train, and farmers collected seeds and other essential goods for their farms there. The farmers also used the trains to transport their produce to market. Wages for the workers in the quarry were also delivered by train, and another important commodity was collected by the public houses of the area – barrels of Guinness!

In a time when cars were a rare sight and even bicycles were not too plentiful, the train as a method of transport was very important. Lots of people used the train to travel to and from Templemore for the weekly shopping, and the train was the only way to get to GAA matches. Mícheál Ó Muircheartaigh wrote about how, when radios were scarce and the telephone had not been invented, the return of the train would be the first news of a match result for the people back home. Indeed, he said that when the train was still a few hundred yards away from the station the crowds waiting would have a fair idea of the result, depending on whether the flags were out the windows or not to be seen. Great crowds would always be waiting for the arrival of 'the news'.

The biggest and busiest time in the year for the station was during the winter beet harvest, which started in late October and lasted until March. All the beet in the area was transported to the nearest sugar-beet factory in Thurles. Yes, for the younger reader, that is how sugar is made. Most of the beet was brought to Lisduff by horse and cart, with each farmer having his own train wagon to fill. A wagon could take around ten cart loads. Wagons were working around the clock and horses worked all through the night. At any one time there could be thirty or forty horses drawing beet to the station.

The station closed in 1962.

CHAPTER 5

TOHER SCHOOL

The roll books and other school records and reports were moved from Toher School at the time it closed in 1998. Unfortunately there no longer exists a complete set of records and roll books. However, there is a comprehensive amount of information, a selection of which is outlined as follows:

(a)　List of all full-time teachers from 1840 to 1998.

(b)　Corporal punishment book, 1908 to 1910.

(c)　Early roll-book entries and details for adults who attended Toher school around 1902 and 1903.

(d)　Girls' roll book, 1867 to 1909.

(e)　Examination roll (and promotion sheet) for boys and girls, 1892 and 1899.

(f)　Primary School Certificate examinations.

(g)　Teachers' daily reports and Inspectors' reports from 1890s.

(h)　Irish Folklore Commission of 1937.

(i)　Clonmore School.

(j)　Templemore CBS.

(k)　Toher school pupils listing from all available roll books from 1901 to 1998.

TEACHERS

The original school in Toher was built in 1839 with the financial help of local Protestant and Catholic clergy, along with neighbouring farmers, notably the Doolans and Greeds, who gave the land for the new school. Similar to other schools at the time, applications were made to the Board of Education for the teachers wages along with desks and seating. Prior to this, another school must have been located there as it was connected to the Board of Education in 1832.

The teachers were:

1840: Patrick Doyle

1841-1873: Dominic McNamee (Principal), Johanna McNamee (Work Mistress)

1873-1892: Johanna Fogarty (*née* McNamee), John Burke and James Kennedy

1899-1897: Peter Flynn

1897-1909: Joseph Downey

1909-1950: Johanna Ryan (Principal), (Mrs O'Meara, married name)

1923: Became a two-teacher school

1923-1940: Myra Gavin (Assistant)

1947: Maire Brennan (Assistant), Brid Hennessy (Assistant)

1950: Peggy Ryan (Assistant), (Mrs Gleeson, married name)

1951: Anna Tighe (Assistant)

1952: September 1952, one-teacher school , Josephine McCraughen

1953: December 1953, Margaret Bourke (Principal), (Mrs Fogarty)

1955: Anna Butler (Principal)

1956: Alice Kennedy (Principal), (Mrs Bergin)

1966: Two-teacher school

1966-1995: Margaret (Peg) Fogarty (*née* Bourke) (Assistant)

1997: Miss Ryan replaces Mrs Bergin

1998: January-June, Mary Butler

The school closed in June 1998.

CORPORAL PUNISHMENT BOOK

During a review of the roll books for Toher school, I came across a register of the school's Corporal Punishment Book. This was an official register and contains instructions and guidance notes from the Office of National Education in Marlborough Street, Dublin. The guidance notes were printed inside the cover of the register as follows:

1. Corporal Punishment should be administered for grave transgressions – never for failure in lessons.

2. The Principal Teacher should inflict the corporal punishment. An interval of at least 10 minutes should elapse between the offence and the punishment.

3. Only a light cane or rod may be used for the purpose of inflicting the corporal punishment. The boxing of ears, the pulling of hair and similar ill treatment are absolutely forbidden and will be visited with severe penalties.

4. No teacher should carry a cane or other instrument of punishment.

5. Frequent recourse to corporal punishment will be concluded by the commissioner as indicating bad tone and ineffective discipline.

6.   The particulars required by the headings shall be entered in the book before inflicting the punishment.

7.   The Principal teacher must submit the book to the manager on the occasion of his first visit to the school after every case of punishment.

P.E. LEMASS, M.J. DILWORTH
Secretaries
Office of National Education, Marlborough Street, Dublin

Author's Note: *For a laugh, read the above to your children.*

There were only twenty-seven entries into the register, on a couple of pages; the rest of the book was blank. The years recorded were 1908, 1909 and 1910. The offences recorded were largely under three or four headings, namely 'idleness', 'coming in past play hour', 'horseplay in class' and 'negligent at work'. The nature of the punishment was recorded as either 'one slap' or 'two slaps'. I don't think I will cause any offence or embarrassment by naming these pupils, and there were a few who were regular entrants over the three years of the records: Henry Fitzpatrick, Susan Shelly, Johanna Carroll, James Kiely, Murty Kiely, Joseph Grimes, Tim Shelly, Pat Loughnane, Thomas Grimes, William Fitzpatrick, Pat Grimes, Alphonsous Deegan, J. Bergin, Kathy Fogarty, Lizzie Fogarty and Nora Carroll.

EARLY ROLL BOOKS

The roll books of Toher school make very interesting reading, and a valuable source of information. Although a number of the roll books are missing, there are still great treasures to be found within their pages.

   The earliest roll book that I found starts in the year 1867, and contains information about the pupils such as 'dates of entrance', 'age of child', 'religious denomination', 'occupation or means of living of parents', 'number of days present in school' and 'examination results'.

   The roll book is divided between girls and boys, but it is not clear if they were taught separately. The entries for the girls are from the period 1871 to 1907, although the entries between 1895 and 1907 appear very sparse, unless there was a dramatic downturn in the numbers in that period. The entries for the boys cover the period 1902 and 1903. On first review of this roll book, I was somewhat taken aback when looking at the pupils' ages. They span from three years to forty years old! However, upon further review I noted that some people attended evening school. In summary, the roll book is actually a record of the girls' primary school attendees and a record of the evening school attendees, who are all men from the age of fourteen to forty.

TOHER EVENING SCHOOL (MALES)

DATE OF ENTRANCE: OCTOBER 1902

NAME	AGE	TOWNLAND
Michael Carroll	18	Toher
Daniel Morrissey	22	Clonboo
John Hanrahan	25	Toher
Michael Feehely	31	Toher
John Guider	40	Lissanure
James Maher	30	Toher
Thomas Greed	30	Clonboo
Philip Maher	23	Toher
John Butler	26	Clonboo
Michael Greed	26	Clonboo
James Greed	31	Clonboo
William Loughnane	24	Toher
Jeremiah Maher	29	Toher
Edward Butler	19	Toher
Denis Butler	24	Toher
Thomas Butler	22	Clonboo
Martin Lanigan	19	Clonboo
Thomas Deegan	16	Clonboo
Tobias Maher	16	Toher
Patrick Feehely	17	Toher
Michael Maher	19	Toher
Richard Grimes	20	Clonboo
John Loughnane	25	Toher
Peter Deegan	17	Clonboo
Martin Guilfoyle	40	Clonboo
Martin Morrissey	29	Clonboo
Thomas Feehely	26	Toher
John Deegan	19	Clonboo
James Fermoyle	36	Clonboo
Patrick Morrissey	21	Clonboo
James Carroll	25	Toher
John Carey	27	Clonmeen
Thomas Butler	17	Toher

Thomas Meaney	40	Clonboo
Edward Kennedy	30	Lissanure
Joseph Greed	22	Lissanure
Daniel Talbot	21	Tullow
Martin Butler	30	Toher
Joseph Carey	19	Lissanure
John Lawlor	17	Lissanure
John Carroll	18	Toher
Michael Meaney	26	Clonboo
Michael Talbot	18	Tullow
John McCann	25	Templetuohy
James Delaney	19	Tullow
Pat Day	27	Clonmeen
Michael Brophy	17	Clonmeen

DATE OF ENTRANCE: OCTOBER 1903

William Grimes	14	Clonboo
Edward Maher	14	Clonboo
John Hanrahan	23	Toher
Philip Maher	23	Toher
John Butler	26	Clonboo
Michael Clarke	19	Clonboo
Toby Maher	19	Toher
Thomas Butler	17	Toher
Murty Kiely	15	Toher
Edward Butler	19	Toher
James Delhaunty	17	Toher
James Shehan	26	Toher
Patrick Feehely	19	Toher
Edward Kennedy	31	Lissanure
Denis Deegan	15	Clonboo
James Fermoyle	34	Clonboo
Thomas Feehely	27	Toher
Joseph Carey	20	Lissanure
William Whelan	16	Clonboo
Joseph Clarke	16	Clonboo
Daniel Lawlor	19	Toher
James Bowe	27	Tullow

Patrick Delaney	19	Tullow
Thomas Clarke	25	Clonboo
Mick Prendergast	30	Clonboo
Thomas Butler	22	Clonboo
Patrick Day	26	Clonmeen
John Carey	29	Clonmeen
John Grimes	15	Toher
Michael Talbot	19	Tullow
John Lawlor	19	Toher
Patrick Brien	20	Tullow
Thomas Talbot	17	Tullow

Author's Note: There are duplications in the above two lists and there are inconsistencies in the age details etc, but these are the contents of the records reviewed.

GIRLS' ROLL BOOK

DATE OF ENTRANCE	PUPIL NAME	AGE	TOWNLAND
1867	Anne Loughnane	12	Clonboo
1868	Johanna Guyder	7	Lissanure
	Anne Guyder	8	Lissanure
1869	Johanna King	11	Clonmeen
1871	Mary Maher	7	Lissanure
	Margaret Burke	12	Tullow
	Anne Burke	7	Tullow
	Ellenor Burke	10	Tullow
	Mary Moloy	7	Clonboo
	Catherine Guilfoyle	14	Clonboo
1872	Mary Burke	16	Tullow
	Johanna McNamee	24	Clonboo
	Anne M Guyder	8	Lissanure

	Catherine Moran	8	Toher
	Mary Fitzpatrick	15	Toher
1873	Margaret Greed	7	Clonboo
	Mary Flinn	7	Clonboo
	Margaret Moran	7	Toher
	Catherine Burke	16	Clonboo
	Catherine Burke	18	Tullow
	Bridget Greed	10	Clonboo
	Mary Costigan Butler	18	Tullow
	Ellenor Ryan	10	Clonboo
	Catherine Treacy	7	Lissanure
	Bridget Butler	8	Gragavalla
	Sarah Burke	14	Tullow
	Mary Carey	10	Lissanure
	Margaret Guider	15	Lissanure
	Alica Burke	10	Tullow
1874	Julia Davy	11	Clonboo
	Bridget Bourke	7	Clonboo
	Marianne Ryan	7	Toher
	Bridget Nolan	8	Clonboo
	Maria Nolan	10	Clonboo
	Anto Moloy	7	Clonboo
	Mary Butler	6	Toher
	Sarah Ryan	6	Derraloughta
	Johanna Bowe	6	Lissanure
	Margaret Hoolahan	7	Tullow
1875	Catherine Guider	5	Lissanure
	Eleanor Hoolahan	13	Tullow
	Julia Ryan	13	Toher
	Mary Murphy	9	Lisdaleen
	Catherine Murphy	7	Lisdaleen
1876	Margaret Loughnane	8	Lissanure
	Margaret Treacy	10	Tullow

	Kate Nolan	17	Clonboo
	Mary Lawlor	6	Lissanure
	Mary Moran	5	Toher
	Eleanor Treacy	6	Lissanure
	Margaret Carey	7	Lissanure
	Nanno Burke	6	Tullow
	Lissie Phelan	6	Tullow
	Marianne Feehely	8	Toher
1877	Eleanor King	7	Clonmeen
	Johanna Ryan	11	Lissanure
	Bridget Butler	5	Toher
	Eleanor Bourke	6	Tullow
	Johanna Moloy	7	Clonboo
	Marianne Treacy	6	Lissanure
	Mary Meaney	8	Clonboo
	Sarah Meaney	6	Clonboo
	Margaret Meaney	7	Clonboo
	Mary A. Ringwood	6	Toher
1878	Elizabeth Bergin	11	Dromard
	Mary Clarke	6	Clonboo
	Ellen Guider	6	Lissanure
	Ellen Delhaunty	6	Clonmeen
	Mary Kennedy	6	Lissanure
1879	Ellen Skehan	7	Lisdaleen
	Norah Carroll	7	Toher
	Grace Martin	9	Lisdaleen
	Anastatia Cullen	13	Clonboo
	Norah Maher	7	Lissanure
	Margaret Lawlor	7	Lissanure
	Margaret Keys	12	Dromard
	Mary Keys	15	Dromard
	Johanna Maher	5	Lissanure
	Catherine Walsh	6	Toher
	Johanna Darmady	6	Lissanure

1880	Mary Luindlan	13	Tullow
	Bridget Carey	7	Lissanure
	Sophia Ringwood	7	Toher
	Johanna Guider	15	Lissanure
	Anne Bourke	15	Tullow
	Margaret Guider	18	Lissanure
	Norah Murphy		Lisdaleen
	Lizzie Feehely	11	Dromard
1881	Bridget Lawlor	6	Lissanure
	Ellen Clarke	6	Clonboo
	Alica Morrissey	6	Clonboo
	Johanna Bowe	6	Killina
	Mary A Ryan	5	Dromard
	Margaret Bergin	8	Dromard
	Bridget Bergin	12	Dromard
	Annie Bowe	9	Dromard
	Mary Prendergast	6	Sorrellhill
	Margaret Feehely	6	Toher
	Kate Lowry	9	Dromard
	Ellen Keys	12	Dromard
	Mary A Davy	9	Dromard
	Mary Costigan	15	Lisdaleen
1882	Ella Morrissey	6	Clonboo
	Johanna Doolan	6	Clonboo
	Bridget Lee	5	Sorrellhill
	Ellen Carey	6	Lissanure
	Bridget Meehan	12	Dromard
	Annie Fitzpatrick	9	Tullow
	Margaret Fitzpatrick	11	Tullow
	Bridget Keys	7	Dromard
	Margaret Bowe	6	Lissanure
	Johanna Ryan	7	Templetuohy
	Annie Costigan	9	Toher
	Kate Costigan	11	Toher
	Mary Quinlan	10	Dromard

	Mary Ann Ryan	15	Derraloughta
	Bridget Bourke	16	Tullow
	Kate Bergin	14	Lismorough
1883	Julia Hayes	18	Lismorough
	Mary A Walsh	6	Toher
	Mary Bowe	7	Lissanure
	Ellen Lawlor	6	Lissanure
	Mary Hennessy	7	Tullow
	Ellen Prendergast	6	Sorrellhill
	Nanno Treacy	6	Lissanure
	Ellen Carroll	9	Toher
	Winfred Keenan	8	Sorrellhill
	Kate Meehan	8	Dromard
	Kate Stapleton	7	Dromard
	Mary Carroll	5	Toher
	Catherine Guider	14	Lissanure
	Lissie Stapleton	9	Dromard
1884	Kate Delaney	7	Dromard
	Mary Larkin	6	Tullow
	Margaret Molloy	6	Clonboo
	Mary Delaney	14	Dromard
1885	Mary Larkin	6	Tullow
	Ellie Larkin	9	Tullow
	Mary A Morrissey	7	Clonboo
	Margaret Clarke	5	Clonboo
	Margaret Doolan	7	Clonboo
	Margaret Lanigan	5	Clonboo
	Maria Costigan	7	Toher
	Kate Meaney	7	Clonboo
	Ellen Stapleton	6	Dromard
	Margaret Darmady	5	Lissanure
	Mary Morrissey	6	Clonboo
	Nanno Bourke	16	Tullow

	Mary Moran	14	Toher
	Bridget Butler	14	Toher
	Eleanor Bourke	14	Tullow
1886	Annie Bowe	6	Lissanure
	Kate Loughnane	6	Toher
	Martha Ringwood	7	Toher
	Margaret Larkin	8	Tullow
	Mary J. Kearney	16	Dromard
	Margaret Meehan	8	Dromard
	Mary Laffan	8	Dromard
	Mary Bergin	10	Dromard
	Mary A Meehan	10	Dromard
	Kate Meehan	11	Dromard
	Mary A Bowe	8	Killina
	Mary Talbert	6	Tullow
	Norah Maher	15	Lissanure
	Mary Kennedy	14	Lissanure
	Mary Clarke	14	Clonboo
1887	Catherine Clarke	6	Clonboo
	Ellen Butler	6	Toher
	Mary A. Doolan	6	Clonboo
	Johanna Treacy	5	Lissanure
	Annie Carey	7	Lissanure
	Sarah Costigan	7	Toher
	Bridget Bowe	6	Lissanure
	Lissie Darmady	6	Lissanure
	Mary Greed	6	Clonboo
	Ellen Shelly	6	Tullow
	Mary Ryan	19	Dromard
	Norah Feehely	7	Toher
	Anne Murphy	8	Lisdaleen
	Mary A. Treacy	15	Lissanure
1889	Julia Butler	6	Clonboo

	Winfred Clarke	6	Clonboo
	Anne Lawlor	7	Lissanure
	Lissie Greed	6	Clonboo
	Johanna Greed	6	Clonboo
	Johanna Maher	14	Lissanure
	Catherine Walsh	15	Toher
	Kate Pyne	8	Sorrellhill
	Lissie Feeley	7	Toher
	Bridget Stapleton	7	Dromard
	Mary Prendergast	14	Sorrellhill
1890	Ellen Deegan	6	Clonboo
	Ellen Feeley	6	Toher
	Ellen Clarke	16	Clonboo
1891	Mary Loughnane	10	Lissanure
	Mary Delhaunty	15	Tullow
	Ellen Lawlor	7	Dromard
1892	Norah Shelly	7	Tullow
1893	Mary A. Laffan	10	Dromard
	Johanna Delaney	13	Dromard
	Norah Deegan	6	Clonboo
1894	Bridget Stapleton	9	Dromard
	Bridget Teacy	7	Lissanure
	Kate Delahunty	8	Toher
	Mary Shelly	6	Tullow
1895	Katie Carroll		Lissanure
	Ellen Butler	13	Toher
	Mary Walsh	15	Toher
	Mary Butler	9	Clonbough
	Hannah Cahill	13	Dromard
	Johanna Stapleton	9	Dromard
	Ellen Loughnane	8	Toher

	Mary A. Doolan	13	Clonboo
1896	Sarah Costigan	15	Toher
	Maggie Cahill	10	Dromard
	Mary Kiely	10	Lissanure
	Lizzie Darmody	14	Lissanure
	Bridget Maher	8	Clonbough
	Maggie Loughnane	7	Toher
	Maggie Kiely	14	Lissanure
	Mary Deegan	6	Clonbough
	Katie Butler	7	Toher
	Mary Shelly	6	Lissanure
1898	Norah Talbert	11	Tullow
	Maggie Doherty	11	Longorchard
	Norah Bowe	8	Lissanure
	Mary Grimes	10	Clonboo
	Lizzie Brophy	7	Toher
	Mary Davy	14	Toher
	Norah Meade	12	Tullow
	Statia Talbert	14	Tullow
1899	Annie Talbert	8	Tullow
	Maggie Talbert	6	Tullow
	Bridget Carroll	10	Toher
1900	Susan Shelly	5	Toher
	Johanna Carroll	6	Toher
	Annie Loughnane	6	Toher
1901	Annie Stapleton	7	Dromard
	Katie Grimes	9	Clonboo
1903	Katie Bergin	6	Dromard
	Maggie Ryan	6	Clonboo
	Julia Talbot	6	Tullow
	Mary Carroll	6	Clonboo

	Katie Lacy	13	Templetuohy
1904	Ellie Treacy	12	Clonboo
	Mary Treacy	11	Clonboo
	Annie Delaney	13	Tullow
	Johanna Lacy	14	Rossmore
	Mary Ryan	6	Clonboo
	Catherine Shelly	7	Toher
1905	Maggie Delaney	7	Tullow
	Anastatia Ryan	12	Clonboo
1907	Winfred Kennehan	9	Clonboo
1908	Katie Grimes	13	Clonboo
1909	Lena Ryan	6	Clonboo
	Bridget Murray	14	Lismorrougha
	Norah Whelan	6	Lismorrougha
	Bridie Whelan	4	Lismorrougha
	Myra Gavin		Clonboo
	Lizzie Whelan	7	Clonboo

EXAMINATION ROLL (AND PROMOTION SHEET)

Without going into the vast amount of information contained in theses rolls, the examination roll breaks down the classes, which are interesting. In 1892, there were no classes above fifth class with twenty-nine pupils in Toher school, but by the end of the decade in 1899, there was Sixth Class, with two stages, and thirty-eight pupils.

Most of my grandfather's generation attended during this decade so it is useful to identify the other pupils in their classes.

EXAMINATION ROLL, 31 OCTOBER 1892.
NAME OF MANAGER: REVD JAS HICKEY PP. TEACHER: PETER FLYNN.

CLASS	PUPILS	AGE	NOS OF DAYS IN SCHOOL
Infants	Matthew Butler	6	126

	Joseph Carey	6	111
	Denis Deegan	5	126
	Denis Butler	5	124
	Norah Deegan	6	125
First	Daniel Lawlor	8	103
	Thomas Deegan	7	130
	Michael Clarke	7	175
	Michael Gallagher	7	128
	Mary Butler	7	115
Second	James Clarke	8	174
	Thomas Butler	9	122
	Johanna Greed	9	148
	Mary A. Doolan	11	119
	Ellen Deegan	8	122
Third	Edward Butler	10	125
	John Deegan	10	111
Fourth	Thomas Kean	12	134
	Julia Butler	10	129
	Winifred Clarke	10	165
	Annie Lawlor	10	100
	Lizzie Greed	10	151
Fifth	Denis Butler	12	111
	Daniel Maher	11	113
	Catherine Clarke	12	138
	Ellen Butler	12	136
	Johanna Treacy	11	107
	Lizzie Darmody	12	134
	Mary Greed	12	125

EXAMINATION ROLL, 31 DECEMBER 1899.
NAME OF MANAGER: REVD JAS HICKEY PP. TEACHER: JOSEPH DOWNEY.

Infants	Richard Carroll	6	142
	James Kiely	6	204
	Pat Butler	5	163
	Susan Shelly	5	187
	Johanna Carroll	5	163
	Annie Loughnane	6	114
First	Michael Shelly	7	164
	Maggie Talbot	6	135
Second	Mick Myrens	7	114
Third	Peter Deegan	13	100
	John Maher	8	111
	Pat Cahill	9	100
	John Grimes	8	100
	William Grimes	11	100
	Bridget Maher	12	113
	Katie Butler	9	159
	Mary Deegan	8	138
	Norah Bowe	9	119
	Mary Shelly	8	115
Fourth	Denis Shelly	11	120
	Murty Kiely	10	167
	William Fogarty	11	100
	Mary Davy	15	149
	Maggie Loughnane	11	111
	Annie Talbot	8	133
Fifth 1st Stage	Mary Shelly	12	100
2nd Stage	Denis Butler	11	113
	Thomas Butler	11	177
	John Lawlor	11	112

Sixth 1st Stage	Thos Deegan	14	102
	Matthew Butler	12	101
	Pat Feehely	13	103
	Norah Deegan	12	124
2nd Stage	James Clarke	15	116
	Edward Butler	16	104
	Maggie Doherty	13	134
	Norah Talbot	12	121
	Ellen Deegan	15	116

PRIMARY SCHOOL CERTIFICATE EXAMINTATIONS

When talking about exam results nowadays, we usually regard the Leaving Cert as one of the most important exams in which to achieve a good result. The Junior Cert, which replaced the Immediate Cert some years ago, must also get a mention. Nowadays, a greater proportion of students continue on to third-level education by attending one of the many Universities or Higher Education Institutes and it could be said that it has become the norm that students progress to third level.

However in the Ireland of the first half of the twentieth century, the Primary Certificate was the normal and most commonly sought-after examination. The three subjects taken in the Primary Exam were Irish, Sums and English. The pass mark in each subject was 80 and the maximum mark was 200 in each subject. Before that, in the years of the nineteenth century, the exams taken were Reading, Writing and Arithmetic.

The other big glaring observation from the roll books in the 1930s, '40s and '50s, was the attendance records of the pupils. The days when pupils were absent usually coincided with good weather, or when turf had to be cut, hay saved or corn trashed. My own father's school year was often interrupted by up to two or three weeks at a time, when work had to be done on the farm at home. This could happen four or five times a year. But fair dues to him for getting a very good mark of 170 out of a maximum of 200 in Arithmetic!

TEACHERS' DAILY REPORTS AND INSPECTORS' REPORTS

Several other nuggets of information were found in the Teachers' Daily Reports, which had to be prepared and then checked by the Inspector. Apart from the pupils' examinations and attendance records, the physical condition of the school and its contents such as desks and forms were noted. The Inspectors' visits and their subsequent reports would have made for undoubtedly stressful times for the teachers. In the reports that I have seen from the 1890s period, the contents were detailed and sometimes hard-hitting, with nothing spared by the Inspector. An example of the summary sections of one such report went as follows:

> Only 29 pupils were qualified by attendances to be examined for Results purposes.
>
> There were none in Senior Fifth or in Sixth Class.
>
> The school is in a very low state of efficiency, and although this is chiefly to be ascribed to the gross negligence of the Teacher that resigned last year, yet I think something more might have been done by the successor to improve the Third Class, the Fourth Class Geography and the Fifth Class generally.
>
> Three new desks have been provided by the Manager, and the school has been floored.
>
> A new map of Ireland is needed.
>
> Signed by the District Inspector

Another example went as follows:

> The state of proficiency in general is low.
>
> The answering was particularly backward in Grammar and Geography: and Spelling especially in Third Class also required more careful instruction. Writing is taught with very fair success and Needlework is good.
>
> The prevalence of an epidemic (the flu) during the past year and the situation of the school, where the pupils were employed at home more continually than usual during the late harvest season. This no doubt contributed unfavourably to the work of preparation for this examination.
>
> The pupils are not sufficiently free from the habit of whispering which has the effect of prompting. Their powers of attention are also not properly cultivated and they are accustomed apparently in the teaching to wait for individual directions.
>
> The school room is in need of repairs. A new floor and new desks should be provided. There is only one large map, that of the world.
>
> Signed by the District Inspector

IRISH FOLKLORE COMMISSION

In 1937, the Department of Education, in conjunction with the Irish Folklore Commission and the teachers of the National Schools throughout the country, organised the collection of parish oral traditions. The teachers were directed to invite the senior pupils in their schools to collect traditions from their parents and from any other persons in their neighbourhood. In hindsight, the timing of this initiative, on the eve of so many changes in our country, has provided a fantastic record of our heritage and traditions. Just to give a brief context, which will still be remembered by the older generation.

At the time, in the mid-1930s, the world was entering into the Second World War, and Ireland was also under going its own changes. It was a time of emigration, scarcity of work, and poverty. The level of poverty was very high in many areas of rural Ireland; many people were still earning their livelihood from the land, and most farms were small holdings. Rural electrification arrived in the late 1940s. The scourge of the tuberculosis (TB, as it was widely known) was only controlled in the 1940s, having claimed so many of our citizens. It is also worth remembering that it was only in 1926 that school attendance was made compulsory for children between the ages of six and fourteen years of age.

Altogether the Folklore Collection of 1936-1937 contains more than 500,000 pages, which document our culture and heritage. These are preserved in the archives of the Irish Folklore Commission. The following is one such story from Toher School, submitted by Patrick Hanrahan, as told to him by Pat Kenehan of Tullow, Templetuohy:

The Enchanted Stone

One day while workmen were blasting stones on Pat Kenehan's land, a jumper broke in a rock and they could not get it up. It is said that there is some gold hidden under that rock because about midnight a little man with a lamp is seen at that stone. Some splinters of gold flew out of the stone and the men picked it up and put it in their pockets and when they went to get it, they found that the gold was gone.

CLONMORE SCHOOL

Clonmore school was attended by a number of children who lived between the cross of Clonboo and the cross of Toher. Some people like Mary Grimes (later Mary Fermoyle) went to Clonmore school, as she lived down in Graffan before moving to Clonboo. Clonmore school was built in 1884 and was opened as a National School on 12 January 1885. One third of the cost of the school came from local contributions and the other two-thirds was provided by the Commissioners for Education of the Government in London. Canon Meagher, parish priest of Templemore, collected the contributions from the community, because Killavinogue was joined to the parish of Templemore, although previously it was connected to Templetuohy. The stones for the building of the school and boundary walls were quarried in the Charters and the work was carried out by local craftsmen.

Before 1884 there was a small school known as 'the shed', which was built by Revd Thomas O'Connor in 1848. It was situated at the end of Paddy Martin's shop. There was no state grant for this school and the teachers did not receive a salary, only what fees they could collect from the pupils. In 1863 this school was recognised as a National School and from then on it came under government supervision and the teacher was paid a small salary.

Ireland, at this time, was just recovering from the effects of the Great Famine. The people were poor and destitute and the population of the parish which, before the Famine was 3,580, was reduced to 1,190 by the time the next census was taken in 1871. The Fenians (1848 and 1867) made an attempt to raise the people from this servitude. Parnell and Davitt were 'fighting' to get the land of the country back for the people.

The conditions of the country were reflected in the conditions of the school. The furniture usually consisted of a stool for the teacher and possibly a long form for the pupils. Most of the pupils stood around in a circle or sat on the floor. In winter it was very cold and damp. One notices also from the early register that most of the families in the parish were labourers.

The school opposite the community centre catered for the boys of the parish only. There was a similar school for the girls at Moyner's Cross. This one was older than the boys' school.

When the new school opened in 1884, Mr McDonald, who had been teaching in the old boys' school, became Principal and taught the boys, who were all in one room. The girls were taught by Miss Moore and Miss Molly Meehan in the other room.

The register for the early years of the school shows the following families: Prender, Clonboo; Cahill, Dromard; Pyne, Sorrell Hill; Guider, Charters; Martin, Moyners; Bowe, Dromard; Meehan, Dromard; Keane, Dromard; Clarke, Dromard; Brien, Charters; Cody, Dromard; Myrons, Dromard; Quinlan, Dromard; Kennedy, Graffin; Davy, Dromard; Leahy, Dromard; Tierney, Dromard; Fitzpatrick, Clonmore; Greed, Skehana; Molloy, Clonboo; McMahon, Graffin; Ryan, Graffin; Joyce, Graffin; Howe, Charters; Treacy, Dromard; Dowling, Dromard; Morrissey, Dromard; Mullally, Moyners; Stapleton, Dromard; Grey, Graffin; Clarke, Ballysorrell; Deegan, Dareens; Bannon, Graffin; Byrne, Sorrell Hill; Butler, Clonboo; Cain, Dromard; Maher, Ballysorrell; Carroll, Dromard; Downey, Charters; Fermoyle, Dromard; Bergin, Dromard; Doheny, Strogue (Blacksmith); Fogarty, Moyners; Ryan, Dromard; Delahunty, Dromard; Maher, Pollough; Nolan, Dromard; Delaney, Dromard; Lonergan, Moyners; Ryan, Ballysorrell; Triehy, Clonmore; Deegan, Sorrell Hill; Maher, Moyners; Haugh, Charters; Deegan, Ballysorrell; Fogarty, Killavinouge;

Fitzpatrick, Dareens; Lee, Clonboo; Laffan, Dromard; Casey, Ballysorrell; O'Neill, Graffin; Roe, Ballysorrell; Shelley, Ballinafad; Murphy, Dareens; Walsh, Dromard; Meara, Graffin, and Gleeson, Dromard.

Pat Meagher became Principal of the boys' school on the retirement of Mr McDonald. Catherine Meagher was Principal of the girls' school and Mary J. Martin became assistant in 1912. Catherine Meagher, who lived in Clonboo, also retired that year (1912) and was replaced by Johanna Ryan from Loughmore. Miss Ryan later became Mrs Allen. Miss Bride Kavanagh took Mary Martin's place on 13 November 1916. On 1 April 1922, Miss Hallinan from Co. Cork came to teach with Mrs Allen in the girls' school. Her appointment coincided with the foundation of the State. From then on, the names on the school register are written in Irish.

The boys' school and the girls' school were amalgamated on 1 April 1929, when Pat Meagher retired and Mrs Allen became Principal. Nora Culligan from Clare came to replace Mrs Egan on 1 May 1929. The number of pupils on the roll at that time were: boys, thirty-two, and girls, thirty-seven. Of this number, eight girls were over fifteen years of age. Mrs O'Sullivan remained teaching in Clonmore until her death in August 1949, when she was replaced by Anna Larkin (O'Brien). On Mrs Allen's retirement in 1956, her son Brendan became Principal.

Some photos of the school classes were reproduced for the 1984 centenary celebrations. The 1923 girls' class included the following: Mary Loughman, Han Ryan (Hill), Molly Butler (Clonboo), Molly Lonergan, Molly Nolan, Nan Stapleton, Molly Shelly, Katie Carey, Magie Ryan, Sarah Nolan, Biddy Lonergan, Brigid Gleeson, Nora Downey, M. Bergin, Nan Shelly, Brigid Gleeson, Josie Carey and Kate Gleeson (Everard).

The boys' class of 1942 included: Dan Bourke, John Butler, Gerry Kean, Ml Fitzpatrick, John Fitzpatrick, Bill Fitzpatrick, Mick Mockler, Pat Delaney, Jim Delaney, Donal Mackey, Mick Fitzpatrick, John Fogarty, Gerry Butler, John Quinn, Tom Quinn, John Nolan, W. Meehan, Eddy Butler, Denis Meehan, Denis Walsh, Tom Bohan, Denis Martin, Jim Quinn and Peter Greed.

Clonmore school will shortly celebrate its 125th year, and preparations are underway to mark this occasion with a publication about the school and its environs, so there is no need to dwell on it further here. But above you will see familiar Clonboo and Toher surnames from the snapshot of classes of pupils who attended Clonmore school. Toher school, especially the early years, gives a lot of familiar surnames who are now resident in townlands all around Clonmore.

TEMPLEMORE CBS

After my primary school education, I went to the Christian Brothers' School in Templemore. The Christian Brothers decided to come to Templemore in 1932 and arrived there on 18 September 1933. On 2 October 1933, Canon O'Brien erected the Stations of the Cross and consecrated the house to the Sacred Heart. Work on the house and grounds continued for several years.

The first secondary school was set up in the Town Hall as a temporary arrangement on Wednesday 16 August 1933. About fifty pupils were in attendance on this first day. The boys were arranged into two classes, one under Br O'Brien and the other under Br Flynn. Most of the pupils had come from 6th Class in the local primary school but very soon other pupils started to come from the surrounding National Schools. The numbers grew and the need for a new school was apparent.

In July 1934, the plans for the new school were approved and local builders Duggan Brothers of Richmond, Templemore were awarded the contract for the sum of £2,454. During my college summer holidays I worked in Duggans for a couple of years; great firm, solid grounding and an excellent experience. It was a great start into the construction business for me. I have Neil Scott (RIP) to thank for my introduction to quantity surveying and for the work experience in Duggans. On 23 September, Archbishop Harty laid and blessed the foundation stone for the new building.

There are other books and publications written about the CBS in Templemore and I do not intend to write too much here, only to mention a few items. When I started in 1975, Br Pat Seaver had just become the Superior. At that time only Br Norris and Br Skeehan were in the secondary school. I have to mention hurling, as it was such an important and focal part of the school. You could say that at that time, Templemore CBS was Tipperary's answer to St Kieran's of Kilkenny or the famed St Flannan's of Ennis. In 1978, we beat them all to win the school's first Harty Cup, along with winning the All-Ireland Colleges hurling final the same year. On the way to winning the All-Ireland that year, we beat school hurling powerhouses such as Coláiste Iognáid Rís (Cork), Farranferris (Cork), North Mon (Cork), St Flannan's (Ennis) in the Harty Final, and St Peter's (Wexford) in All-Ireland Final. Martin Bourke from Clonmore was captain that year and led from the front as he always does. Br Perkins was a strong motivator and fed the lads loads of oxtail soup, while John Costigan, with All-Ireland senior medals in his back pocket, was the man who fine-tuned that team with tremendous passion and dedication. He is a man steeped in hurling and has served his county loyally at all levels, from his playing days to the position of County Chairman. Now the hurlers were not too bad either. All the local parishes were represented: Loughmore/Castleiney by Pat McGrath, Pat Treacy, Frankie McGrath, Peter Brennan, Jody Sweeney, Pat Cormack, Jim Maher, Dick Stapleton and Tim Stapleton; Borrisoleigh by Bobby Ryan and Mick Ryan; Templemore by Noel Farrelly (RIP), John Hanley and Noelie Fogarty; Clonakenny by Brendan Russell; Drom by Jim Kennedy, and Errill by goalkeeper Pat Joe Hassett. Clonmore had the captain, Martin Bourke, midfield powerhouse Mick Ryan (of the Hill), sharpshooter Eamonn Cody from Ballysorrell and 'never stand back from anything' corner forward Joe Bourke from Dromard.

There is no doubt the success of hurling in the school resulted from the sheer hurling knowledge, the hard work and the total commitment of the teachers and staff of Templemore CBS. Of course the options for playing sport were not that plentiful either. Wednesday afternoon was for sports and the choice was simple enough – either hurling or chess!

I started secondary school in 1975, and the following also started that year: Alan Hanley, Paddy Hennessy, Seamus Hassett, Pat Joe Hassett, Tony Allen, John Wall, Richard Butler (Railway View), John Butler (Barna), John Bourke, Martin Browne, John Brennan, Joe Kavanagh, Frank Coffey, Pat Quinlan, Tim Connolly, David Cambie, Michael Casey, Seamus Cahill, Davy Cummins, Joe Keating, John Corbett, Michael Clohessy, Paddy Corbett, Eillei Coffey, Gerard McGrath, John Denny, Francis Denny, Donal O'Dwyer, Tommy Doyle, Tony Hynes, Johnny McDonnell, Joe Delahaunty, J.J. Dunne, Sean Farrell, Pat Gleeson, Gerry Fogarty, Tommy Gleeson, Liam Gorman, Sean Geary, Sean Og Lynch, Gerard Maher, Augustine Maher, Jim Meehan, Jim Moloney, Dominic Maher, Johnny Murray, Christy Nolan, Raymond Power, Brian King, Eddie Roche, John Paul Ryan, Eddie Ryan, Tom Ryan, Gerry Ryan, Sean Ryan, Seamus Ryan, Michael Reilly, John Russell, Eugene Stapleton, Philip Shanahan, Tony Sheedy, Richard Stakleum, Eddie Treacy, Tony Wixted and Brendan Cahill.

TOHER ROLL BOOK (BOYS & GIRLS)

There are a number of comments to be made by way of explanation, before you start to look at the various roll books for Toher National School.

> A pupil whose first name is registered in the roll book may well be known or remembered by a different first name nowadays.

> The earlier years of the roll book entries were recorded in the old Gaelic script, meaning that the accuracy of the translation can't be guaranteed.

> The school opened in 1840 and closed in 1998. Unfortunately a number of the roll books are missing from various periods and especially for the period 1840 to 1900.

> Most of the pupils from roll number 190 up to the last pupil registered at roll number 724, are recorded and detailed below.

> There are a number of known errors recorded in the initial registration of some pupils.

Although most pupils fall into the category of having Toher as their first school, there are a number of pupils who transferred from other schools. These other schools are noted below in brackets after the pupils' names, where applicable. In other cases, where the exact date of entry to the school could not be found, the pupil's class is noted instead of the townland. In these roll books, the townland is not recorded.

In the early years, separate roll books were kept for boys and for girls. There is much duplication of numbers, as both teachers appear to operate their own number referencing. However, even in later years, when a joint numbering system was in use for the combined pupil registration, there are several examples of the same number being recorded for more than one pupil. There are also a number of conflicting and erroneous entries and inaccurate details. It is fair to say that we all can make mistakes, even teachers! I have recorded, to the best of my ability, all the information that was found in these roll books. Apart from recording the correct Irish translations, there are also a great number of years recorded in the old Gaelic lettering.

REGISTER NO.	ENTRANCE DATE	NAME	TOWNLAND
190			
191	January 1901	Edward Butler	(Sixth Class)
192	January 1901	Ellen Deegan	(Sixth Class)
193			
194			
195			
196			
197			
198	January 1901	James Clarke	(Sixth Class)
199			
200			
201			
202			
203	January 1901	Thomas Deegan	(Sixth Class)
203	January 1901	Norah Deegan	(Sixth Class)
204			
205	January 1901	Michael Clarke	(Sixth Class)
206			
207			
208			
209			
210	January 1901	Mary Shelly	(Fifth Class)
210	January 1901	Matt Butler	(Sixth Class)
211	January 1901	Katie Carroll	(Fourth Class)
212			

213	January 1901	Bridget Maher	(Third Class)
213	January 1901	John Lawler	(Fifth Class)
215	January 1901	Dennis Deegan	(Fourth Class)
216	January 1901	Denis Butler	(Fifth Class)
217	January 1901	Katie Butler	(Third Class)
218	January 1901	Maggie Loughnana	(Fourth Class)
218	January 1901	Tobias Maher	(Fifth Class)
219	January 1901	Mary Shelly	(Third Class)
220	January 1901	Thomas Butler	(Fifth Class)
221	January 1901	James Delahunty	(Second Class)
222			
223	January 1901	Patrick Feehely	(Sixth Class)
223	January 1901	Mary Kiely	(Sixth Class)
224	January 1901	Anne Loughnana	(Infants)
224	January 1901	Denis Shelly	(Third Class)
225	January 1901	Williams Grimes	(Third Class)
227	January 1901	Joanna Carroll	(Infants)
228	January 1901	Edmond Maher	(Second Class)
228	January 1901	Norah Talbert	(Sixth Class)
229	January 1901	John Maher	(Third Class)
229	January 1901	Maggie Doherty	(Sixth Class)
230	January 1901	Norah Bowe	(Third Class)
230	January 1901	William Fogarty	(Third Class)
231	3 May 1911	Susan Shelly	Toher
232	January 1901	Patrick Cahill	(Third Class)
233	January 1901	Murty Kiely	(Third Class)
233	January 1901	Mary Carey?	(Fourth Class)
234	January 1901	John Grimes	(Third Class)
235	30 January 1899	Michael Myrens	Clonboo
236	25 July 1903	Thos Myrens	Clonboo
236	January 1901	Annie Talbert	(First Class)
237	10 February 1900	Patrick Butler	Clonboo
237	January 1901	Margaret Talbert	(First Class)
237	April 1901	Maggie Ryan	(Infants)
238	30 January 1899	Michael Shelly	Toher
239	27 January 1906	James Kiely	Lissanure
239	April 1901	Annie Stapleton	(Fist Standard)

240	10 February 1900	Richard Carroll	Toher
240	January 1902	Maria Carroll	(Infants)
241	April 1901	Julia Talbot	(Infants)
242	10 June 1901	Josephine Toal	Clonboo
242	January 1901	Peter Deegan	(Fourth Class)
243	24 June 1901	Katie Grimes	Clonboo
244	25 July 1903	Timothy Shelly	Toher
244	16 July 1901	Patrick Loughnane	Toher
245	25 July 1903	James Grimes	Clonboo
245	27 August 1901	Mary Maher	Clonboo
246	25 July 1903	Patrick Loughnane	Toher
246	9 September 1902	Katie Bergin	Drumard
247	3 May 1911	Catherine Shelly	Toher
247	25 May 1903	Katie Shelly?	Toher
248	April 1901	William Bergin	(Third Standard)
249	July 1901	Thomas Stapleton	(First Standard)
250	22 April 1901	Joseph Dowling	Dromard
251	25 July 1903	Andrew Bergin	Dromard
252	April 1901	Daniel Bergin	(First Standard)
253	26 March 1904	Patrick Grimes	Clonboo
254	31 March 1906	Henry Fitzpatrick	Toher
254	April 1901	Patrick Toal	(Infants)
255	31 May 1906	James Fitzpatrick	Toher
256	3 May 1911	Nora Carroll	Toher
256	4 February 1908	John Bergin (Clonmore)	Dromard
257	9 December 1903	Patrick Costigan(Brittas)	Toher
258	17 October 1910	William Fitzpatrick	Toher
259	3 May 1911	Lizzie Whelan	Tullow
259	29 June 1907	Murty Kiely	Tullow
260	25 October 1904	Martin Deegan (Clonmore)	Clonboo
261	25 October 1904	Daniel Deegan (Clonmore)	Clonboo
262	29 June 1907	Joseph Grimes	Clonboo
263	28 November 1904	Edward Byrne (Templemore)	Ballysorrell
264	29 June 1907	Martin Kiely	Tullow
265	11 September 1905	Thomas Byrne (Clonmore)	Ballysorrell
266	6 November 1905	Thomas Laffan (Clonmore)	Dromard
267	5 January 1906	John Regan (Clonmore)	Sorrellhill

268	3 April 1904	Daniel Kiely	Lissanure
269	11 June 1907	Daniel Fitzpatrick	Toher
270	11 June 1906	William Carroll	Toher
271	28 June 1904	Richard Paddle	Urlingford
272	17 April 1907	Patrick Shelly	Toher
273	14 May 1907	Maurice Callahan (Templetuohy)	Toher
274	14 May 1907	Edmond Callahan (Templetuohy)	Toher
275	20 May 1907	Thomas Grimes	Clonboo
276	23 September 1907	Timothy Toal	Clonboo
277	21 January 1908	Daniel Egan	Clonboo
278	4 February 1908	William Ryan (Templetuohy)	Tullow
279	4 February 1908	John Ryan (Templetuohy)	Tullow
280	6 April 1908	Thomas Kiely	Lissanure
281	7 April 1908	Daniel Bourke	Tullow
282	6 May 1908	Daniel Hennessy	Tullow
283	2 February 1909	Timothy Ryan	Toher
284	April 1909	Lena Ryan	(First Standard)
285	2 March 1909	James O'Neill (Clonmore)	Lisduff
286	2 March 1909	Patrick O'Neill (Clonmore)	Lisduff
287	16 March 1909	Alphonsus Deegan (Clonmore)	Sorrellhill
288/289	19 April 1909	Patrick Fitzpatrick	Toher
290	3 May 1911	Nora Whelan	Lismorougha
291	3 May 1911	Bridie Whelan	Lismorougha
292	3 May 1911	Myra Gavin	Clonboo
292	22 June 1909	Fran M. Toal (Tullamore)	Toher (head const)
293	October 1909	Myra Gavin	(First Standard)
294	13 October 1909	John Ryan	Toher
295	25 October 1909	Patrick Ryan	Clonboo (shopkeeper)
296	18 January 1910	Patrick Fitzpatrick	Toher
297	18 January 1910	Bridget Fogarty	Tulla McJames
298	18 January 1910	Lizzie Fogarty	Tulla McJames
299	18 January 1910	Kathy Fogarty	Tulla McJames
300	18 January 1910	Annie Fogarty	Tulla McJames
301	18 January 1910	Ellen Fogarty	Tulla McJames
302	17 May 1910	Thomas Ingram	Templetuohy
303	30 May 1911	James Moran	Toher
304	8 May 1911	Mary Moran	Toher
305	9 May 1911	Bridie Fitzpatrick	Toher

306	26 April 1911	Michael Bergin (Clonmore)	Dromard
307	19 April 1911	Laurence Grimes	Clonboo
308	9 October 1911	Nano Egan	Clonboo
309	13 November 1911	William Rooney	Toher
310	15 February 1912	Michael Deegan (Clonmore)	Sorrelhill
311	13 May 1912	Johanna Ryan	Toher
312	28 May 1912	Bridget Bergin (Clonmore)	Dromard
313	10 June 1912	Johanna Moran	Toher
314	15 July 1912	John Whelan	Dromard
315	9 September 1912	Joseph O'Regan (Clonmore)	Sorrelhill
316	11 September 1912	Thomas Deegan (Clonmore)	Sorrelhill
317	13 May 1913	John Carey	Toher
318	16 June 1913	Patrick Kennedy	Lissanure
319	27 April 1914	Lizzie Moran	Toher
320	4 May 1914	James Greed	Ballinafad
321	25 May 1914	Thomas Feehily	Clonmeen
322	30 November 1914	James Murray (Errill)	Lismorougha
323	30 November 1914	Denis Cummings (Errill	Lismorougha
324	12 March 1915	Katty Grady	Clonboo
325	26 April 1915	Mary Greed	Ballinfad
326	15 May 1916	Mary Hennessy	Tullow
327	15 May 1916	Josephine Hennessy	Tullow
328	15 May 1916	John Hennessey (Templetuohy	Tullow
329	22 May 1916	Bridget Darmody	Lissanure
330	22 May 1916	Patrick Darmody	Lissanure
331	29 May 1916	William Greed	Clonboo
332	13 June 1916	Daniel Hennessey (Templetuohy)	Tullow
333	19 June 1916	Margaret Ryan	Toher
334	21 June 1916	Tobias Maher	Clonboo (Mason)
335	21 June 1916	James Fermoyle	Clonboo
336	4 September 1916	Ellie Maher	Templemore
337	12 March 1917	Christopher Flood	Killavinogue
338	12 March 1917	Nora Flood	Killavinogue
339	12 March 1917	Veronica Gavin	Clonboo
340	7 May 1917	Mary Anne Flood	Killavinogue
341	18 June 1917	Patrick Costigan	Toher
342	1 October 1917	John Deegan	Clonboo
343	27 November 1917	Bridget Flood	Killavinogue

344	8 April 1918	Maggie Kennedy	Lissanure
345	22 April 1918	Patrick Shelly	Lissanure
346	22 April 1918	John Shelly	Lissanure
347	30 April 1918	Thomas Moran	Toher
348	13 May 1918	Martin Fitzpatrick	Lissanure
349	18 June 1918	Edward Guilfoyle	Clonboo
350	1 July 1918	Toby Maher	Toher
351	1 July 1918	Michael Maher	Toher
352	5 May 1919	Joseph Ryan	Toher
353	6 May 1919	Mary Anne Darmody	Lissanure
354	25 April 1921	Maggie Maher	Toher
355	9 June 1919	Con Costigan	Toher
356	1 July 1919	Mary Carroll	Toher
357	7 July 1919	Maggie Fermoyle	Clonboo
358	15 September 1919	John Joe O'Meara	Toher
359	24 May 1920	Katie Maher	Toher
360	7 June 1920	Katie Shelly	Lissanure
361	19 July 1920	Maggie Flood	Killavinogue
362	6 September 1920	Henry Bergin	Toher
363	31 January 1921	Julia Murray	Lismuragha
364	21 March 1921	Josephine Darmody	Lisannure
365	1st March 1921	Patrick Greed	Clonboo
366			
367	2 May 1921	James G. O'Meara	Toher
368	2 May 1921	Ellen Loughnane	Toher
369	9 May 1921	Katie Guilfoyle	Clonboo
370	30 May 1921	James Greed	Clonboo
371	30 May 1921	Mary Greed	Clonboo
372	30 May 1921	Josie Greed	Clonboo
373	17 August 1921	Lizzie Greed	Clonboo
374	31 October 1921	Mary A. Fitzpatrick	Lissanure
375	25 April 1922	Maggie Maher	Clonboo
376	26 September 1922	Joseph O'Meara (Teacher)	Clonboo
377	1 October 1922	Michael Shelly	Lissanure
378	1 October 1922	John Maher	Toher
379	16 October 1922	Bridget Barret	Toher
380	16 October 1922	Christina Flood	Killavinogue

381	20 May 1923	Nora McDermott	Lissanure
382	7 May 1923	Nora McDermott	Clonboo
383	7 May 1923	Evelyn Ryan	Toher
384	21 May 1923	Donal Hoban? (O'Bou)	Toher
385	10 September 1923	Bill Carroll	Clonboo
386	10 September 1923	Bill Shelly	Lissanure
387	10 September 1923	Eilish Kelly (Errill)	Clonboo
388	1 October 1923	James Hassett/Hayes?	Clonboo
389	24 September 1923	Margaret Guider	Toher
390	24 September 1923	Eliz Lanigan	Clonboo
391	1 October 1923	Kate Hayes	Clonboo
392	29 October 1923	Kate Loughnane	Toher
393	1 April 1924	Donal/Dan Maher	Toher
394	5 May 1924	Mary Fermoyle	Clonboo
395	5 May 1924	Kate O'Meara (Teacher)	Toher
396	26 May 1924	Brid Maher	Toher
397	28 May 1924	Kate Feehily (Errill)	Clonboo
398	2 June 1924	Patrick Clarke	Clonboo
399	16 June 1924	James Hoban? (O'Bou)	Clonboo
400	9 September 1924	Ann Kinnane? (Shanakill)	Clonboo
401	1 October 1924	James Guider	Toher
402	3 November 1924	Donal Whelan/Phelan(Errill)	Lismouragha
403	11 May 1925	Martin Clarke	Toher
404	25 May 1925	Brid Maher	Toher
405	25 May 1925	Mary Clarke	Clonboo
406	7 September 1925	Ann Bergin	Toher
407	19 April 1926	Michael Talbot	Toher
408	23 April 1926	Siobhan Guider	Toher
409	10 May 1926	Sile Maher	Toher
410	17 May 1926	Murt Kelly	Toher
411	18 May 1926	Donal McDermott	Lissanure
412	8 June 1926	Mary Loughnane	Toher
413	2 May 1927	Mary Gleeson	Clonboo
414	17 May 1927	Peg Carroll	Clonboo
415	25 May 1927	Mary Guider	Killana
416	4 July 1927	Donnacha Fitzpatrick	Lissanure
417	7 May 1928	Stephen Talbot	Tullow
418	4 June 1928	Michael Loughnane	Toher

419	4 June 1928	Mary Bowe	Toher
420	8 April 1929	Mick Carroll	Clonboo
421	10 June 1929	James Kelly	Lissanure
422	18 June 1929	Michael Hayes	Clonmeen
423	18 June 1929	John Hayes	Clonmeen
424	24 June 1929	Mary Maher	Toher
425	5 May 1930	Mary Guider	Toher
426	2 June 1930	Mary Kelly	Lissanure
427	16 June 1930	Mary Carroll	Clonboo
428	15 September 1930	Eamonn Butler (Rathdowney)	Toher
429	18 February 1931	Cathal Delahunty (Clonmore)	Toher
430	13 April 1931	Eileen Clarke	Clonboo
431	13 April 1931	Joseph Kirrane/Kinnane?	Clonboo
432	1 May 1931	James Hayes	Clonmeen
433	1 May 1931	Jimmy Maher	Toher
434	21 September 1931	Siobhan McGrath	Clonmeen
435	21 September 1931	Mary McGrath	Clonmeen
436	19 October 1931	Nell O'Meara	Tullow
437	2 November 1931	Martin Clarke (Templetuohy)	Kylena
438	17 May 1932	Kate Kiely	Tullow
439	30 May 1932	Bill Loughlin/Loughnane	Toher
440	3 October 1932	Patrick Kiely	Toher
441	10 October 1932	Kate McGrath	Clonmeen
442	1 May 1933	Pat Hanrahan	Tullow
443	1 May 1933	James Brophy	Lissanure
444	1 May 1933	Pat Carroll	Clonboo
445	1 May 1933	Siobhan Brophy	Toher
446	19 March 1934	Ambrose Brophy	Toher
447	16 April 1934	Margaret Kiely	Lissanure
448	16 April 1934	Mary Hayes	Clonmeen
449	23 November 1934	Sorcha McGrath	Clonmeen
450	14 May 1934	Margaret Loughnane	Toher
451	30 April 1934	Una Carroll	Clonboo
452	11 March 1935	Eamonn Kiely	Lissanure
453	13 May 1935	Robert McGrath	Clonmeen
454	3 June 1935	Tom Maher	Lissanure
455	30 March 1936	Brid Hayes	Clonmeen
456	11 May 1936	Billy Grimes	Clonboo

457	11 May 1936	Tommy Grimes	Clonboo
458	25 May 1936	Margaret Kiely	Lissanure
459	25 May 1936	Kate O'Shea	Toher
460	16 November 1936	Kate McKeown	Toher
461	23 November 1936	Siobhan O'Shea	Toher
462	3 May 1937	Johnny Butler	Clonboo
463	31 May 1937	Patrick Kiely	Tullow
464	4 April 1938	Jack Carroll	Clonboo
465	4 April 1938	Michael Brophy	Lissanure
466	5 April 1938	Ann Hayes	Toher
467	11 April 1938	Teresa Kiely	Lissanure
468	5 September 1938	Kate Hayes	Clonmeen
469	5 September 1938	Mary Maher	Lissanure
470	1 May 1939	Evelyn McGrath	Clonmeen
471	1 May 1939	Bridget Shelly	Toher
472	23 May 1930	Paddy Grimes	Clonboo
473	28 August 1939	Teresa McGrath	Clonmeen
474	29 April 1940	Mary Kiely	Lissanure
475	17 June 1940	Billy Brophy	Lissanure
476	28 October 1940	James Fitzpatrick(English)?	Lissanure
477	28 October 1940	Donnacha Fitzpatrick?	Lissanure
478	28 October 1940	Martin Fitzpatrick?	Lissanure
479	1 April 1941	Brid Butler	Toher
480	21 April 1941	Peggy Hayes	Clonboo
481	17 May 1941	Bill Hayes (Moyglass)	Lissanure
482	3 June 1941	John Maher	Lissanure
483	10 November 1941	Frank Fogarty(Graigue)	Lissanure
484	13 April 1942	Michael Grimes	Clonboo
485	20 April 1942	Andy McGrath	Clonmeen
486	20 April 1942	Ann McGrath	Clonmeen
487	20 April 1942	Mary Butler	Toher
488	4 May 1942	Andy McGrath	Lissanure
489	28 June 1943	Ann McGrath	Clonboo
490	28 January 1943	Mary Butler	Clonboo
491	28 June 1943	Mary Brophy	Clonboo
492	30 August 1943	Eamonn Caudy (Littleton)	Toher
493	30 August 1943	Evelyn Kiely (Littleton)	Clonmeen

494	1 September 1943	Siobhan Costigan	Toher
495	22 March 1944	Eileen Maher (Loughmore)	Clonboo
496	22 March 1944	Thady Maher (Loughmore)	Clonboo
497	22 March 1944	Danny Maher (Loughmore)	Clonboo
498	3 April 1944	Ann Costigan	Toher
499	12 June 1944	Joan Maher	Clonboo
500	23 October 1944	Mary Moore	Lissanure
501	9 April 1945	Eamonn Maher	Clonboo
502	16 April 1945	Tom Butler	Toher
503	23 April 1945	Brid McGrath	Clonmeen
504	11 June 1945	Tom Moore	Lissanure
505	18 June 1945	Bob Carroll	Clonboo
506	27 August 1945	Patrick Costigan	Toher
507	18 February 1946	Michael Butler	Toher
508	19 March 1946	Donnacha Fitzpatrick	Toher
509	1 April 1946	Mary Doolan	Clonboo
510	1 April 1946	Sorcha Kiely?	Clonboo
511	1 October 1946	James McGrath	Clonmeen
512	6 May 1947	Eilish Guider	Clonmeen
512	6 May 1947	Peter Hayes	Clonboo
513	5 May 1948	Mary Costigan	Toher
514	12 April 1948	Eamonn Butler	Toher
515	12 April 1948	Jimmy Grimes	Clonboo
516	18 May 1948	Billy Grimes (Clonmore)	Clonboo
517	1 July 1948	John McGrath	Clonmeen
518	3 April 1948	Martin Costigan	Toher
519	3 April 1948	Jim Ryan (Clonmore)	Dromard
520	3 April 1948	Liam/Bill Ryan (Clonmore)	Dromard
521	16 May 1949	Frances Ryan	Lissanure
522	17 June 1948	Ann Moore	Lissanure
523	11 July 1949	Eileen Grimes	Clonboo
524	12 September 1949	Martin Carroll	Clonboo
525	13 March 1950	Angela McGrath	Clonmeen
525	25 February 1952	Liam/Bill Beggan (Thurles)	Lissanure
526	16 October 1950	Connie Costigan	Toher
527	15 May 1951	Timmy Moylan	Toher
527	1 June 1960	Fergal Ryan	Toher

528	15 May 1951	Johnny Moylan (Killadooley)	Toher
528	12 September 1960	John Carroll(?) Farmer	Clonboo
529	22 September 1952	Patricia Carroll	The Derries
529	13 September 1960	Ann Loughnane	Toher
530	23 March 1953	Patrick Moore	Lissanure
531	25 March 1953	Gerry Driscoll	Lissanure
532	22 June 1953	Catherine Ann Costigan	Toher
533	26 April 1954	Martin Moylan	Toher
534	26 April 1954	Sorcha Carroll	The Derries
535	1 October 1954	Dan Guider	Clonboo
536	18 April 1955	Paddy Moran	Toher
537	20 June 1955	Johnny Hanrahan (Templetuohy)	Lissanure
538	20 June 1955	John Guider	Clonboo
539	5 September 1955	Treasa Costigan	Toher
540	12 September 1955	Mary Hanrahan	Lissanure
541	12 September 1955	Mary Loughnane	Toher
542	3 September 1956	Joe Moylan	Toher
543	29 April 1956	Sean Moran	Toher
544	27 May 1957	Jim Hanrahan	Lissanure
545	28 May 1957	Mary Guider	Clonboo
546	1 October 1957	Jim Maher (Garda)?	Toher
547	9 April 1958	Eileen Loughnane	Toher
548	17 June 1958	Jim Moran	Toher
549	1 July 1958	Peggy Driscoll?	Lissanure
550	25 May 1959	Mairead Moore	Lissanure
551	19 April 1960	Jim Maher	Toher
552	19 April 1960	John Loughnane	Toher
553	9 May 1960	Ger Moylan	Lissanure
554	10 May 1960	Tom Moran	Toher
555	13 April 1961	Esther Fermoyle	Clonboo
556	13 April 1961	Mick Maher	Toher
557	6 February 1961	John Ryan (Graigue)	Lissanure
558	13 April 1961	Pauline Guider	Clonboo
559	6 February 1961	Carmel Ryan	Lissanure
560	20 February 1962	Helen Fermoyle	Clonboo
561	14 May 1962	Breda Loughnane	Toher
562	3 December 1963	Con Moylan	Lissanure
563	1 May 1963	Eileen Bowe	Lissanure

564	1 May 1963	Margaret Ryan	Toher
565	1 July 1963	Breda Clarke	Clonboo
566	11 September 1963	Kathleen Driscoll	Lissanure
567	2 March 1964	Maire Bowe	Lissanure
568	23 April 1964	Mary Moylan	Lissanure
569	23 April 1964	Michael Loughnane	Toher
570			
571	1 April 1964	Ger Moran	Toher
572	7 September 1964	Billy Loughnane	Toher
573	1 October 1964	Michael Clarke	Clonboo
574	1 October 1964	Tom Guider	Toher
575	13 October 1964	Sally Moylan	Lissanure
576	1 April 1964	John Guider	Toher
577	1 July 1965	Kathleen Guider	Clonboo
578	6 September 1965	Johnny Ryan	Toher
579	1 October 1965	Breda Maher	Toher
580	2 May 1966	Peggy Loughnane	Toher
581	23 May 1966	Anne Clarke	Clonboo
582	13 June 1966	Mary Tynan	Clonboo
583	5 July 1966	Breda Hassett (Errill)	Lisduff
584	5 July 1966	Denis Hassett (Errill)	Lisduff
585	6 September 1966	Mary Healy	Clonmeen
586	6 September 1966	Tom Healy	Clonmeen
587	5 September 1966	Patrick Lanigan (Templetuohy)	Lisdaleen
588	6 September 1966	Donie Bowe	Lissanure
589	2 November 1966	Maura Bergin	Longorchard
590	9 January 1967	Jack Butler	Clonboo
591	1 March 1967	Kathleen Maher	Toher
592	4 April 1967	Breda Tynan	Clonboo
593	4 April 1967	Pat Joe Hassett	Lisduff
594	3 July 1967	Anne Ryan (Clonmore)	Dromard
595	6 July 1967	Geraldine Driscoll	Lissanure
596	3 July 1967	Mick Ryan (Clonmore)	Dromard
597	6 September 1967	Tom Clarke	Clonboo
598	3 July 1967	Tom Ryan (Clonmore)	Dromard
599	5 September 1967	Jane Bergin	Toher
600	16 October 1967	Jimmy Bergin(Moyne)	Toher

601	1 May 1968	John Bergin	Toher
602	3 September 1968	Tomas Bergin	Longorchard
603	3 September 1968	Catherine Ryan	Dromard
604	7 January 1969	Liam Fogarty	Longorchard
605	1 April 1969	Seamus Maher	Toher
606	15 April 1969	Kathleen Loughnane	Toher
607	1 July 1969	Margaret Tynan	Clonboo
608	26 April 1965	Sile Maher	Toher
608	2 September 1969	Noirin Bergin	Longorchard
609	2 September 1967	Patricia Loughnane	Clonboo
610	6 October 1969	Michael Moylan	Lissanure
611	8 April 1970	Seamus Fogarty	Longorchard
612	15 May 1971	Statia Tynan	Clonboo
613	1 June 1971	Ned Butler	Clonboo
614	1 September 1971	Maura Fogarty	Longorchard
615	1 September 1971	Tomas Deegan	Clonboo
616	1 September 1971	Francis Davey (Graigue)	Clonmeen
617	19 April 1972	Tommy Hayes	Clonmeen
618	11 April 1972	Seamus Hassett	Lisduff
619	17 April 1972	Mary Ryan	Toher
620	1 July 1972	Veronica Campion	Lisduff
621	2 October 1972	Miriam Deegan	Clonboo
622	1 July 1973	Mark Campion	Lisduff
623	4 July 1973	Liam Grimes	Clonboo
624	3 September 1973	Sean Hayes	Clonmeen
625	7 May 1974	Catherine Butler	Clonboo
626	1 July 1974	Jim Ryan	Toher
627	5 November 1974	Anna Statia Fogarty	Longorchard
628	8 April 1975	Timmy Bergin	Longorchard
629	1 July 1975	Treasa Fox	Lissanure
630	1 July 1975	Cliona Hanrahan	Lissanure
631	1 July 1975	Brigid Ryan	Toher
632	1 June 1976	Catherine Tynan	Clonboo
633	1 July 1976	Vincent Campion	Lisduff
634	5 July 1976	Karen Fox	Lissanure
635	1 September 1976	Margaret Butler	Toher
636	6 September 1977	Sean Grimes	The Derries

637	2 February 1977	Margaret Fogarty	Longorchard
638	1 July 1977	Paul Campion	Lisduff
639	1 July 1977	Paul Deegan	Sorrellhill
640	3 October 1977	Marty Deegan	Clonboo
641	4 April 1978	Catherine Stapleton	The Derries
642	4 April 1978	Eamonn Fogarty	Longorchard
643	4 April 1978	Willie Bergin	Longorchard
644	4 April 1978	Pat Butler	Clonboo
645	1 May 1978	Laurence Grimes	Clonboo
646	3 July 1978	Catherine Costigan	Toher
647	3 July 1978	Kathleen Fox	Lissanure
648	5 September 1978	Sam Stapleton	The Derries
649	2 July 1979	Mary Butler	Toher
650	2 July 1979	Tom Tynan	Clonboo
651	2 July 1979	John Tynan	Clonboo
652	3 September 1979	Kevin Fox	Lissanure
653	1 May 1980	Maire Grimes	Clonboo
654	1 September 1980	Eilish Deegan	Sorrellhill
655	1 September 1980	Padraig Costigan	Toher
656	1 September 1980	Jacinta Hartigan	Toher
657	1 April 1981	Siobhan Egan	Toher
658	1 September 1981	Padraig Hartigan	Toher
659	1 September 1981	Sorcha Maher	Lissanure
660	1 September 1981	Tomas Maher (Templetuohy)	Lissanure
661	1 September 1981	Eilish Maher	Lissanure
662	3 May 1982	Mary Maher	Lissanure
663	1 September 1982	Donncha Maher	Clonmeen
664	1 September 1982	Brian Delahunty	Toher
665	1 September 1982	Matt Butler	Clonboo
666	1 September 1982	Tomas Costigan	Toher
667	1 September 1982	Stephen Fox	Lissanure
668	6 September 1982	Phonsie Deegan	Sorrellhill
669	11 April 1983	Caitriona Egan	Toher
670	1 September 1983	Josephine Maher	Lissanure
671	1 September 1983	Michael Driscoll	Toher
672	5 September 1983	John Maher	Ballysorrell
673	10 January 1984	Paula Butler	Toher

674	1 May 1984	Eileen Costigan	Toher
675	6 June 1984	Ann Hassett	Lissanure
676	6 June 1984	Brendan Davey	Clonmeen
677	3 September 1984	Liam Danaher	The Derries
678	10 September 1984	Brendan Guider	Clonboo
679	8 January 1985	Lorraine Egan	Cowpark
680	16 April 1985	Padraig Danaher	Derries, Errill
681	2 September 1985	Con Costigan	Toher
682	2 September 1985	Aidan Deegan	Clonboo
683	2 September 1985	Ann Costigan	Toher
684	7 April 1986	Catherine Guider	Clonboo
685	7 April 1986	Veronica Kirwan (Clonmore)	Dromard
686	7 April 1986	Rebecca Kirwan (Clonmore)	Dromard
687	7 April 1986	Kieran Kirwan (Clonmore)	Dromard
688	7 April 1986	Patrick Kirwan (Clonmore)	Dromard
689	7 April 1986	Derek Kirwan (Clonmore)	Dromard
690	1 May 1986	Claire Hassett	Lissanure
691	1 September 1986	Pat Clarke	Lisdaleen
692	1 September 1986	Tom Deegan	Sorrellhill
693	3 November 1986	Kevin Clarke(Blanch'stown)	Lissanure
694	3 November 1986	Paul Clarke (Blanchardstown)	Lissanure
695	1 September 1987	Patrick Egan	Cowpark
696	1 September 1987	Damien Bergin	Lissanure
697	1 September 1987	Timmy Guider	Clonboo
698	1 September 1987	Yvonne Cawley (Dublin)	Lissanure
699	1 September 1987	Emma Kirwan	Lissanure
700	11 January 1988	John Hassett	Lissanure
701	11 April 1988	Martin Costigan	Toher
702	1 September 1988	Mary Clarke	Lissanure
703	1 September 1988	Lorraine Hartigan	Toher
704	6 June 1989	Paul Guider	Clonboo
705	1 September 1989	Lorcan Egan	Cowpark
706	1 September 1989	John Costigan	Toher
707	1 March 1990	Louise Davey	Clonmeen
708	12 March 1990	Emma Bergin	Lissanure
709	3 April 1990	Mary Campion	Clonmeen
710	7 June 1990	Treasa Hartigan	Toher

711	3 September 1990	Denis Deegan	Sorrellhill
712	3 September 1990	Mary Deegan	Sorrellhill
713	2 September 1991	Geraldine Campion	Clonmeen
714	1 September 1992	David Costigan	Toher
715	1 September 1992	Elaine Clarke	Lissanure
716	25 September 1992	Aidan Nolan (Clonmore)	Clonmore
717	3 May 1993	Patricia Campion	Clonmeen
718	1 September 1993	Sylvia Madden	Dromard
719	9 May 1994	Dan Guider	Clonboo

DAILY REPORT BOOK.

1. _____ Toher _____ NATIONAL SCHOOL. Roll No. 613

Townland, _____ Clonboo _____ Parish, _____ Templetuohy _____

Barony, _____ Ikerrin _____ County, _____ Tipperary _____

Poor Law Union, _____ Thurles _____ Electoral Division of Poor Law Union, _____ Templetuohy _____

2. **Nearest Post Town,** _____ Clonmore _____ Distance and Direction from the School _(Statute Miles.)_ 3

3. Area of Site _____ Acres, _____ Roods, _____ Perches.

4. Whether is School Vested or non-Vested? _Non Vested_

5. If vested, whether in the Commissioners or in Local Trustees? _Non vested_

6. From what Funds built? _Local Contributions_

7. In what year? _____

8. If only Rented as a School-house, amount of Rent? _None_

And by whom paid? _____

9. Precise date of its opening as a School, _1832_

10.   Do.   as a National School, _____

11. Internal Dimensions of each School-room, in feet .

Length.	Breadth.	Height.
22	16	9

12. Number of desks and forms, 4 ; length, 10 feet — inches

Separate Forms, 2 ; length, 10

13. Is there a recognized School Committee? If so, of how many Members does it consist? } _No_

And how often are its Meetings held? _____

14. If the School has a Patron as well as a Manager, give the Name, Religious Denomination, and Address of each.

Patron.	Manager.
	Rev P Murphy PP
	Templetuohy
	Templemore

15. (a) Has the Teacher a Free Residence? _Yes_

(b) Was the Residence of the Teacher provided by } _No_
means of Loan or Grant from the State?

(c) If Residence is not entirely rent-free to Teacher, } _No rent charge_
state the amount of Rentcharge paid by him

GRANTS MADE BY THE COMMISSIONERS OF NATIONAL EDUCATION.

Toher _____ **National School.**

Date	NATURE OF THE GRANT	£	s.	d.
1917	Brought Forward	3905	8	7½
Quarter end Sep 30	Salary for three months £16. 0 0		6 9	
	Stoppage for Pension 10 : 13 3	10	13	3
	War Bonus	2	12	0
	Requisite	1	10	0
Quarter 31st Dec.	Salary for three months £11. 0 0		6 9	
	Stoppage for Pension £10 13 3	10	13	3
	War Bonus	2	12	0
	Requisites		10	0
Jan 16th 918	On acc/. Salary	5	9	3
Feb 15	Salary £3 . 0 0			
	Barrel G. 5 16. 0			
	Bonus 2. 8. 0	11	4	0
	Requisites		10	0
March 4th	Salary on acct	5	0	0
	Bonus	2	0	0
April 12th	Balance of Salary	6	0	0
	Bonus	1	12	0
May 12th	Salary on acct	5	0	0
	Bonus	1	12	0
June 12th	Salaray	5	0	0
	Bonus	2	0	0
	Requisites for Quarter ended June	2	0	0
July 12th	Salary	5	0	0
	Pension	5	13	3
	Bonus	1	12	0
	Requisites		10	0
Aug 12th	Salary + Bonus	6	12	0
Sep 12th	Salary + Bonus	7	0	0
Oct 12th	Salary + Bonus	7	5	3
	Requisites	1	0	0
November 13	Salary + Bonus	6	12	0
Dec 12th	''	8	16	3
	Requisite	1	0	0

GRANTS MADE BY THE COMMISSIONERS OF NATIONAL EDUCATION.

_____ National School.

Date	NATURE OF THE GRANT	£	s.	d.
	Brought Forward			
Dec 15th '23	Salary, Bonus & arrears	36	0	0
Jan 16th (1924)	Salary Bonus & arrears	17	1	4
	Requisites	1	0	0
Feb. 14th	Salary	14	0	0
Mar "	"	14	0	0
April 14th	Salary £17 . 7 6			
	Pension 16 . 11 . 2			
	Capitation. 6 . 5 . 0 = £22 . 16 . 2	22	16	4
May 16th	Salary	18	0	0
June 16th	"	18	0	0
July 13	" 21 . 2 . 6			
	Pension 20 . 15 . 9	20	15	9
	Requisites	3	10	0

CHAPTER 6

EARLY MEMORIES, OLD CUSTOMS & OTHER YARNS

VERY EARLY MEMORIES

My grandmother Sarah Doolan was born just before the last millenium, on 20 August 1897. In her final years and long before she passed away, she often recalled how many changes she had seen in her lifetime. I have always held a deep interest and respect for tradition and ways of old. You have to admire the self-sufficiency that existed and the community spirit and sense of belonging that was evident in days gone by. All those attributes still exist in people today, but how we live today is very different and there are so many additional factors to contend with: the pace of life, the luxury and variety of food, the search for new inventions to improve our comfort and enjoyment of life, along with the power and need (maybe greed) for money. My grandmother always marvelled at the new gadgets that came along. Remember, when she was born, the 'pony and trap' was the main mode of transport and before she died we had sent several missions to the moon and into other places in the universe. It's all relative, but I wonder how many changes my daughter Sarah will see in her lifetime. She was born in the year 2000 and when I am in my nineties I hope to talk to her about the changes we will both have seen, please God.

This is a random chapter and as previously noted, I have a great love of old traditions and ways of life that previously existed in Ireland. Apart from admiring the ingenuity and practical methods and uses of everyday materials, you also have to remember that like us today, the people were only trying to make life easier for themselves. There was little or no waste; everything from the goose's wing by the open fire to the barrel catching rainwater had a use or a job to do.

Among the very early memories I have of growing up on the farm at home were two events: thrashing corn and the killing of a pig. Corn was thrashed to separate the grains of corn from the chaff (straw). The grain was stored in a barn before being collected by the co-op or used by grounding it for feed on the farm. I remember big, high loads of barley grain in the barn. The cutting and thrashing of corn was a community event. Each farmer's corn was thrashed with the help of neighbours from all around, and then you would help out on the next farm, and so on. Labour, not machinery was the main method of doing the work on a farm. Most farm jobs were done with farm animals, notably the workhorse and to a lesser extent the donkey, including ploughing, tilling, sowing, cutting and thrashing corn, going to the creamery, cutting and saving the hay, bringing home the turf, etc. As a social gathering, thrashing corn lasted several days and the nights were filled with dancing and craic.

Killing the pig was a different story. I remember a pig being killed in one of the outhouses and buckets of salt being used to cure it. When I say cure the pig, I don't mean make him better. The salt was used to preserve the meat and to ensure it stayed fresh for enough that we could eat it all. We had bacon and pork for a long time, but it never put me off bacon. We had just got the latest gadget at the time, called a freezer. It was a large chest-type freezer and I think most farm families had them.

Today all food is traceable back to source, a DNA-type system to identify the history of the piece of steak or the lamb chop that you are that you are buying in the supermarket. The farmer who owned and reared the animal is often named on the food packaging. As consumers we demand this information. The same applies to vegetables and other foodstuffs. However, we didn't need any paperwork or any such system. As you were having your dinner in the kitchen, you knew that the roast beef had been out in the front field about three days earlier, or that you had pulled the carrots out of the ground yourself that very morning.

Unfortunately, a sad and true story must be mentioned here. When sheep have multiple births or there are subsequent problems with the ewe, it often happens that a baby lamb needs a bit more care and attention. Sometimes the ewe may not have enough milk herself to feed all of her lambs. In such cases one of the lambs had to be fed with cow's milk from a large glass lemonade bottle (we used glass before plastic) with a big teat fitted to the end. I used to heat up the milk, put it in the bottle and take it out into the flock of sheep. I'd call the lamb's name, Dickie in this instance, and she would race over to me to get her nourishment. She'd drink that bottle of milk in less than a minute. After no time at all I would not even have to call her name; she would run to me whenever I appeared near the field. When I got home from school, if the sheep were in one of the lower fields, she would be waiting by the wall. I did a great job and Dickie thrived and became a fine lamb. The sad part came on the day she had to go to the factory. Heartbroken, I didn't eat lamb or mutton for some time afterwards. I had several other farm-animal pets; other lambs but also calves and the odd foal. I also went through a phase of keeping pet rabbits but the bloody foxes used to break in and kill them. If only I had Michael O'Brien from Bohola with his fox terriers, we would not have foxes within twenty miles!

Myself and Ned used to have great craic with the young calves. We had suckler cows and twice a day the cows would be brought into the milking parlour and the calves would be brought out from the store or barn to suck milk from the cows. When they were finished, the cows would be put back out into the fields while the calves would be put back into the barn. The calves would sleep there on the straw beds. The barn was a big enough space. Myself and Ned used to set up jumps like a showjumping arena at one end of the barn and then we would each select a calf and make it run and jump the obstacles. We felt it was a good way to keep the calves fit ! I don't know if this was the reason, but when the calves were let out into the fields at springtime, they used to run like mad around the fields and the open spaces for about an hour after they were released. They'd be leping and jumping like crazy, kicking the hoofs upwards. We used to try and hold onto their tails for a long as we could but that wasn't long.

OLD CUSTOMS AND TRADITIONS

People lived their lives governed by the world around them. They had to play the cards they were dealt in life and get on with it. There was a certain amount of ignorance or lack of knowledge about the goings on in the wider world. People got all their information from the immediate community or parish in which they lived, along with the news they got from radio, later television and stories from visitors. It was a big occasion if a trip or journey had to be made to Dublin or Cork or Limerick. Life was also regular, with any change being as a result of an unexpected event, such as sickness. Everybody went to Mass at a certain time and sat in the same pew each Sunday. There would be a day in 'town' shopping, a weekly game of cards (or more often than once a week at Christmas time), etc. If there was any break from the regular outings, it was immediately apparent to the rest of the community that there was something wrong. News would soon travel until the cause was identified. 'Ah I see Jimmy Ryan was not at Mass today [nobody in his pew].' 'Oh that's right, his sister the nun is home and they are going to Mass in Holycross this afternoon because the Novena is on there.'

Older people were and are much cleverer that the younger generation will ever be. They observe the world around them and learn, whereas nowadays, we need to have proof and need reassurance in terms of scientific evidence. We also go along with the popular view. Peer pressure has never been as strong. There is a comfort in the support we receive, along with an inherent confidence, which is great for our young people to have. However, there is a sense of an 'easy ride', in that the hard lessons are not learned by the youth because the parents want to do everything for them. There is always a sense of responsibility.

Maybe the balance of nature has been disturbed or changed forever in built-up areas, but in the countryside my grandmother had several 'signs' that told her of future events. I can't remember all of them, but weather predictions were an important and helpful to have. When the smoke from the chimney came down around the yard, there was rain on the way. When the swallows were flying low in the evening, it was going to rain the following day. Birds and farm animals also provided signs by their habits and behaviour.

I heard a story recently about the travelling people (they were known as 'tinkers' around home) and their ability to predict weather and other events well into the future. They could tell the signs of nature, and their lifestyle was such that they had to be watchful of extremes of weather to provide for themselves or make plans to change location. One story goes that soon after a new clan leader had been appointed, he was asked by some of the family to tell them if the coming winter was going to be cold or mild. Not knowing the old customs and signs to look out for, and not wanting to let his clan down, he decided to ring the met office on the quiet. The met office said it was too far away to say if the winter would be cold or mild but the chances were that it would be cold. He went back to the families and told them with forthright authority that the forthcoming winter would be cold. So they all set about collecting firewood in preparation for the cold winter.

A few weeks later the clan leader was again asked if the winter would be cold or mild, so he again rang the met office and this time the met office told him that the winter would in fact be a cold one. He went back and told the families to go out and collect more firewood, which they did, until they had a massive pile of timber. A few more weeks passed and again the leader was asked if the winter would be cold or mild. Again he rang the met office and this time he was told that the winter would be very cold indeed. He told the families to go back out and collect every bit of firewood they could get their hands on, which they did. After a few more weeks he again rang the met office after another question about the winter. So, when the met office told him that it was going to be the coldest winter on record, the leader asked how they knew this, and he was told, 'Sure the tinkers are going mad collecting firewood.'

SEASONS AND RELIGIOUS DATES

Lent is another tradition that is dying, or maybe losing its significance in modern Ireland. In bygone years, Lent had a real element of penance about it. The penance went past just Lent and Easter, in that nobody was to allowed eat meat on a Friday throughout the year. Even before that, complete fasting on a Friday was the normal Church requirement. Nowadays, Church teaching says that the days of abstinence only relate to Ash Wednesday and Good Friday. These days of fasting allowed one full meal and two collations. One collation could amount to two ounces of food;

the other collation could be eight ounces of food. Later, some bishops permitted a biscuit with a cup of tea at night. Doctor Con Lucey, Bishop of Cork, was one such bishop and a bakery in the city produced a large substantial biscuit that became known as a 'Connie Dodger'.

All those between the ages of twenty-one and sixty who were in good health and not engaged in laborious work were bound, under the pain of mortal sin, to fast. While meat was not allowed on any Friday during the year, in Lent it was not allowed on Wednesdays either.

RTÉ, the only radio station (and later the only television station), only played classical music along with news bulletins on Good Fridays, with no ads or films allowed.

St Patrick's Day always occurs during Lent, on 17 March. Apart from celebrating our patron saint and the man who is honoured for bringing Christianity to Ireland it is a day for the tradition of 'wetting the shamrock', or in recent times 'drowning the shamrock' might be more appropriate, as the day has got a bad reputation by those who overdo the drinking part of the festivities. It is a day to be Irish and to celebrate that fact.

People often associate certain days with events relating to weather and dates, such as a date when geranium flowers must not be put outside (due to risk of frost attack) or a date by which time summer flowering bulbs must be planted. St Swithin's day on 15 July carries an amusing reputation:

> St Swithin's Day – if it should rain
> For forty days it will remain.
> St Swithin's Day – if it be fair
> For forty days t'will rain no more.

The story goes that St Swithin was a theologian and adviser to King Egbert of Wessex. He became Bishop of Winchester in 852 and died there in 862. Nine years later there were plans for exhumation, to remove his remains to a new Cathedral on 15 July. Torrential rain and thunderstorms postponed the event and a legend began that the saint was crying about the delay.

Hallowe'en, the last night of autumn and eve of winter, is one of the four season festival celebrations. There are several customs associated with this time of the year, mostly pre-Christian and pagan traditions. For children growing up in the country it was a great night, with loads of games to play. Remember the scene: one television station, dark evenings and not much to do apart from whatever games you could play with the most recent toys you had been given (the most recent toys being from the previous Christmas).

Fruit played a big part in Hallowe'en celebrations for children, not for nutritional purposes but for games and activities. A big basin, or ideally a small steel bath, was essential. Into the basin of water would go lots of stuff, including apples, oranges, nuts, pears and bananas. The apple would have the top cut off to make it more difficult to pick out of the water. You'd be down on your knees on the floor and, with a towel nearby, you'd dive into the basin of water to pick the fruit. Nuts and smaller items that floated would be easy, as you could put them into your mouth, but larger items were harder to get a grip on with your teeth. The prize each time was that you could eat whatever you picked out. Putting money into the basin was something the adults did to tease the children. This was usually done after all the fruit was gone. More water was added to replace the water that was spilled around the floor at this stage and also to make the dive for the coins more difficult. After we finished getting the coins out we would be drenched, the floor of the kitchen would be flooded, we would have swallowed water and got water up our noses and after all that the basin would not have much water left.

Another game was 'snap apple', which involved hanging an apple from the ceiling on a piece of string. We would line up with our hands behind our backs and tried to get a grip on the apple to take a bite. There would be a time limit on everyone's go. If you got a start at all on the apple you were away.

A cherry on top of a hill of flour was a messy game. You had to slice away pieces of the mountain as close to the cherry as you could, without dislodging the cherry from the top of the heap of flour. Whoever let the cherry fall had to pick the cherry up with their teeth which meant putting your head down into the collapsed pile of flour. Usually you would get a bit of help, with a push down of the head into the flour, just as you were picking up the cherry.

The original custom of dressing up in fancy dress and going out with the 'Pooka' singing songs and collecting nuts and fruit is carried on today, albeit with a different custom of 'trick or treating'. Originally the fruit and nuts that you would collect would be used to play the games mentioned above, but of course nowadays the custom is to collect sweets or money without doing anything to earn it. The dressing up years ago was in costumes made by your mother or older sister, or even by yourself with a bit of shoe polish. Nowadays there are still outfits made by parents and children, but fancy-dress outfits of cartoon and action characters sold by toy stores are more common and less hassle. They are also 'cooler' and more sophiscated, for the fashion-conscious six to eight year old.

Christmas time brought its own customs and traditions, like card games of 25 and 45 (depending what part of the country you were from). Our house was strictly a 25 house. There was and still is a game of cards on Christmas night, when a 'nine of twenty-five' takes place. There is a traditional representation to the game, with the slot held by a previous player that passed away being taken by a subsequent generation. It is not always easy to get nine.

Other traditions and memories are remembered for a whole range of issues and belong to a time when affluence was not as evident in the country. This had not as much to do with the individual wealth of people but rather society as a whole. Everybody was struggling and the opportunity to save or spend was not an issue. I remember waking up on St Stephen's Day so sad, because it would be a full year before I would see new toys again. Mel Murphy's shop at the end of the Main Street in Templemore, at the Roscrea end, would have toys in the window every year for Christmas. Murphy's was a grocer shop and we shopped there. At Christmas time their sitting room on the right-hand side was turned into a toy store. You would go in with your mother on Christmas Eve to do the Christmas shopping and pick out a toy or a game. I remember you could go through the shop under the hatch or sometimes Mrs Murphy (Mel's mother) would let you go in the front door of the house on the right of the shop and you could go straight into the sitting room, or, to us, Aladdin's Palace. Needless to say the current crop of kids would not believe such stories and could not possibly comprehend a world without Smyth's or Toys'r'Us, etc.

The day after Christmas, St Stephen's day was a day to 'hunt the wren'. St Stephen was the first martyr, who died in AD 34. Tradition says that soldiers were following Stephen and he hid in an ivy bush. As the soldiers came close, a wren rustled in the bush; the soldiers then spotted Stephen and took him away and killed him. After this time, every year men and youths go out and hunt the wren and parade through the towns and villages with the dead bird on a stick carried over their shoulders. A song is sung that goes like this:

> The wren, the wren, the king of all birds,
> On Stephen's day, he was caught in the furze,
> Although he was little, his family was great,
> Rise up, landlady, and give us a 'trate'.
> I whooshed her up and I whooshed her down,
> And I whooshed her into Roberstown.
> I'll dip my head in a barrel of beer,
> And wish you all a Happy New Year.

The 'wren boys', as they were known around home, became an adult version of the children who went out trick or treating at Halloween time. It is now a tradition that is almost, if not entirely, extinct. It has also been a long number of years since a real wren was caught and carried on a stick around a village or town. In later years some groups did the rounds, going from house to house in the parish collecting for charities and good causes, but it was the poor drivers you would have to feel sorry for, as the performers would gratefully accept the 'hospitality' of the house along with any donations to the charity.

SELF-SUFFICIENCY

Country customs and traditions, when we look back on them nowadays, were a necessary part of everyday life. My grandmother's generation were totally self-sufficient. All their food was homemade from the baking of bread, the sowing of vegetables, the milking of cows and laying of hens. Animals such as chickens, cattle, pigs, lambs, geese, ducks, and a turkey for Christmas, were all reared on the farm. The woman's role and work on the farm was a tough. Along with getting stuck into the day-to-day physical work, she also had the washing of clothes with washboards and the churning of butter. A washboard is something that the modern woman or modern man would find hard to comprehend. It was a serrated or ribbed board about three feet long by twelve or fifteen inches wide. The wet clothes would be rubbed up and down at a fast pace and the ribbed surface would clean them. In those days also, men would put on a new collar on their shirt rather than change the shirt itself. The collars were detachable and they would always get a good starching and be shining white for Mass on Sunday.

I have never seen butter churned but it was hard work. The skin and cream from the top of the milk was removed and put into a butter churn. A constant stirring of this milk would eventually lead to butter. Ned Fogarty was the creamery manager in Templetuohy. The creamery was on the Toher/Clonboo side of Templetuohy about half a mile this side of the village. I remember people taking milk there from all the farms on our road. Actually, Neddy Guilfoyle and others used to take the churns of milk up to the creamery on an ass and cart. The milk was all taken in and then a milk tanker would collect the milk from the creamery and take it to the co-operative for processing into the various products. Nowadays the milk tankers collect from the farmers directly.

'Saving' hay was always a big event and one in which the weather played a big part. The farmer was always watching the weather and trying to get a good time to cut. If you could get four or five days of good, fine weather, with a bit of sun and a breeze, you could get the hay saved. Going back to early times, before the help of tractors and machinery, hay was cut with a scythe, which was a very awkward and difficult tool to use. You would not want to be clumsy with this tool. It had a timber handle about five-feet long, with two handles to hold, and the blade was roughly four-feet long and curved in shape. Cutting the hay was done by one strong movement of a wide sweep, with correct timing being essential. Long swards of hay would be cut and the top part left to dry. The hay would then be turned with a hayfork to let the other side dry. It might have been necessary to turn the hay again, but when it was fully dry it was put into rows along the length of the field. A couple of rows were joined together and a 'tram' of hay was made. This was a heap of hay about six feet in diameter and about eight-feet high. As the tram settled down over a couple of days it would reduce in height to five or six feet. After a few more days it would be brought into the hay barn. On my summer holidays down in Co. Limerick, the stack of hay was called a 'vine'. In later years, various implements on the tractors were used to cut with mowers and turn with rakers, and hay was 'baled' instead of being trammed. A bale of hay is a rectangular box shape about a foot and a half by three feet by a foot thick, tied together with two lengths of baling twine. When the hay was baled we would have to 'stuck' the bales. Usually the bales were stucked in twos or fours, by standing them up on their edges and assembling them against each other on a V-shaped bridge. Like the tram of hay, the stucked bales would not get wet, as the rain would run off the surface.

MONEY

A small amount of money went a long way when we were growing up. For a start, it may sound strange, but we really didn't have any need for money as there wasn't anything to buy compared to nowadays, where money is an essential ingredient for living in the same way we need water and oxygen. We live in a commercial way of life, where, as my economics lecturer used to proclaim, 'the consumer is king' and 'the language of communication is money.'

Before the advent of decimalisation and later the euro, the currency was 'old money'. The euro arrived in 2002 in an attempt to harmonise all money across the continent of Europe, although somebody forgot to tell Britain, as they decided to stay outside the 'Eurozone'.

In February 1971 Ireland adopted a currency of punts and pence. The former pound was replaced by the punt. There was 100 pence in the punt. This currency was only in existence for about thirty years and it replicated the British currency of sterling pounds and pence. The new decimal system made it a lot easier to calculate your values and conversions compared to the old money system as described below. The older generation at the time of changeover were sceptical and took a bit of time to adjust. When the euro arrived in 2002, a lot of the 'new' older generation were heard saying, 'There is no value in the new currency as your pound [the new euro] goes nowhere these days.' In this decimal system the new penny was worth the equivalent of 2.4 old pence.

The various currencies fluctuated in value relative to each other and led to unstable variations, easily affected by a variety of issues such as political changes and economic performances. When the euro started, the Irish punt was valued at one euro and twenty-seven cents.

But going back to the start of Irish currency. In 1825, the then Irish currency was abolished by Britain and replaced with English currency. With the advent of the Irish Free State in 1921, Ireland secured a degree of economic and monetary independence from England. In that context, the Irish Government subsequently appointed a Currency Commission to oversee the designing, minting and printing of new Irish coins and banknotes. Such a task was completed by 1928 when Irish coins and banknotes were put into circulation. This was the start of old money.

Prior to the birth of the punt, money was denoted by the symbols £, s and d. These were the first letters of *librae, solidi* and *denarii*, which were the names of the Roman pound, the Roman gold coin, and lesser Roman coins.

The £ s d coins comprised half crowns (2/6); florins (2/-); shillings (1/-); six-penny bits (or tanner in slang) 6d; 3d; pennies (1d); halfpennies (½d) and farthings (¼d). There was also a gold coin called a sovereign, which was worth one pound, but there were no sovereigns in circulation for many decades. There was also a ten-shilling note. There was a silver coin called a crown which was worth five shillings, but that coin also went out of circulation. There were twenty shillings in a pound, twelve pennies in a shilling, twenty-four pence to the florin, thirty pence to the half crown, and 120 pence to the ten shilling note. A pound was worth 240 pennies. There was also a coin called a guinea, which was worth twenty-one shillings. All in all a fair amount of change to calculate for a shopkeeper with no calculator or cash register. Is that why the older generation are sharper with figures and can recite their maths (or in those days, sums) tables so well compared to the current-day whizz kids who need a calculator to add and multiply simple figures?

Thinking back on the usage of money in our language, a lot of slang, sayings and songs have survived to the current day. I suppose if you hadn't got the money, you might as well make other use of it. I've gathered a few examples, which might help you to recall other ones:

A Penny Farthing was an old bicycle, where the front wheel was four or five feet in diameter and the back wheel was less than a foot in diameter. The wheels looked like the difference in size between a farthing and a penny.

To 'spend a penny' meant going to the toilet, and still does, because public toilets used to have locks on them which needed a penny to open them.

The Ha'penny Bridge, a pedestrian bridge over the Liffey in Dublin, is free to use nowadays, but in days gone by it was the first official toll bridge, long before national toll roads.

'Look after your pennies and the pounds will look after themselves' … 'Pennywise and pound foolish'. Both of these sayings had merit, one in relation to being careful about small amounts of money, and the other warning against concerning yourself with small amounts of money, only to not to realise that you are wasting large amounts of money. I hope the children are reading this!

The poor farthing was the lowest-valued coin, being worth ¼ of a penny, and so it was often used in less-than-luminous expressions, such as, 'I haven't got two farthings to rub together' or 'not worth a brass farthing'.

Other general sayings include, 'A penny for your thoughts', someone 'turns up like a bad penny', and to be 'In for a penny, in for a pound'. The list goes on and on.

In terms of songs and rhymes, the old ones for times of the year include:

EASTER

Hot Cross Buns
Hot Cross Buns

One a Penny, two a Penny
Hot Cross Buns

CHRISTMAS

Christmas is coming,
The goose is getting fat.
Please put a penny in the old man's hat.
If you havn't got a penny, a ha'penny will do.
If you haven't got a ha'penny, a farthing will do.
If you havn't got a farthing, then God bless you.

The sixpence seemed to get a special place in a lot of rhymes, all of which we learned in school. I remember two of them that are still in use. The first one always reminds me of one of our own fields at home called 'the crooked stile field':

There was a crooked man, who walked a crooked mile.
He found a crooked sixpence, beside a crooked stile.
He bought a crooked cat, who caught a crooked mouse,
And they all lived together, in a crooked house.

(Nowadays being 'crooked' means you might have to go to Dublin Castle not as a guest but to a tribunal!)

Sing a song of sixpence, a pocket full of rye,
Four and twenty blackbirds baked in a pie.
When the pie was opened, the birds began to sing.
Wasn't that a dainty dish to set before a king?

Money was always scarce especially, in rural Ireland, the main reason being that the farmer had no regular income. The one great asset the farmers had was their ability to produce almost all their own food. They owned the land, thanks mainly to Parnell and Davitt, and the labour was supplied by themselves and their families. In those days, all the family worked on the farm. As long as they were physically able, older family members worked in the fields at sowing crops, and again at harvest time, when all hands were called upon. The land was tilled with farm implements such as spades and shovels, while the plough, scuffler, grubber, harrow and cart were drawn and pulled by the farm horses. Milk and butter were supplied by their own cows and meat was supplied from the farm stock, including pigs and fowl, along with wild animals that were hunted on the lands and woods. The wool from the sheep was spun by the women folk and excess of goods were sold at local markets.

An important product was the humble egg. Every farmer's wife kept a good stock of fowl: hens, chickens, bantams, ducks, geese and sometimes turkeys. The goose was the traditional Christmas food long before the turkey, especially in less affluent times and in poorer areas. Along with the food value of the fowl, the egg production value was often of even more benefit. The eggs were always in demand and formed a part of most cooking recipes. Eggs were sold and exchanged with merchants in turn for other food items and goods such as tea, shoe laces, polish, cutlery, flour, delph, etc. During times of high levels of egg production, the farmer's wife would be in surplus with the merchant, and this situation would balance out during the non-laying season.

One story that Niall Tobin tells (indeed, one of my favourites), is about the regular inclusion of an egg in the schoolboy's breakfast. Two brothers are going to primary school. The first boy arrives five minutes late for school, and when the teacher asks him why he is late, he says, 'I was havin' my breakfast.' Then the teacher asks him what he had for his breakfast, to which he replied, 'I had an egg.' Five minutes later, the second boy arrives to school, and when the teacher asks him why he is late, he says, 'I was havin' my breakfast.' Then the teacher asks him what he had for his breakfast, and the boy replies that he also had an egg. Then teacher then says, 'Your brother had an egg for his breakfast and he was here five minutes before you', to which the boy replies, 'Did I have a spoon, did I?'

SHEEP DIPPING AND SHEARING

The earlier mention of a sheep dip may have provoked thoughts of one of those creamy 'dips' you get in a supermarket for dipping your Pringles or raw carrot strips into, but not in this case. These were sheep with worms to be precise. 'Oh, thanks for sharing that information with us', I hear you say, but at the time sheep dipping was great crack.

The purpose-made trailer, which was attached to a tractor, was tank-like in form, or even like a portable small-size swimming pool, about 4ft wide and 6ft long, with a depth of a couple of feet. There was an entrance at one end with a ramp up to the tank and an exit gate at the other end. The idea was simple: fill the tank with a disinfectant to remove or cure the worms, push the sheep up the ramp and into the tank, let them swim around in the liquid, give them a good steeping in the tank and then, when they were well and truly 'dipped', open the exit gate and let them out. That's how you dip sheep.

Shearing sheep was another great day. Just when you had all the sheep in the field identified by various markings such as a wool or fleece mark, a stick or bit of wire that might be stuck to the sheep's coat, they would all be sheared and end up look-ing identical. Sheep shearers were skilled operators, barbers in the making. The wool would all be bundled up into balls or bales and sold. It was a great relief for the sheep, as obviously they were sheared at the start of summer after carrying a heavy coat for the winter. Immediately after the shearing, all the sheep made lots of noise as they baa-ed and looked for their unrecognisable lambs. After losing their fleece some sheep would also get colds and the flu at this time, if the weather turned cold – only joking!

We used also cut the tails off lambs at a couple of months old … you've heard of oxtail soup! Tails were a constant dirt collector and always getting caught in bushes, so they had to be cut off. It was no problem; just a quick cut, just like cutting your nails … Well maybe not exactly, but you know what I mean. I suppose it was more like burning the horns off calves.

WEATHER

Weather is one of the most talked-about topics of conversation in Ireland. It is today as it always was. Indeed the summers of 2007, 2008 and 2009 have been some of the worst in my living memory. I don't know what the statistics are until the end of the summer, but there has been so much rain and little sunshine that it must be one of the worst summers in a long time. My Mother always told me that there was a severe and prolonged period of cold weather around the time I was born, end of '62 and early '63. We went through a very cold period earlier this year and the comparisons were made with the '60s. I was over in Spain for one of the weeks of the builders' holidays at the end of July. I met a friend of mine, also in the building industry in Ireland over there and he said to me, 'here in Spain, nobody talks about the weather, but at home we talk about nothing else'.

In years gone by, the people didn't have the benefit of satellite technology to monitor weather patterns or track storms and weather fronts coming towards land from the sea. As we all know, regardless of all the technology at their disposal, the weather forecasters still get it wrong. Also, with the undoubted changes in climate and atmospheric conditions, the ability to accurately predict the weather in the medium to long term is going to get more problematic and challenging. So hopefully science can keep ahead of the environmental advances and give us the necessary time to put in place the protection measures necessary into the future to safeguard our existence. There is no doubt that more and more dramatic and dangerous weather incidents take place nowadays than in the past.

Going back to the past, there was of course bad weather, and the people learned the signs and watched out for behaviour patterns of animals and birds, along with signals from the moon and the sky. Everybody had various signals and depending on the yarn that was told, the signal or sign could be good or bad and other people would have variations of the same sign. Nonetheless, observing the weather and foretelling the signs were important for the people who earned their livelihood from the land. The ones that I was told about are, in my opinion, well-founded signs that rain is coming. They were that rain is not far away when 'smoke from a chimney comes down around the yard' and 'when swallows fly low around the yard'. The other sign that I remember is that if you looked out at the quarry in Lisduff from outside our house and if you could clearly see it, then rain was not far away (the opposite being that if it was hazy in the distance then the weather was going to be good and warm). It was always a correct sign. In Templemore I heard someone say a similar thing about the Devil's Bit mountain with a slight variation, 'if you can see it then it's going to rain and if you can't see it, then it's already raining'. Another sign that my grandmother always said, was that rain was on the way when the soot fell back down onto the grate from the open-fire chimney.

As we've read, folklore says that if it rains on St Swithin's Day it will rain for forty days. I think it rained in 2009 on 15 July and most days since then for the rest of the summer! Other countries have similar folklore about continuous rain based on it raining on a particular date, so the Irish are not unique in this regard. The French have a date of 19 July and the Germans have a similar yarn about 19 July.

We have several superstitions about rain but here are a few, some of which are totally daft:

...dogs eating grass.
...cats washing their ears or cats sneezing.
...swallows flying low.
...pine cones closing up.
...smoke from chimneys rising to the right, spreading and descending.
...a new moon lying on its back.
...fleas biting ferociously.
...cows huddling together on low ground.
...ants getting agitated and climbing walls.
...roosters crowing at night.
...crows sheltering low in trees.
...donkeys braying louder and twitching their ears.
...soot falling into the fire grate.
...magpies feeding alone.
...red skies appearing at night.

I recently came across this verse from *c*.1834, which summarises a lot of the foregoing weather signs:

'Signs of Rain'

The soot falls down, the spaniel sleeps,
And spiders from their cobwebs creep.
Last night the sun went pale to bed,
The moon in halos hid her head.
A boding shepherd heaved a sigh,
To see a rainbow span the sky.

The walls are damp, the ditches smell,
Closed is the pink-eyed pimpernel.

Loud quacks the ducks, the peacocks cry,
The distant hills are looking nigh.

Hark how the chairs and tables crack,
Old Betty's joints are on the rack.
The frog has changed his yellow vest,
And in a russet coat has dressed.

Whatever the signs, the topic of weather still remains and it will always be a central theme in any conversation in rural Ireland. It is, after all, something that affects our daily lives, what we wear and how we go about our days. It is also a simple opener to any conversation with a friend or a complete stranger. Thank God for the weather.

LESSONS FOR LIFE

A little bird lies frozen cold, dying in the cold weather, a bull comes along and shits on top of the bird, the little bird thaws out and starts to sing loudly, a cat comes along and digs the bird out of the shit and eats the bird.

Lessons Learned:
Not everyone that shits on you is your enemy.
Not everyone that digs you out is your friend.
Remember, when you are in the shit and you get out of it, keep your mouth shut.

Then the same bull drops a load of shit. Along comes a turkey and gobbles it all up. With strength from the bullshit, the turkey flies to the top of the tree but in time she comes back down.

Lesson Learned:
Bullshit might get you to the top but it will not keep you there.

A LEAP YEAR

The twenty-ninth of February occurs every four years. By tradition, the leap year date is one of the rare days when women can go down on one knee and propose to men. It occurs every four years, or to be more precise, every 1,461 days.

The tradition of women proposing to men on 29 February is believed to have started in fifth-century Ireland, when St Bridget complained to St Patrick about women having to wait so long for men to propose. St Patrick then said the custom could be reversed on this day in the leap year. Our world and our lives are full of traditions and customs. Men proposing to women instead of the other way around is just that, a tradition or a custom.

In 1288, Scotland passed a law allowing women to propose in that year. Any man who declined a proposal in a leap year had to pay a fine, ranging from a kiss to payment for a silk dress or a pair of gloves.

The leap year was actually invented by Julius Caesar after his astronomers told him that the year was not 365 days long but 365.25 days long. Caesar settled on adding an extra day to every fourth year. In 1582, Pope Gregory XIII changed the Catholic calendar again after it was discovered that the remainder after each year was closer to 0.2425 of a day – a small difference that added up over time. To combat the slight shift, Pope Gregory removed ten days from October that year between the fourth and the fifteenth. The British Empire changed to the Gregorian system by removing ten days from September in 1752.

The system is still not quite accurate, with the dates drifting by three days every 10,000 years. A century year is only a leap year if it exactly divisible by 400, so the year 1900 was not a leap year, while the year 2000 was a leap year.

CLOCKS IN HOUSES

Clocks in houses long ago were a rare item compared to nowadays, when time is told from mobile phones, on regular watches or on radio programmes. In the time before clocks, people told the time from the location of the sun and used time dials, etc., when the clouds were clear. Meal times were always at regular intervals and even the diet and food that were eaten were fairly predictable. There was always meat eaten twice on a Sunday, the main roast for lunch and some form of cold meat for the tea-time meal. It is fair to say that eating during the day is now based around convenience and speed, with fast-food and deli outlets the main suppliers to our hunger needs.

The problem with clocks in the houses years ago was that the time was rarely accurate. This was due to the custom of people moving the clock forward and backwards for various reasons. The mother would move the clock forward to make sure the family were in time for Mass or another event, while the son might move it back knowing that his mother had moved it forward. The moving back and forward would leave a visitor to the house to ask the common question, 'Is that clock right?' The answer would be, 'Never mind that clock it's a half an hour fast.' I think we got our first clock at home with Green Shield Stamps.

There was a story I heard one time about a woman who won a cuckoo clock in a bazaar. It was a great novelty and an excellent timekeeper. One night, soon after they got the clock, when they were not yet used to the little bird popping in and out, one of the teenage sons was out at a disco and stayed out too late. He had been warned by his parents to be home before twelve midnight. The son arrived home almost at 3a.m. and was quietly going up the stairs when his mother called out from her bedroom:

'Is that you Jimmy?'

'Yes mother.'

'What time is it?'

'Oh, just twelve o'clock.'

'Good boy, that's not too late.'

At this very moment, the clock struck 3a.m. and out popped the bird and called out 'cuckoo' three times. As quick as you like, Jimmy did the only thing he could, he called out 'cuckoo' a further nine times and then went to bed. All's well that ends well. Jimmy was a lucky lad thanks to his quick thinking.

I can remember a scene, like it was yesterday, of my grandmother Sarah Doolan sitting by the open fire, under a Sacred Heart lamp in total stillness with not a sound disturbing the quietness apart from the odd cracking sound from the fire and the solemn ticking of the clock. I'm sure it is a scene well remembered by many readers of a mature age who grew up in the countryside.

WATER SUPPLIES

The main supplies of water in the locality were by means of hand pumps attached to shallow wells. These were supplied by the county council and located through-out the parishes. There was one such well at the end of Toby Maher's lane in Toher. There was another in Clonmore village opposite the church, which became a weekly meeting point after Sunday Mass. Farmers had their own wells and this sup-plied the water for the stock and for the house usage.

DOGS

Every farmhouse had a sheepdog to help bring in the cows or herd the sheep. Some good dogs could bring in the sheep on their own. As for the cows, they were on a regular routine and would nearly come in for milking on their own. As everyone knows, sheep follow sheep, and if you can get one sheep to go in a certain direction the chances are the others will follow.

In a story a bit like that of Cú Chulainn, a farmer lost his sheepdog and he hired a young fella that had a fantastic turn of speed on foot. The farmer decided to take some sheep to the local fair and told the young fella to round up all the sheep and take them to the quarry so that he could pick out the best ones. When the farmer got to the quarry, all the sheep were there and the young fella was there on guard at the entrance. When the farmer was checking through the flock he noticed a hare in the middle of the sheep. He asked the young fella how the hare got into the flock. The young fella had never seen a hare before and said, 'is that what it is, and he was the one who gave me more hardship than all the rest combined'.

The first dog arrived in Finnstown in mid-December 2006 – a black cocker spaniel pup. Her name is Holly, appropriately named for the time of year, and she was ten weeks old when she arrived. She is a pure bred, with a family tree to resemble any of the families contained in this book. Anne's uncle and aunt in Rockville Centre, Long Island, New York had a golden/light-brown cocker spaniel named Clancy, which we loved when we visited there in the early '90s. Everyone loves Holly and for good measure she now has an assistant, aptly named 'Silly'.

RECOLLECTIONS OF JOHNNY BUTLER

One of Pat's assignments during his second-year projects in Mary Immaculate Teacher Training College was to interview my father about rural life in Ireland during the '40s, '50s and '60s. Thanks to Pat, I have included excerpts from the transcript here, which give further insights into farming life at the time.

Pat: *What age did you leave school to start farming?*

Johnny: Fourteen, from full-time school, or semi-full-time we'll say … I used to go in more or less on the wet days and stay home the fine days. That was around 1946.

P: *What's your earliest memory of working on the farm, good or bad or indifferent?*

J: Oh my earliest memory was maybe when I was about eight or nine. I used to have to tend in the evening time, we thinned crops and tended crops, on our knees. I also used to have to go to the bog to catch turf when I was about nine years of age.

P: *And were these jobs you used to look forward to or dread?*

J: No, I never looked forward to them and I never liked them. I never liked farming years ago; t'was too tough and there wasn't a bob to be got out of it. You couldn't get a bob out of my mother or father.

P: *What equipment had you at the time?*

J: There was no tractors at that time, or very few anyway. We didn't get a tractor 'til 1961. I started to plough with a pair of horses, an ordinary till plough, when I was fourteen, and you walked all day from eight o'clock in the morning 'til half six or seven in the evening and you'd be as tired as a dog after it. Especially when you were only a young teenager. It was hard going.

P: *I'd well believe it.*

J: And then, we tilled with a zig-zag harrow, they used to call it, a cultivator and a roller and so on – all horse pulled. We always had two horses. Some of the smaller farmers might have only one horse. They'd borrow one, what was known as cooring. They used to coor with neighbours if they hadn't a second horse, but we always had two horses.

P: *I want us to talk now about the sense of community in farming circles. I know that a certain number of farmers used to take turns taking the milk to the creamery and that. Did we get involved in that?*

J: Ah yeah, Maher's and ourselves, we used to go every second week to the creamery. Apart from going to the creamery there was a very neighbourly system. If you had a spare man on the day they'd be tramming hay you'd send them to a neighbour or you'd help a neighbour at harvest time and things like that. We were helping each other all the time.

The harvest was a very important time because people usually got money on credit or got goods and credit during the year and they paid for it in the harvest. That was the usual run of the thing back in the '40s and the '50s. When the harvest came, it had to be cut with a reaper and a binder pulled by horses. It had to be stooked in the field, and it had to be let dry and then it was drawn in and reeked and then threshed. All the local neighbours were called; Maher's and a few others would be involved with the cutting and the stooking and the drawing in but then when it would come to the thrashing, you'd need about twenty men there to operate the thresher. So they would come from a wider area maybe, a second townland. We were from Clonboo, and a certain number of people came from Toher, maybe more from Killivinogue as well from Clonmore, places like that.

P: *Work in lieu of you helping them? Or would you have to pay them?*

J: No you'd go to their threshings as well. You were all month going to the thrashings, day after day, after day.

P: *We have forty acres here of barley and we're able to do it in a day now – roughly how long would it take the whole process then?*

J: Well, when I was young, we used to grow wheat and barley and oats and sugar beet, and mangles and turnips and potatoes. That was all done in about twelve or thirteen acres. That's all we'd have tilled. We'd have livestock as well, but thirteen or fourteen acres, so we'd have roughly six or seven in cereals and the rest'd be in the root crops. But it was an awful lot of work. We're mostly talking in Irish acres at this stage of course. Usually when you were ploughing here, you were doing well if you ploughed half an acre in a day. So you're talking about thirty days, taking in wet days and snowy days and all the rest of it. With an early spring or late winter you were talking about twenty-five or thirty days ploughing alone. You started ploughing maybe in January or February, if the weather permitted, and you wouldn't be sowing until. We'd sow the wheat first, the barley second and the oats last and then we sowed the sugar beet, the potatoes, the mangles and the were turnips last. The turnips weren't sown until June, or swedes we used to call them.

The sowing was always by horse-pulled machine with the result that there was twenty times more seeds sowed than was needed, so you had to thin it out as you went along and that had to be done by hand as well. You might give a month thinning between turnips and mangles. The beet and the potatoes had to be weighed as well. It'd be known now, I suppose, as organic farming. Jack thinned turnips for days during the summer at home and for neighbours for money – so much a drill.

P: *It was yourself and your father mostly?*

J: We always had a couple of men working here as well.

P: *And was it different men every year?*

J: Ah no no. They were mostly long term. There was one man here gave twenty years near enough. Ah sure we had nothing and they had nothing and that was the way it was.

P: *Just going back to what we were saying about going to the creamery and the thrashing and that – would you say that was a social outlet?*

J: Thrashing was a social outlet and some of the people would give us a dance in the house the night after the thrashing. I remember one night we were in Sorrillhill and there was a dance. Tom Quinn, the Lord have mercy on him, was playing an accordion. You'd dance till three o'clock in the morning, then you'd be thrashing in a field at eight the next morning again.

P: *When would you say things start changing?*

J: Ah sure it started changing in the '60s because then the combines started coming in – small combines. But it was a gradual process

P: *And when did we get a tractor here?*

J: 1961. It was only a little two cylinder, twenty or thirty horsepower or something like that. There were only twelve-inch ploughs at that stage.

P: *You mentioned earlier there about the bog. I can remember from my own childhood having to go to the bog to catch turf – was it much the same for you?*

J: Oh the bog was big. You usually gave three weeks in the bog, maybe end of April, early May. I would go to the bog and catch turf, wet turf in my hands, as it came off of the slane and I'd put it on the barra. I started doing that about nine years of age and at fourteen I was wheeling. I didn't get promoted to the slane till I was sixteen or more.

We used to sell about six lorry loads of turf every year. The strange thing about it is, we sold what we cut turf in April. We'd try and save it, my mother and a lot of them would give a hand at the saving of it, and then we'd drag it home and sell it. Then we'd go back, maybe between the saving of the hay and the harvest, and we'd cut a few more days and that was for our winter fire. It would often be October before we'd draw that turf home out of the bog. We used to have at least two men that we paid in the bog in the summer I'd be catching and there'd be a lad cutting and a lad wheeling, maybe two sometimes. There was an awful lot of it and it was very labour intensive.

P: *Was it something you'd just do yourselves or would you ever club together with other farmers?*

J: Umpteen times, when I was eleven and twelve years of age, when I'd come home from school I'd just grab a bit to eat and get an ass and horse and draw out turf till the dark that night. It was tough going. That's why I turned against farming and bogs and everything in my time, because I got too much of it when I was young.

P: *You have been a pioneer all your life. How did you socialise, as a farming community? Nowadays we've Macra na Feirme. Was there something similar back then?*

J: Well, there was an agricultural class in Toher school, I don't know, maybe in the mid to late '40s, and I attended that for a whole winter. What was known as the young farmers' club was set up, one of the first young farmers clubs in the country. It was set it up here in Toher and that was the forerunner for Macra na Feirme

The farmers' club used to run a dance every year in Rathdowney in the month of September. It was always a great success. I was about fifteen or sixteen when I went to my first dance in Rathdowney. We saved what bit of money we made out of that and we got a corn sower and a manure spreader, which was to be used by the members of the of the young farmers' club. Well, for the general use of the farmers around the place.

We used to run this dance every year, so that was a big social occasion, and it always came in the middle of the thrashing. We'd be at the dances at Rathdowney on a Sunday night, and Monday morning at the thrashing. So all the talk would be the dance the night before and who took home who, and who was looking after who and so on.

I used to go to the dancing about once a fortnight. I'd very seldom go to Rathdowney or Templemore or Templetouhy, a lot more in Borisoleigh and different places. They were all in the halls. If you wanted a drink you'd have to go to a pub. In Templemore the town hall was the main place for dances. The dances were from nine to three, and I often saw the hall packed at half past nine. And you'd dance six hours there, as hard as ever you could I remember coming home one night on a bicycle and it rained so hard my shoes filled with water and they overflowed as I cycled.

We also used to hurl. There was hurling every Sunday for the summer and most of the winter in that field out there opposite the door. They weren't organised games, just a few of the locals. We'd have five one week and maybe ten another week.

There was a little lay by there, below at the Banjo's, where we used to play skittles and pitch and toss in the summertime.

P: *We have the tradition of the card game here of a Christmas night. When did that start or can you remember?*

J: Ah, that started around, I'd say, 1957 or '58. It's around fifty years since it started (so 'tis still going still going strong as they say)but I'd say there was a few years missing here and there. See, I only got married in 1961, and I remember Mary was here the Christmas before, at the card game. That's my first memory of it so maybe 'twas going on a few years before that.

P: *Tipperary had a good hurling team back then. Would you go to many of the matches?*

J: When I got a car in 1953 I used to go to matches all right … I'd pick up four or five lads of a Sunday morning, and I'd charge them a pound each and we'd drive off to Cork or to Limerick. So I collected four or five quid for a gallon of petrol; at that time you used to be able to buy four gallons of petrol for thirteen or fourteen quid.

The '61 All Ireland was the first one that I was at I think. I'm not sure now, maybe the '71. I was at the '56 league final, I won't ever forget that. They were playing Wexford and there was a storm blowing the same day. Tipperary were playing with the wind in the first half and they were leading by something like fourteen points at half-time. Wexford came out with a new team in the second half and they scored four goals on Reddin. It was the beginning of the end as far as Reddin was concerned.

Ah, Wexford beat them. I remember coming out of the canal end that evening, and I forget who was with me (Johnny Hennessy, I think, and Ned Fogarty) and Patrick Clarke, the Lord have mercy on him, was up the road in the middle of a crowd of women up from Wexford and they arguing over the match, only pure laughing at them making a pure cod of them. That's my first memory of Croke Park.

P: *If you didn't get to the match, would you listen to it on the radio here?*

J: We didn't have a radio in the early times. There was a man who lived down in the double house below Finn Whelan and he used to have a radio. We used to go down there to listen to the matches. He had to sit beside it all day, because he'd be tuning it the whole time to keep it going. We didn't get electricity here until about 1957. It was a big change.

P: *Back to farming. I've seen photos of the fair in Templemore and I've seen the square just full of livestock. How did that organise itself, was there an auctioneer there or did everyone do their own?*

J: I used to have to go to in fairs in Templemore, Roscrea, Thurles, Rathdowney and Urlingford. They used to be every month. I had an uncle living over in Kyle. I used to have to go to the fairs with him. That was always on a Monday and I'd usually go somewhere on Sunday night, maybe to a dance, and I'd have to be up at half three in the morning. My aunt and my uncle, Lord have mercy on them all, would have the breakfast ready and the calves would be fed by that time too. We'd walk the cattle on the road from Kyle to Rathdowney. We'd probably be in Rathdowney about six o'clock in the morning. I remember been in Rathdowney one morning in the square at six o'clock and the sun and moon were shining.

They'd make deals and then the cattle would be sold. You would just stand there and somebody who would be interested in the cattle would come up and ask you how much you were asking for them. You'd say so much, and they'd bid you so much and you'd haggle away. Jobbers, as they were known, would try to buy and sell any kind of a thing. If you were trying to make a few bob you'd avoid them.

All the cattle were transported to the Dublin market by train. Rathdowney was particularly awkward because the railway station was three miles from the town, in Ballybrophy. In Templemore, when you sold cattle, you had to take them down to the station yourself and get them loaded and get your ticket marked. When the person bought the cattle off you, he usually gave you a ticket and said the cattle were to be loaded on the Dublin side or the Cork side of the train track.

In Rathdowney it was different. There you would sell the cattle and the man who bought them might have bought many cattle and at a certain time of the day, you'd take the cattle to such a spot where there'd be a collection point. Maybe he'd be after buying fifty cattle and he'd get them all together, say outside the church, and he'd have somebody hired to take them to Ballybrophy and load them.

P: *Was there ever a case where you'd fail to sell and you'd have to walk them home again?*

J: Yeah, 'twas usually no bother to walk them home as they'd know the road themselves. It would be early in the morning and of course the roads weren't all well tarred. Maybe we'd come to the conclusion we'd keep them another month or maybe someone might come up to the house and buy them. The mart started in Templemore in 1955 so it would have been pre '55 that I'm talking about there.

P: *There's one other thing I wanted to ask you about. I've read in a few books that every farmer used to have to help out the local parish priest and the local teacher. Was that in your time or before your time?*

J: Well, when I was going to school there was no central heating and there was just a fire at one end of the school. Each family having children going to the school would bring a load of turf to the school for the fire for the year. As regard the parish priest, people used to give the priest turf and they used to give him chickens and different things. It wasn't organised. I don't ever remember giving anything to pre-ists. We paid the collections alright but I don't remember giving anything in the line of turf or anything like that.

P: *Thanks very much, that'll do nicely.*

J: Ok, no problem.

GOOD NEIGHBOURS

A Dutch farmer is out shooting one day, in all his hunting gear, heavy mountain jacket, warm hat, steel toe boots, gun and his dog. He walks for hours but sees nothing, until the dog sniffs a pheasant and the chase is on. The dog rises the pheasant and it flies up over a hedge; the man aims and fires, the pheasant drops. The Dutch man is delighted, and goes to retrieve his pheasant, when he is met by a man coming out of the field where the pheasant has dropped. The man is German and declares that the pheasant fell across the border and he now owns the pheasant. The Dutch man is going mad and pleads his case, but to no avail. Eventually, the Dutch man suggests a way of deciding who keeps the pheasant, but says that it will be a challenge of courage and strength. The German does not want to back down from such a proposal, as he has pride in his nationality. The Dutch man suggests that each of them in turn give the other a kick up the private parts, and the man that makes the less noise will keep the bird. The Dutch man goes first and gives the German an unmerciful kick. The German crawled over in pain, but keeps the howls of pain to himself, although he has tears flowing down his face in agony. Eventually the German gets up and says, 'There you are, that is brave, now my turn.' And the Dutch man says, 'It's ok, you can keep the pheasant!'

CHAPTER 7

HURLING & MORE

HURLING

Hurling is one of the oldest field games in the world. As they say, 'the Irish were playing hurling when the sons of Greece were growing up'. Mícheál Ó Muircheartaigh recently said in a documentary that All-Ireland Hurling final day should be a national holiday to replace St Patrick's Day, as the Irish learned how to hurl long before they learned how to pray. In fact, the first mention of hurling in Ireland was in Cong, Co. Mayo in 1272 BC, as found in the Book of Leinster. It would be 3,000 years later that the GAA would be formed.

'Hurling at its best is a beautifully balanced blend of silken skills and fierce man-to-man combat, a spectacle of sport that beggars description', is how the journalist Paddy Downey once tried to define the sport that a lot of people around home do nothing but talk about and discuss, especially during the summer months. It is a bit different nowadays, but years ago, unless you could discuss hurling, politics or farming, there was no need to go to the local pub:

Some sportsmen love the dog and gun
Some like the coursing hound,
And others when the day is done,
Will seek the golfing ground;

My heart in haste would scorn to taste
The pleasures from such drawn,
In the sport I toast is a hurler's boast
A well-grained ash camán.

In ancient times when Éire reigned
A Nation great and grand,
When Oscar's and Cú Chulainn's fame

Was spread throughout the land;

On Tailteann plain with might and main,
In contests fiercely drawn,
What else could grace the pride of place,
But the well grained ash camán?

The game of hurling is very much part of Irish myth and legend. The most famous story, and the one we all were fascinated by when we were growing up, was about Setanta. There is no doubt that he would be a definite for the team of his millennium and an automatic for the All-Stars' team. The story is set in the Iron Age – the age of the Celtic people. It was a time when a code of honour was the main way of life; you lived and played honourably.

The story goes that Setanta left his father's home in Dundalk to visit his uncle King Conor MacNessa, who lived a few miles outside the town of Armagh. To shorten the journey he took his hurley and sliothar. As he set off, he pucked the ball up into the air ahead of himself and then he ran and caught the sliothar as it came back down. It shortened the trip and young Setanta showed his class as a fine hurler. He had skill, speed, accuracy, stamina, precision and first-touch perfection, which, combined, make up the ingredients for the perfect hurler.

In due course he reached his destination, only to discover that his uncle had gone to a feast in his friend Culann's castle. Setanta followed on to the party but got a shock when he arrived. The castle was guarded by a fierce hound that viciously approached Setanta at speed. With a coolness borne of the supreme confidence of a master, Setanta steadied, took aim and sank the sliothar in the throat of the hound. The hound fell to the ground, howling and roaring.

The guests at the feast inside the castle heard the howling of the dying hound and came out to see what had happened. The owner, Culann, was horrified. He was a blacksmith and the hound guarded his castle and now he had no guard. But on that day honour prevailed and Conor MacNessa announced that since Setanta had killed the hound he would now take its place. His uncle said that as he was good enough to kill the guard dog, then Setanta must be good enough to replace it. And so Setanta was renamed Cú Chulainn, the hound of Culann. He is immortalised in legend.

There are lots of other stories and legends, but another that I like is the story about King Labraidh Loinsigh. Labraidh was born with two afflictions. First of all he had horse's ears that were so bad that he always wore a special hat that covered his ears from the public, even he was playing hurling. The second affliction that he was born dumb and could not speak a word. He remained dumb until one day when playing hurling he got a fierce belt on the shin. So great was the pain that he shouted out loud in agony. The words spoken were not recorded – just as well by all accounts. His speech defect was cured. Word spread throughout his kingdom and the game of hurling had bestowed upon it a special place of honour. The problem of the ears, however, was not solved.

One of the greatest strengths that the game of hurling has is the fact that it is an amateur sport. All players are on an equal footing. They play for the love of the game, for the honour of the little village. There is a widespread belief and justifiable requirement nowadays that players should be well looked after by way of compensation and payment of all necessary expenses, and there should be no qualms about this, in my opinion. But you have to be careful not to go down the slippery slope of professionalism. Hurling does, I think it will always, yield enough satisfaction to players of the game to ensure its survival and enhance its reputation as one of, if not *the*, top field games in the world. The GAA should ensure it retains its role in the promotion and development of the sport and treat players properly rather than appearing to live up to its alternative name of 'GAA – Grab All Association'.

The road signs on the various county boundaries along the Cork–Dublin main road read, 'Welcome to Tipperary: The Home of Hurling'. This title, 'The Home of Hurling' is of course accurate, if for no other reason than the fact that the GAA was founded or born in Tipperary. Wherever you are born is naturally your home. So it was, that around 3p.m. on Saturday 1 November 1884, a small group of men (at least seven and possibly as many as fourteen) met in the billiard room of Miss Hayes's Hotel in Thurles, and there founded the Gaelic Athletic Association. Some of the founding members were: Michael Cusack, a teacher by profession, from Clare; Maurice Davin, an outstanding athlete who won the world championship at the hammer-throw event, from Carrick-on-Suir; Thomas Croke, later to become Archbishop of Cashel, from Mallow; John Wyse Power, a Waterford journalist; John McKay, a Belfast journalist; J.K. Bracken, a stonemason from Templemore; Joseph Ryan, a solicitor in Thurles and Callan, and Thomas McCarthy, a police officer in Templemore.

Michael Davin was the first President and Michael Cusack was the first secretary of the GAA. Archbishop Croke was a skilful and wise negotiator and solved a lot of the initial problems in the early days. The founding meeting, after electing the officials, also proposed to ask Archbishop Croke, Charles Stewart Parnell and Michael Davitt to become patrons of the association. The fact that two of the founding members were journalists helped greatly to send a positive message to promote the newly established GAA.

There are two poems, or prayers depending on your outlook, that are hurling made simple to a lot of people. Well, for me at least, they always define what is good in the sport. When you hear someone say, 'they didn't care if their team won or lost provided it was a good game', the chances are that in the game of hurling there may be a little truth in these words.

The Hurler's Prayer

Grant me Lord, a hurler's skill,
With strength of arm and speed of limb,
Unerring eye for the flying ball,
And courage to match whate'er befall.

May my stroke be easy and my aim be true,
My actions manly and my misses few;
No matter what way the game may go,
May I rest in friendship with every foe.

When the final whistle for me has blown,
And I stand at last before God's judgement throne,
May the Great Referee when He calls my name,
Say, You hurled like a man; You played the game.

This is the second poem about hurling that I like. It is not as well known as the last, more famous verse, but it covers a hurler's lifetime, indeed the lifetime of any person:

The Hurler

When the buachaill óg is born, all relations come to see,
With gushing admiration full, what name now will it be?
But the sire is not too worried, could be Jack or Bill or Mick,
The problem is much different – Now will he swing a stick?

He creeps and crawls then stands and walks and learns to take a tumble,
As he wobbles round the kitchen floor, he causes many a rumble;
He fastens on to a wooden spoon midst cutlery and delph,
With glint in eye, he swings it high, a proper hurling elf!

Time passes as it always does and then his first camán,
He raps his mother on the shin, 'Now get out on the lawn!'
Dad has a lot of patience for the proper grip and swing
We could have here a genius now like Mackey, Keane or Ring.

Then to the schoolyard hurly burly and exciting lunchtime game,
As he braces for the clash of ash his teammates shout his name;
His hands and body feel the sting of ash from stronger fellow,
But in his heart he makes a vow – I never will be yellow!

With tennis ball against the wall he fine hones down the skill
That will in heat of battle shine and loyal supporters thrill.
The lift and strike from left and right, the sideline cut and flick,
He will always thank the gable for many a hurling trick.

He goes into his bed at night still slightly 'fraid of dark,
But his dreams they are all happy ones of playing in Croke Park;
Of dashing forward in the fray to score that vital goal,
He wakes up hoping that in life he'll realise that role.

His first time in club colours is a day he won't forget,
He wouldn't have more butterflies for the first trip on a jet.
As he pulls on numbered jersey he is part of hurling lore
And shares the pride and spirit of all who went before.

And when in battle muscles ache, lungs hammer on chest wall,
He really cannot give up; he has to chase that ball.
He senses old club heroes are there above the fray,
Urging on the present lot, 'Bring home that cup today!'

He loses many games in life, a lot more than he wins,
And always takes the blame himself for some foolish hurling sins.
He forms many friendships new from within the GAA,
And they blossom with maturity until that final day.

And when the ref blows full-time and the game of life is o'er,
His pals and teammates gather round to see him from the shore.
They wrap him in club colours and they wish him bon voyage
And through the mists of mourning they see a bright mirage

Of a youthful hurler in his prime and he dashing o'er the sward
Going for to make a score then back to help rearguard
Urging on his teammates for that little extra spurt
And he always spoke encouragement; he was never mean or curt.

As the clods fall on his coffin they remember his great joy
To always turn out for club since he was just a boy.
Though his body has gone back to earth his spirit it will stay
To lift the parish players for many a long day.

And when they field out loyally from passing year to year,
They'll always give their utmost, supporters they will cheer.
And when the going it gets though they hear above the fray,
A voice recasts from hurling's past, 'Bring home that cup today.'

TIPPERARY HURLING

Hurling is full of great stories and funny incidents, partly because it is full of characters, but it is the infamous incidents that are recorded in the folklore of the GAA. One of my favourites is the incident in the Cork dressing room before a Munster Hurling final against Tipperary in the early '60s. The trainer, 'Tough' Barry had finished giving his team talk when the great Christy Ring stood up and gave a scarifying verdict of their opponents, his language flavoured with some choice words that opened the priest's eyes a bit. When Christy had finished talking, the priest interjected, 'My dear Christy, I'm sure you did not read those words in the New Testament.' Christy immediately replied, 'Father, the man who wrote the New Testament never had to play Tipperary!'

Most people in Tipperary used to associate events in their lives with hurling matches. 'So and so got married the day before the Munster final when Tipperary beat Cork in Killarney.' That was in the glory years of the '50s and '60s, when the memories were sweeter and more regular. Recent years have been barren in relative terms, although we hold on to the memories as best we can. Kilkenny and Cork have kept their traditional position of dominance, both provincially and in All-Ireland titles. Clare have made the breakthrough and kept it going, while Wexford have been second best in Leinster for the past few years, having won the All-Ireland in 1996. Waterford have come close, winning Munster in 2002, 2004, 2007 and 2010. In recent years Offaly have been in the doldrums, having won two All-Irelands in the '80s and two in the '90s. Limerick won three consecutive under-21 All-Irelands at the end of the '90s and should have made the well-deserved breakthrough at senior level. A combination of too many small forwards and internal rows has denied some fine hurlers from the Treaty City ultimate hurling glory. Galway has also produced nice teams of skilful and pacey hurlers without delivering a proper proportion of success. They won their second All-Ireland in 1980 after a fifty-seven-year gap and then won again in 1987 and 1988. Like us all, we would say that that team should have won more All-Irelands than it did.

The current Kilkenny team (2005-2010) is by far the best hurling team that I have ever seen play the game. Indeed, they may go down as the best hurling team of all time. They have won the last four All-Ireland hurling finals and are on the cusp of a fifth, which is some achievement in the modern era, or any era. Even as a Tipp man I have to say, we are lucky to have seen them play.

AUTHOR'S NOTE

This paragraph – a last minute addition – give me the chance to record Tipperary's twenty-sixth All-Ireland hurling title, after a great match in the final with Kilkenny on 5 September 2010. Going for an unprecedented fifth title in a row, Kilkenny were second best and could not match the hunger, intensity and skill of Tipperary on the day. It was a tremendous victory for Tipperary, who won on a scoreline of 4-17 to 1-18. Lar Corbett, with three goals, was the man of the match, but other contenders on the day included Brendan Maher, Padraic Maher, Paul Curran and young Michael Cahill, who also had fine games. Kilkenny never got the lead in the match. Noel McGrath gave a sublime defence-splitting hand pass to Lar Corbett for his second goal – great stuff. Lar's first goal was hip to hip beside Noel Hickey (Kilkenny), a high dropping ball at the edge of the square, grabbed out of the air – turn and strike, net rattling, sheer class!

I thought Tipperary's hurling and their overall performance was as good as anything I have seen. From the great defence and midfield play, to Lar's three goals, to the great speech by Eoin Kelly and the rendition of 'The Galtee Mountain Boy' by Pat Kerwick, it was magic. Not only did they prevent the great Kilkenny team from achieving the 'drive for five', but it re-established Tipperary's place at hurling's top table. It also offers hope to other counties who will undoubtedly be encouraged to give it a lash in 2011 and in the coming years. Apart from the great match and the great result for Tipperary, the day was memorable in other respects. It was great to witness the standing ovation that Henry Shefflin received when he had to go off injured after just twelve minutes. Tremendous respect was shown for this great player, from both sets of supporters, as he came off the field. The other memorable part of the day for me was that I was there at the match, with my son Sean and my father Johnny, along with my brothers Pat and Matt. Kilkenny are a great team and will always be acknowledged as such, with their legacy secure. It also shows how brilliant Tipperary were on the day, to beat them. Great day, great memory!

In the roll of honour, the counties of Kilkenny (thirty-two), Cork (thirty) and Tipp (twenty-six) have won over 70 per cent of all titles. Since the turn of the new millenium no other team has won the All-Ireland.

Of my own memories, I remember the 1971 All-Ireland between Tipp and Kilkenny. Babs played most of the second half without his boots and socks. Tipp won a great scoring game by a score line of 5-17 to 5-14. Tadgh O'Connor from Roscrea captained the team. Some Tipperary hurling legends played on that team: Mick Roche, Len Gaynor, Francis Loughnane, Noel O'Dwyer, Roger Ryan, Liam King and John Flanagan.

In 1971, the All-Star team was relaunched after a gap of three years. The team was: Damien Martin, Tony Maher, Pat Hartigan, Jim Treacy, Tadgh O'Connor, Mick Roche, Martin Coogan, Frank Cummins, John Connolly, Francis Loughnane, Michael 'Babs' Keating, Eddie Keher, Mick Bermingham, Ray Cummins and Eamonn Creagan.

The first All-Ireland that I went to was in 1973, when Limerick beat Kilkenny on what was a very wet day but a great day for Limerick. Looking back now, it is hard to believe that Limerick would not win another All-Ireland in the intervening years. That was an altar-boys' trip to the All-Ireland that Fr Flynn organised for us. We were supposed to get a bus from Templemore but it broke down on the way to collect us and we went on the train instead. Fr Flynn put us on the train in Templemore station and he drove by car to Dublin himself. When we arrived in Heuston Station (or King's Bridge station as it was originally known), there was Fr Flynn waiting to meet us, having arranged a bus to take us to Croke Park. Now I know we had a few stops at stations on the way to Dublin from Templemore but luckily for Fr Flynn speed cameras and penalty points were not in such common usage at the time.

Limerick had a great team, including Pat Hartigan, Eamonn Creagan, Richie Bennis, Eamonn Grimes, Frankie Nolan, Jim O'Brien, Phil Bennis, Ned Rea and Sean Foley. I had a particular affection for these Limerick hurlers as I often went to see them playing club hurling while on my holidays in Knockainey, Co. Limerick. I used to go to my Aunt Ann's house for a few weeks over a few summers during the 1970s. Her son Michael Callaghan took me to matches. One day, which I remember well because most of the Limerick team were playing and I got loads of autographs, was a double header of the Limerick county semi-finals. Claughan were playing Patrickswell in one match and South Liberties were playing Ballybrown in the other.

The All-Star team of 1973 was mainly made up of Limerick and Kilkenny players, all household names: Noel Skehan, Phil Larkin, Pat Hartigan, Jim O'Brien, Colm Doran, Pat Henderson, Sean Foley, Richie Bennis, John Galvin, Joe McKenna, Martin Quigley, Mick Crotty, John Quigley, Kieran Purcell and Eddie Keher – five from Limerick, six from Kilkenny, three from Wexford and one from Waterford.

Apart from the earlier memories, we do have family events that coincide with happy hurling memories. We got married two weeks after Tipp won the All-Ireland in 1989 and we had a bit of hurling mentioned in speeches and it figured in aspects of the day. Well it got a fair number of mentions – after all, we had waited eighteen years since 1971. Bobby Ryan from Borrisoleigh was captain of that team, and he went to Templemore CBS like myself. Joe Hayes played midfield and he stayed in the same house as me when I was in college in Limerick. But all that is for a different day and a different book…

Our eldest daughter, Aoife was born on 5 October 1991, a month after Tipperary won the All-Ireland. Tipp beat Kilkenny with the help of an opportunist goal by Michael Cleary from a free in what was a low-scoring match, 1-16 to 0-15.

We were also there in Killarney when Richie Stakleum lifted the cup after the Munster final replay and declared 'the famine' to be over. After travelling down through west Limerick – a load of us in the Volkswagan van – there was good crack on the way home. Richie Stakleum was in my class in Templemore CBS. It was one of the great matches, and it went to extra time in the replay, with Tipp winning on a score line of 4-22 to 1-22. Pat Fox and the magical Nicky English were to the fore.

Tommy Dunne, who was on the team when Tipp won in 2001, was another student of Templemore secondary (which is now called St Mary's, as the Christian Brothers left Templemore and the boys' and girls' schools amalgamated some years ago). Seven players from the winning Tipp team won All-Stars awards: Brendan Cummins, Philip Maher, Eamonn Corcoran (J.K. Brackens), Tommy Dunne, Eddie Enright, Mark O'Leary and Eoin Kelly. Tommy Dunne also won Hurler of the Year award in 2001.

The year that you are born always seems to be associated with hurling as mentioned earlier, so although I could not remember any of the matches myself, 1962 was a good year for Tipp. I was born at the very end of 1962, two days short of 1963. Tipp won the All-Ireland by beating Wexford in a thrilling match by all accounts.

Tipp played Limerick in Cork in the '62 Munster semi-final, and led at the interval by 2-7 to 0-4. Wholesale changes by Limerick early in the second half had the desired effect, as their youthful side took control of the exchanges to take the lead. Tipp equalised, and then Donie Nealon put Tipp ahead with a point. Four minutes from time, referee Jimmy Smyth prematurely blew the final whistle, with Tipp leading by 3-12 to 4-8. After some discussion the game was restarted. P.J. Keane equalised for Limerick. Just before the final whistle Tipp forced a seventy, but Mickey Burns's effort was just wide. In the replay, a totally different match provided a clear win for Tipp on a score line of 5-13 to 2-4, where Jimmy Doyle 'cleaned up' and Theo English, along with Liam Devaney, had stormers.

Waterford beat Cork in the other semi-final, in a game that was Christy Ring's last championship game for Cork. In the Munster final, Waterford did not live up to their pre-match expectations and were well beaten by Tipp on a score line of 5-14 to 2-3.

The All-Ireland final was a thriller. Tipp got off to a great start, with two goals in the first eighty seconds, by Tom Moloughney and Sean McLoughlin. After twenty-five minutes the sides were level, but Tipp finished the first half leading by 2-6 to 1-6. It was a ding-dong struggle in the second half, with the lead changing from side to side. In the end Tipp had two points to spare on a score line of 3-10 to 2-11. Liam Connolly and Tom Ryan of Toomevara replaced Tom Grace and captain Jimmy Doyle early in the second half. In the end it was said that the super fitness of the Tipp squad was the difference between the teams. A crowd of 75,039 watched the match, in the largest attendance at an All-Ireland hurling match in the '60s.

By the way, 84,856 attended the 1954 All-Ireland final to see Cork beat Wexford in a low-scoring 1-9 to 1-6 match, but Wexford got their revenge in 1956, beating Cork by 2-14 to 2-8 in front of another massive crowd of 83,096. Just imagine how full the trains were and the whole logistics of the occasion with money taken at the gate.

The Tipp team in 1962 had some big-name players. Donal O'Brien was in goal, and the full-back line of John Doyle, Michael Maher and Kieran Carey became well known for their less-than-welcoming treatment to incoming forwards (always fair but hard). The name of Hell's Kitchen was used to describe the goalmouth area of the field that these three boys patrolled. The half-back line of Matt Grace, Tony Wall and Mickey Burns were skilful stickmen, along with the midfield pairing of Theo English and Liam Devaney. The half-forward line of Jimmy Doyle, J. 'Mackey' McKenna and Tom Ryan took a bit of watching, as did the inside line of Donie Nealon (who was Texaco Hurler of the Year in '62), Tom Moloughney and Sean McLoughlin.

Jimmy Doyle was a sub on the 1971 team and came on to get his sixth All-Ireland medal. Jimmy was one of the greatest forwards of all time. His speed to the ball, his deft first touch and control of the ball, his keen sense of positioning, the speed of lift and strike in one flowing movement, and above all his deadly accuracy, combined to make him one of hurling's greatest. He was on all the millennium teams and was from the famous Thurles Sarsfields club.

The previous mention of Mickey Burns reminds me of the story about a young fella who once asked his trainer how he could be as good as Burns. His trainer told him to train every evening when he came home from school after he had his farm jobs done for his father, to run three miles on a cold night, to practice with a ball against a wall for one hour, then to come in, make a bowl of soup and sit in front of the open fire in the kitchen. 'Keep doing this every night,' said the trainer, 'until your "micky burns".'

With the help of Hell's Kitchen, Tipp won seven Munster finals and four All-Ireland finals in the 1960's. John Doyle's record of eight senior All-Ireland medals is only equalled by the great Christy Ring.

THE BEST TIPPERARY TEAM (THAT I SAW PLAYING)

As they say, I am really gilding the lily here by naming the best Tipperary team that I have seen play. My father's best Tipperary team and even my brother's and my son's best Tipperary teams would be very different. Even friends of my own age will not entirely agree with my selection. Anyway here goes :

Goalkeeper: Brendan Cummins

Right Corner-Back: Paul Delaney
Full-Back: Noel Sheehy
Left Corner-Back: Tadhg O'Connor

Right Half-Back: Eamonn Corcoran
Centre Back: Mick Roche
Left Half-Back: Bobby Ryan

Centre Field: Tommy Dunne
Centre Field: Noel O'Dwyer

Right Half-Forward: Francis Loughnane
Centre Forward: Declan Ryan
Left Half-Forward: Lar Corbett/John Leahy

Right Full-Forward: Pat Fox
Full-Forward: Nicky English
Left Full-Forward: Eoin Kelly

Subs: Ken Hogan, Len Gaynor, Philip Maher, John Flanagan, Shane McGrath, Paul Shelly, Colm Bonnar, Declan Fanning, Roger Ryan, Babs Keating, Declan Carr, Liam King, Noel McGrath, Dinny Ryan, Padraic Maher.

Manager: Liam Sheedy

SLIEVENAMON

Apart from being the county's anthem and its favourite song, Slievenamon is of course a mountain range. Located to the north-east of Clonmel town, and standing at 2,368 feet high, Slievenamon, or 'The Mountain of the Fair Women of Feimhinn', was the scene of a legendary romantic contest. Finn McCool, the fella who built the

Giant's Causeway in north Antrim, was unable to decide on a wife, so he perched himself on the summit of Slievenamon and invited all the hopeful young lovelies who were vying to be his bride to race each other to the top. The lucky – and energetic – winner was Grainne, the daughter of Cormac, King of Ireland.

The Giant's Causeway has a connection with Slievenamon. If you ever get up towards the north Antrim coast it is a fantastic place to visit. In recent years I have travelled to the North of Ireland on several occasions for business, golf and relaxation. Although my good friend John Dalton has always told me so, I do believe the Antrim and Down coastlines, along with their golf courses, their folk parks and their charming villages, are equal to anything in Kerry, Wicklow or Mayo.

When I first went to see the Giant's Causeway I thought the rock formation was going to be much larger, but it is a very special sight. It is Ireland's first World Heritage site. As mentioned before, legend says that it was built by the Irish giant Finn McCool as a way of getting to the island of Staffa in Scotland, where his lady love lived. I don't know if this was before or after he had the contest for the ladies running up the mountain in Slievenamon!

The causeway consists of some 40,000 polygonal columns of basalt formed by cooled lava. Most of the columns are six-sided but a happy time can be spent looking for those rare columns with a different number of sides. For instance, there is only one column (I am told, and I didn't find it either) with three sides, and one column with eight sides called the Keystone, because some people think that if it was removed the whole causeway would collapse. Some of the columns mark out interesting formations like the 'wishing chair'. It is said that if you sit here and make three wishes they will come true!

Happy times, when I think of Northern Ireland, and it is usually also a happy occasion when I am singing 'Slievenamon'.

HURLING IN CLONMORE

When Clonmore Juvenile club joined with Templemore, in the mid 1970s, four of us from Clonmore joined the 'townies'. Tom Clarke, Pa Delaney, John Fitzpatrick and myself were taken to regular training sessions, not easy for us culchies. Brother O'Reilly and Batt O'Meara looked after us during the early days. I have to say the other three excelled and were all fine hurlers and were better hurlers than me. My underage career was cut short, but I got another chance at 'Number 1' Level or Junior Level with Clonmore. I remember the day so very well, like it was yesterday: we were playing Knock, the match was played in Castleiney. I remember Mick Smith TD was on the sideline, as all local TDs should be! I remember being asked back onto the team and sitting in the dressing room togged out, knowing very few of the team, seeing the selectors talking about the team. As soon as they had agreed on the team, I remember seeing Denis Noonan immediately searching through the jerseys from the bag and picking out the number 7 and coming over and handing it to me saying, 'put that on'. Mark it down, for me that was a defining moment. I played ok, enjoyed the game and drove on from there. We had a good campaign; myself and Johnny Delaney played well that year. We had a great run and I remember a great game against Templetuohy in Templemore, when myself and Johnny got some great scores from play and from frees. There was a great local crowd on the sideline and in Clonboo, Templetuohy was our nearest neighbouring parish. That was our hurling memory and my favourite time playing. I did go on to play some intermediate games and even some senior games for Clonmore when they moved into the senior championship after winning the intermediate county final. Like all hurlers I regret the 'might have beens' and wish it had been different. Can't get it back … shit, but that's it … so glad to have been there, thank God for that.

It is funny, the hurling association that I had with the three Delaney boys. Myself and Pa played at underage hurling level, while myself and Johnny played Junior and Intermediate hurling together, ending up on the 1987 County Winning Panel, but myself and Tom Delaney introduced hurling to Mayo! It is a long story but genuine, as Michael O'Brien from Bohola will agree and verify. Tom Delaney and I worked together in Swinford, County Mayo, around 1985. Most Thursday nights, we would go up to the local GAA pitch and puck the sliothar around for an hour or so. One evening, the local football team arrived for training so Tom and I had to cut short our puck-around that evening to let the team train. As I walked off the field, one of the footballers came over to me and asked if he could have a look at my hurley. I gave him the hurley and he was delighted as he swung it back and forth on the grass surface. I could not believe it when he told me that he had never previously held a hurley in his hands. For me, that was like meeting an Irish person who had never seen rain!

In terms of hurling achievements, the winning of the 1987 Intermediate Hurling County Final heads the honours list. It was the sixth time that Clonmore had contested a county final, having lost the previous five times. As a parish, Clonmore had won the Mid-Tipperary junior hurling title on five occasions: 1932, 1970, 1974, 1975 and 1978. We then moved on to the intermediate grade and won the Mid title on four occasions, in 1979, 1984, 1986 and 1987.

The Hurlers of Clonmore

There's joy tonight, where bon-fires bright.
Light up the verdant plain;
And hurling men play games again
Round Carden's Wild Domain.
The Blue and Gold as in days of old
Will forever proudly soar,
To recall the names, and the gallant games
Of the men of Sweet Clonmore.

Though beaten by the Fennellys, They conquered Gortnahoe;
And then Moycarkey/Borris went down
Before the Gold and Blue.
Tommy Treacy's name, on that cup of fame,
In the Mid they proudly bore;
Friends from Killea were proud that day
Of the men of Sweet Clonmore.

Then bowed the Boys from Solohead,
The champions of the West;
In the Borris field, the Mines did yield;
Clonmore proved they were the best.
The '87 intermediate team,
The Millar Cup now bore;
There's rejoicing still round Shanakill,
And the homes of Sweet Clonmore.

Captain John Lee played manfully;
Brendan Bane his class did show;
The Larkins and Delaneys are
The pride of Knockinroe;
Dromard's Delaneys, John and Pa,
Who got many a smashing score,
To win the day, with a great display,
For lovely sweet Clonmore.

John Fitzpatrick came from Graffin
And another from Dareens
And James and Michael Cahill are
The boys of Ballyheen.
Mick of the Hill is remembered still
For his Harty feats of yore;
John Costigan's dream, and the Harty team
Were honoured by Sweet Clonmore.

We'll ne'er forget the brave Bourke boys,
Beneath Dromard's fair hill;
There was Martin, Tommy, Seamus, Joe
With brave Paddy, Johnny, Phil,
Martin was the Captain bold
In seventy-eight who bore
The famous Dr Harty Cup
To his school in Templemore.

'Tis true, Clonboo, we're proud of you
With Butler, Deegan, Clarke;
Mick Doyle, Jim Meehan, Declan Bourke,
You all have made your mark
Laherty, Foley, Purcell, Morris, Madden,
Pat Bergin to the fore,

Who played the game, brought honour and fame
To the homes of Sweet Clonmore.

Selectors, trainers and masseur,
Thady Maher and Francis Bourke,
Francis O'Meara, Billy Sweeney
And Danny Moloney did their work.
Then Hurrah for '87.
And those boys who proudly bore
The victorious Intermediate Cup
To the homes of Sweet Clonmore.

The above poem was written to commemorate the historic achievement of the
Clonmore Intermediate Hurling team who won the 1987 County Final. The victory was made all the sweeter as it made up for five previous County Final defeats in
1975, 1978, 1979, 1984 and in 1986. It was a great year for hurling in the parish, and
it was a great year for the parish.

Refer to 'Noonan' in the Houses Between the Crosses section for more on
Clonmore hurling.

CHAPTER 8

THE BUTLER CLAN

1. INTRODUCTION

This is the section about the Butler Clan. The first few pages are about the Butler name, its origins and its arrival in Ireland back in 1177. While we can not find any connection with our famous and previously wealthy Norman Clan, our ancestors have the Butler surname and it is worth recording some of the background information about the Butlers' first arrival on these shores. There is also a bit of a history lesson, which maybe difficult to follow with so many Earls and Dukes to connect together, most of them with the same first names.

Anyway, you can skip that section if you like. Then we get onto the current crop of Butlers and their relations, which is far from the finished or complete record of everybody within the family tree. Actually there are numerous family trees within the Butler Clan. For most of my relations, it will be a start for them to go and develop their own family tree from the seeds which I hope are now sown here for them.

2. THE BEGINNING

The surname Butler, as far as Ireland is concerned, dates from about the year 1220. It arose from the fact that in 1177, Theobald Fitzwalter, a brother of the Bishop of Canterbury, who accompanied Henry II to Ireland, was created Chief Butler of Ireland. The seventh in decent from him was created Earl of Ormond in 1328. In 1391, the head-quarters of the Ormonds was removed from Gowran to Kilkenny Castle. The huge territories that Theobald was granted were mainly in the counties of Kilkenny, Tipperary, Wicklow and Limerick. For centuries a rivalry existed between the Butlers and the Geraldines (Fitzgerald), and it may be said that up to the death of the Great Duke of Ormond in 1668, the effective government of the country was in the hands of one or other of these Norman houses. A branch of the Butlers, for a while in the fifteenth century, took the surname of MacRichard and had an important Chief, in Gaelic terms, however they reverted to the Butler surname after a short while.

The Butlers were very successful in collecting titles, acquiring more than twenty-five separate patents of nobility, including such titles as Mountgarrett, Dunboyne, Ossory, Galmoy and Cahir. In 1328, they became the Earls of Ormond, their principal title, and James, the 12th Earl, was created Duke of Ormond after the restoration of Charles II in 1660. The first Duke of Ormond was Chancellor of the Universities of Oxford and Dublin, Lord Lieutenant of Ireland, founder of the Royal College of Physicians and creator of the Phoenix Park.

Among the numerous Catholic Butlers who were loyal to the Jacobites the most noteworthy were James Butler of Nantes, who was chaplain to Prince Charles Edward (the so-called 'Young Pretender') in the 1745 expedition, and

Pierce Butler (1652-1740), the 3rd Viscount Galmoy, who fought with Sarsfield in all his Irish and French campaigns. The Butlers were patrons of Gaelic-Irish learning and great collectors of Irish manuscripts. When the ancestral castle of Kilkenny was abandoned as the seat of the family, the very large volumes of the Ormond manuscript collection were taken to the National Library of Ireland, where it forms an invaluable source for Irish study, as well as for Butler family history.

Edward Butler (1823-1879) of Kilkenny edited the *Galway Vindicator* during the period of the Young Ireland uprising, and subsequently emigrated to Australia, where he became Attorney General.

To the list of distinguished persons of the Butlers, the name of Sir Theobald, commonly called Sir Toby Butler, should be added. He was Attorney General in the reign of James II and the negotiator and framer of the Treaty of Limerick on the Irish side. He also made a memorable speech in 1703 against the Anti-Popery Act.

THE BUTLER CREST AND COAT OF ARMS

Coat of Arms: A shield divided quarterly, six gold cups on a red shield and two sections of gold and blue.

Crest: A plume of ostrich feathers emerging from a crown with a falcon rising.

Motto: 'As I find'.

Various Surveys of the Butler name going back to the 1800s indicate that Tipperary and Kilkenny have the largest concentration of the surname. In the years 1848-1864 the Primary Valuation property survey shows the following results:

Butler Households
Tipperary: 332
Kilkenny: 382

At this time, within the region of mid-Tipperary, a breakdown of the local Butler households on a parish basis shows the following:

Killavinogue: 4
Loughmore West: 2
Templemore: 2
Templetuohy: 4

SHANAKILL CASTLE

Kilkenny Castle is recognised as the main home for the aristocratic Butler family in Ireland between 1391 and 1935, but Shanakill Castle also deserves a mention. Our relations and our forefathers came to Clonboo in 1820 from Loughmore and prior to Loughmore, we believe they came from near Paulstown.

The name Shanakill is derived from the Irish Seanchill, meaning 'Old Church', and the parish of Shanakill in Co. Kilkenny, a few miles north of Gowran, is named from the medieval parish church, the ruins of which stand close to the castle. The history of Shanakill is inseparable from that of nearby Paulstown Castle and of the Butlers who owned it. This family was descended from Walter (d. 1506), younger brother of Sir James Butler (d. 1487), who was father of Piers, 8th Earl of Ormond. This Walter was descended from Richard Butler, younger son of James, 3rd Earl of Ormond. It was a branch of some importance, as Walter was Sherriff of the county in 1574, his son Sir Richard was knighted in 1605, and his son Edmond was MP for the county in 1634. At this period, there was already a house in Shanakill, presumably a tower house, and contemporary records such as the Fiants show that it served as a dower house and as a residence for junior members of the family.

3. THE HISTORY LESSON

KILKENNY CASTLE AND THE BUTLER ASSOCIATION

One of the most instantly recognised buildings in Ireland, Kilkenny Castle has been an important site since 1172, when the Norman Knight Richard de Clare, called Strongbow, built a wooden tower on this rocky height overlooking the River Nore. The first stone castle was built there twenty years later, in 1213, by Strongbow's son-in-law William Marshall, Earl of Pembroke. Three of the castle's four towers survive today.

A busy and prosperous commercial centre grew around the original Norman settlement, and the present Hightown and Irishtown areas of Kilkenny today date from that period.

The Butler family bought the castle in 1391 and lived there until 1935. The family or some of its members lived there for 544 years. As mentioned elsewhere, they were Earls, Marquesses and Dukes of Ormond. They were a remarkable family, resilient, politically astute and faithful to the Crown and to Ireland as dictated by the politics of the times. These loyalties determined their fortunes and careers, and so too the fortunes of their seat.

The Butlers have resided in Ireland for around 830 years, having come to Ireland in 1171 in the first wave of the Norman invasion. Originally their name was Fitz Walter.

But they changed the family name to Butler because of a royal privilege that the astute Theobald Fitz Walter managed to acquire. In 1185, the King of England made him Chief Butler of Ireland, a title which made him a sort of senior toastmaster at the coronation banquet; he would offer the new king his first cup of wine, which, more importantly, gave him prestige or butlerage (duty or leverage) on all wines imported into both countries. To mark this valuable honour and to ensure its continuation, the family dropped the name Fitz Walter and assumed the name Le Botiller or Butler.

The Walter/Butler wealth and influence quickly increased. They acquired large tracts of land in Tipperary and Kilkenny, and in the final years of the fourteenth century, James Butler, by now also third Earl of Ormond, bought Kilkenny Castle and installed himself as undisputed ruler of the surrounding areas.

Through the centuries, the Butlers went on to live, acquire property, battle and survive. During the middle part of the seventeenth century, the struggle between King and Parliament in England dragged on, and the Butlers were also caught up in struggle. A Confederate Council was set up. This breakaway alliance of Irish and Old English held their alternative parliament in Kilkenny for seven years (1642-1648), trying to determine their own affairs in Ireland. James Butler, twelfth Earl of Ormond had been raised in England as a ward of court and had tremendous personal loyalty to both King Charles I and his son Prince Charles. Ormond was now the King's Lord Lieutenant in Ireland and commander of his army (also during this time, a Butler cousin, Viscount Mountgarret, was prominent in the Confederate Council). Affairs in England defeated them all. After a civil war, King Charles I was executed, and Oliver Cromwell proceeded through Ireland ruthlessly restoring control. In 1650, he attacked Kilkenny, battering the castle's now-missing south wall and one of the towers before the town surrendered.

Throughout the years of parliamentary control and Ormond's exile, Lady Ormond held on tightly to the Butler lands and properties. Letters she wrote to Cromwell stated that they were her inheritance and so could not be forfeit for her husband's treason. Her claim succeeded.

At the end of the seventeenth century, England and Ireland was divided again. King James II had been deposed, and his daughter Mary, with her husband William of Orange, were invited to take the throne. James and William had several battles, and the Butlers were involved in this crucial ongoing struggle for power. The second Duke, James Butler decided to join William's cause, while a Catholic cousin, Lord Galmoy, held Kilkenny Castle and entertained King James there. In 1690, the two Kings met at the Battle of the Boyne. James was defeated. Ormond then recovered his castle and was host to King William soon after.

The Butler estates and titles in Ireland passed to James's brother, Charles, Earl of Arran. He did not claim these, feeling it politically unwise, and so when he died without an heir in 1758, the titles of Duke and Marquess of Ormond became extinct. The title of Earl passed to Catholic cousins in Kilcash, Co. Tipperary. This Kilcash has become a major historical location associated with the Butler name.

By the second half of the eighteenth century, Kilkenny Castle was very badly rundown, reflecting the fortunes of the Butler family and indeed Ireland itself. But outside external pressures, such as the wars in America and France, meant that England had to lobby for Irish loyalty, and so the Penal Laws were relaxed. Walter Butler of Garryricken inherited the Butler titles and lands in 1776, and decided to move into the dilapidated castle in Kilkenny. His son John had married the heiress Anne Wandesford of Castlecomer, and Walter and John spent much of their inheritance on the castle. Along with rerouting new roads and doing the gardens, they also built the stables and courtyards, and finally Walter moved into a newly built house beyond the stables, Butler House. After his father's death, John Butler claimed the title of seventeenth Earl of Ormond, as confirmed in 1791. The Butlers soon re-established their position and prestige. The next Earl, Walter became a companion of the Prince Regent, who subsequently recreated the title of Marquess of Ormond for him. Walter's brother James Butler represented Kilkenny in the Irish Parliament in Dublin for four years, up to the Act of Union in 1800. He was against replacing the Irish parliament with Irish seats in the House of Commons and House of Lords in London, but represented Kilkenny for a further twenty years there.

The nineteenth-century Butlers were typical of their time – very wealthy, with agents who ran their estates very efficiently and effectively. They served with a suitable regiment, married well, and enjoyed their well-organised lives.

In 1826, a major programme of work was begun to restore Kilkenny Castle to its supposed medieval appearance and also to bring it up-to-date as a modern country house with modern conveniences. The east wing was completely rebuilt to house the large family picture collection and the west curtain wall built out to provide more bedrooms.

The eighteenth century in Ireland was the age of the Penal Laws, which were a series of laws designed to ensure Protestant control in Ireland by means of a detailed oath of allegiance to the Crown which Catholics could not take. This effectively excluded then from parliament, from holding any public office, from entering law or from holding a commission in the army or navy. Further laws forbade Catholics from buying land or from renting other than a short lease. The practice of the Catholic religion was also banned. This led to the hedge schools (see Toher school). Overall, this meant that the old Gaelic ways of life were seriously undermined and in real decline.

In the first half of the twentieth century, the Irish state changed and the Civil War took place. Kilkenny Castle was besieged by the Free Staters during May 1922 but the castle was restored to the Butlers after a two-day siege. The changes in Ireland meant that the Butlers had to look at the viability of maintaining their seat in Kilkenny. In 1935, they decided to leave, and so a big auction was held in the castle. For five days all the contents of the castle were auctioned, with the exception of the family's collection of paintings and tapestries.

Apart from a brief period of occupation by Irish troops during the First World War, known as 'the Emergency', Kilkenny Castle stood empty and abandoned. In 1967, Arthur Butler, sixth Marquess and twenty-fourth Earl of Ormond, handed Kilkenny Castle over to the Castle Restoration Committee for the nominal sum of £50.

Because of the expense involved in restoring such as castle, the building was taken into State care, under the Office of Public Works. The early stages of restoration were funded by a generous gift from C.J. Lythe, a London businessman of Irish decent. After treating the fabric of the entire building for dry and wet rot, a phased programme of restoration started. The east tower was re-roofed and completely restored. It opened to the public in 1976.

EARLS OF ORMOND

The following is the list of the Earls of Ormond, from the 1st Earl in 1328 to the 22nd Earl in 1943:

James Butler, 1st Earl, 1328-1337, son of Edmund le Botiller

James Butler, 2nd Earl, 1338-1382, son of James, 1st Earl

James Butler, 3rd Earl, 1382-1405, son of James, 2nd Earl

James Butler, 4th Earl, 1405-1452, son of James, 3rd Earl

James Butler, 5th Earl, 1452-1461, son of James, 4th Earl

John Butler, 6th Earl, 1461- 1477, son of James, 4th Earl

Thomas Butler, 7th Earl, 1477-1515, son of James, 4th Earl

Piers Butler, 8th Earl, 1515-1539, g-g-g son of James, 3rd Earl

James Butler, 9th Earl, 1539-1546, son of Piers, 8th Earl

Thomas Butler, 10th Earl, 1546-1614, son of James, 9th Earl

Walter Butler, 11th Earl, 1614-1632, g-son of James, 9th Earl

James Butler, 12th Earl, 1632-1688, g-son of Walter, 11th Earl

James Butler, 13th Earl, 1688- 1745, g-son of James, 12th Earl

Charles Butler, 14th Earl, g-son of James, 12th Earl

John Butler, 15th Earl, 1758-1766, g-g-son of Walter, 11th Earl

Walter Butler, 16th Earl, 1766-1783, g-g-son of Walter, 11th Earl

John Butler, 17th Earl, 1783-1795, son of Walter, 16th Earl

Walter Butler, 18th Earl, 1795-1820, son of John, 17th Earl

James Butler, 19th Earl, 1820-1838, son of John, 17th Earl

John Butler, 20th Earl, 1838-1854, son of James, 19th Earl

James Edward Butler, 21st Earl, 1854-1919, son of John, 20th Earl

James Arthur Butler, 22nd Earl, 1919-1943, son of John, 20th Earl

THE BUTLER SOCIETY

The Butler Society was founded in 1967 and has published *The Journal of The Butler Society* since 1968. A Butler Rally is held every three years in Kilkenny. There are a number of different families called Butler, some of which can be traced back to origins in different medieval households. The Butler Society sets out to be a one-name society. In Latin, the name was *Buticularius* or *Pincerna*. There used to be many variations in spelling, such as Boteler, Boutillier, Botiller, Butiller and Botyller. Modern variations include Boutler (France), Buttlar (Germany), and Buteler (Argentina).

On 29 August 1965, the late Patrick Butler, 28th Lord Dunboyne, gave an address on 'Butler Family History', in Kilkenny Castle, to the Kilkenny Archaeological Society. The lecture was extraordinarily well attended and a society was proposed. The Butler Society was founded in August 1967.

Members of the Society are given access to submit queries onto the website for others to discuss, and there are a few items that could be relevant based on timescales involve, and these relate to Butlers that emigrated to Australia. We have a few possible emigrants going back five or six generations, so any connection would be a long shot and difficult to establish without further research, but the queries are interesting nonetheless. One reads:

> Tobias Butler, born circa 1835 in Kilkenny and emigrated to Australia before 1860. He married Julia Jackson and their children were born in Australia, Thomas and George in 1860 (assumed twins); Julia born in 1863; John Richard born 1863; Tobias Peter born 1866; Anne Elizabeth born 1868; Stephen John born 1871; John born 1856; Sarah born 1874. George subsequently moved to New Zealand in 1881 and married Agnes (née Hardie) and lived in Dunedin until his death in 1944.

Another entry reads as follows:

> Patrick Butler, born 17th March 1834, probably in Kilkenny, son of John Butler and Catherine Whelan. Patrick's parentage is recorded on the certificate of his marriage to Margaret Brown in Victoria, Australia on 27th March 1864. Seeking records in Ireland. Patrick arrived in Australia on the Saldanha from Liverpool in 1854.

The Butler Rally is held every three years in Kilkenny to coincide with the Triennial General Meeting of The Butler Society. Rallies and gatherings are arranged by members, for members. They tend to be social occasions which offer a great opportunity to get to know more about the Butler family and its past.

Overseas gatherings also take place. In Madrid, the Spanish members have an annual lunch every November. In Germany, the von Buttlar families held a very successful gathering in August 1998 in Berlin and Kassel. Other countries including USA, Canada, Argentina and New Zealand hold occasional gatherings, while members hold regular seminars in Cambridge and Oxford, England.

The news section of the society's journal covers articles and submission made by members. An article covering the death of Charles Butler, Marquess of Ormonde is one such submission:

Charles Butler, 7th Marquess of Ormonde, 31st Chief Butler of Ireland, and President of the Butler Society died in Chicago on 25th October 1997, aged 98 years. He inherited his titles in 1971, two days before his 72nd birthday, on the death of his cousin Arthur. Charles took seriously his responsibilities as head of the senior branch of a large Butler clan and for many years he presided over Butler rallies in Kilkenny with quiet dignity and great good humour. He last travelled from his home in Chicago to Kilkenny at the age of 95 years.

Charles had no son, so it looks as though the Marquessate, created in 1825, is now extinct. However, it is by no means certain who should inherit the much older titles of Earl of Ormond (created in 1328) and Chief Butler of Ireland (created 1171). The latter is the most ancient hereditary title in the British Isles which continues to decend down the male line of any family.

The Mountgarret branch are descended from Richard Butler, first Viscount Mountgarret (died 1571), younger son of the eighth Earl of Ormond. Thus the present (17th) Viscount Mountgarret has a claim to the titles in the absence of any more senior heir male.

One interesting article that I came across in one of the journals of the Butler Society relates to 'The Family of John Butler of Lisduff'. Although there appears to be no connection to this family, I have included a summary here, as they lived so close to Clonbough.

John Butler (b.1773, d.1823) was a farmer of Knockahaugh, Lisduff, Errill, Co. Laois. He married Margaret Davy from Knockahaugh (the Derries). As will be seen, many of their descendants emigrated to Australia and elsewhere. They had nine children:

John (b.1808, d.1874), a farmer of Ballyknockane married Mary Kennedy (b.1805, d.1889) of Lisdaleen. They also had nine children: John, Margaret, Mary, Catherine, Patrick, Ellen, Richard, Edward and Elizabeth.

Patrick (b.1807, d.1881), whose descendants remained in Ireland, was a farmer of Clonmeen. He married Bridget Kennedy of Lisdaleen. One of their seven children, Thomas (b.1839, d.1912), married Bridget Gorman of Castletown and had eleven children.

Michael, a farmer, moved to Aughafan near Mountrath. He married Judy Hennessey of Errill and emigrated to Australia about 1847/48.

William (b.1816, d.1876), also a farmer of Aughafan, married Margaret Marnell of Castletown. Their descendants do not appear to have emigrated.

Martin (b.1819, d.1874), a farmer of Graiguearalla, married first Hanora Dowling and secondly Bridget Egan.

Edward died young at Lisduff.

Thomas married Margaret Kennedy of Lisdaleen and emigrated to the USA around 1847/48.

Mary married John Hennessy of Errill.

Margaret married a Ryan of Rathdowney.

LORD DUNBOYNE

Author's Note: *This section is in the book for the person with a more serious interest in the historical perspective of the family. I have picked up my own extracts from the story of the Butler family coming to Ireland from different sources but the account which follows here is mainly from Lord Dunboyne's speech in Kilkenny Castle. It is difficult to follow and complex in content, with most references made to English titles and honours bestowed on various Butler family members by kings and parliaments. The difficulty is making it relevant to the current generations of Butlers and their relations, now living in and around North Tipperary. No direct ties can be clearly identified, although a few interesting references or coincidences crop up. Before Clonbough and before Loughmore we originally came from Paulstown, County Kilkenny. Several searches in Paulstown all came up blank, with no link found to Loughmore. I have added my own notes and comments along with some added pieces of research to establish some relevance, as appropriate.*

The chief historian of the Butler family is undoubtfully Lord Dunboyne, and his talks and books on the subject are a great help to anyone researching the origins of the family. One of the most important and informative was given in Kilkenny Castle on 29 August 1965. His address on that occasion was very detailed and too long for reprinting here, but for the true historian it is worth noting some of the extracts contained in that speech.

Lord Dunboyne goes back to the real beginning and also divides up the Butler family into the different branches, which is picked up below. We are believed to be from the Paulstown branch. In the Cromwellian period, the Butlers were divided by religion, the Ormonds being Protestants, the Mountgarrets and Dunboynes being Catholic.

Lord Dunboyne went back to before the Butlers came to Ireland in 1171, back to 1150 when, in twelfth-century England, the paternal ancestry of the family is traceable in unbroken succession to a certain Hervey, who was living about 1130. From the *Testa de Nevill*, which was compiled a century later, we know Hervey had a son, Hervey Walter (which suggests a maternal connection with someone by the name of Walter) and a daughter Alice, to whom her father gave a dowry of about 400 acres in Lancashire. Hervey seems also to have had various estates in East Anglia. But the identity of his father, mother or wife has not yet been established. It had been suggested in *The Complete Peerage* book that he may have married an aunt of Thomas Becket, with whose family the Butlers were reputedly connected.

Theobald Blake Butler was a leading authority on the history of the family. He died in the early sixties and his works are in the National Library, Dublin along with the British Museum. His work traced back to doomsday the lands which this family subsequently held in East Anglia and Lancashire, and discovered that no fewer than nine of the sixteen or more holdings which our Hervey was believed to have owned in Norfolk and Suffolk were entered in the *Domesday Book* under the ownership of Walter de Caen. The discovery led him to surmise that the paternal ancestor of the Butlers was Walter de Caen (son of William Malet, who accompanied the conqueror and, being half Saxon, was entrusted with the burial of King Harold after the Battle of Hastings). In his last years, however, Blake Butler was inclined to the view that Hervey, in about 1130, may have acquired much of Walter de Caen's land by marriage, which would make Hervey not a son or grandson, but a son-in-law of Walter de Caen. Further research on the point might prove rewarding, particularly with reference to the most likely candidates of the name of Herve in eleventh-century France and to the Hervey who was Becket's envoy at the Papal Court (1163 to 1166) when he died.

1150-1200

Whether his wife was Walter de Caen's daughter or Thomas Becket's aunt or someone else, Hervey was succeeded by his son Hervey Walter, whose marriage was of considerable consequence to the family that was taking root. His wife was Maud de Valognes, sister-in-law of Ranulph de Glanville, the most powerful of all Henry II's subjects, and Ranulph took a great interest in the upbringing of Maud's children.

One of those children was Hubert Walter. Hubert is commonly remembered as having been instrumental in raising the enormous ransom demanded by Henry VI for Richard Coeur de Lion. But Hubert had other claims to fame and he was immensely prudent and powerful. As to his power and prestige, Hubert had been Bishop of Salisbury and had accompanied Richard on the Third Crusade; he was then Primate, Chief Justicar, Papal Legate and Chancellor. He died in 1205.

THE CHIEF BUTLERS, 1185-1965

(A) THE FIVE THEOBALDS, 1185-1299
Hubert's eldest brother was christened Theobald, presumably after his maternal grandfather, Theobald de Valognes. Theobald Walter was the first of the family to come to Ireland, where, by 1185, he had been created the Chief Butler. The Chief Butlerage of Ireland is the most ancient hereditary dignity still enjoyed by the male heirs of any family in the British Isles, if not in Europe. The right to the office was admitted to reside in Lord Ormonde at the coronation of George IV in 1821 – the last coronation at which there was an official banquet. (William IV did away with the feast.) The prisage of wines was another matter, as it involved the right to about one tenth of the cargo of any wine ship that came into Ireland. This right was also granted to Theobald Walter and continued in his descendents until it was restored to the Crown by an Act of Parliament in 1810. This was an early version of excise duty. It's no wonder I got the love of a nice bottle of red wine, with all that wine to be

drank – one bottle in every ten that came into the country!

Going from father to son, each of the first five Chief Butlers was called Theobald, which causes confusion, especially since each of them was involved in feuds, feared God, fought hard, married well and, except for the first Butler, died young.

Out of his vast estates in Ireland and England, the first Butler founded the Abbey of Wotheney, Co. Limerick, where he was buried, the monastery of Arklow, Co. Wicklow, where the 2nd, 3rd and 4th Butlers were buried, and the abbeys of Nenagh, Co. Tipperary, and of Cockersand in Lancashire.

The 1st Butler married Maud Vavassour from Yorkshire. The 2nd Butler, who died in France, married twice. Through his first wife, Joan, who probably died in childbirth, the 3rd Earl of Ormond inherited further considerable estates in Ireland and England. Through his second wife, Rohesia, the 2nd Butler was the forefather of the Lords de Verdon who did not retain the surname of Butler. The 3rd Butler, who supported his guardian Henry III in the wars with the Barons, married a daughter of Richard de Burgh, ancestor of the Clanricardes.

The 4th Butler fought against the Mortimers at Evesham, sat in the Irish parliaments of Edward I and campaigned under him in Scotland and Wales, before dying at the relatively advanced age of about forty-three and leaving eight sons and two daughters by his widow, Joan.

The 5th Butler stood fifth on the roll of the Irish parliament of 1295 without any territorial designation, which indicates that the Chief Butlerage of Ireland carried with it the status of a Baron at least. He then accompanied Edward I to Scotland when the Coronation Stone was purloined, and he died in 1299, at the age of thirty, unmarried.

(B) THE EPHEMERAL EARL (D.1321)

He was succeeded by his brother, Edmund, aged about twenty-six, as the 6th Butler. Edmund is an enigma. Like many of his family, he was Governor of Ireland, but it was with some reluctance that he accepted the post. While he was Governor, the Scottish invasion of Ireland occurred under the Bruce Brothers but he was said to have bestowed peace on the land and that he was able to travel from his barony at Arklow to Limerick guarded by no more than three horsemen. His services were rewarded by Edward II in 1315 when he was granted the castle and manor of Karryk MacGriffyn and Roscrea. Most of the land in the Clonbough townland was at one time under the ownership of the Earl of Carrick.

(C) EARL OF ORMOND, 1328-1633

Edmund was succeeded as 7th Butler by his teenage son James, a liberal, friendly, pleasant and stately youth. As soon as James was twenty-one he was knighted. A year later he married the King's niece Elaenor de Bohun, and, the following year, in October 1328, he was created Earl of Ormond. As in the case of his father's Earldom of Carrick, the creation charter is missing, but the Earldom of Ormond was probably limited to the heirs male.

A few weeks after he was created Earl of Ormond, James was granted, by Edward III, the regalties and liberties of Co. Tipperary. Ormond himself had extensive and widely distributed properties.

He was succeeded by his seven-year-old son, James, whom the Irish called 'The Chaste'. The 2nd Earl of Ormond spent most of his life in Ireland, where the considerable estates he had inherited were augmented by grants for his good services. He was Governor of Ireland several times, although he refused the post in 1381. In 1382, he died at Knocktopher, aged fifty-one. Like his father, was buried in Gowran.

Gowran, Co. Kilkenny was the principal seat of the family before they moved to Kilkenny Castle, and James, son and successor of the 2nd Earl, was sometimes called Earl of Gowran. This 3rd Earl built a castle there and it was he also purchased Kilkenny Castle from Hugh Despenser between 1391 and 1393. Being fluent in Irish, the 3rd Earl was able to improve his relations with the O'Neills, O'Briens, O'Connors and MacMurroughs, and to forge bonds of amity with the O'Kennedys that brought a measure of peace to North Tipperary for four centuries. In 1405, he died at Gowran. He had several illegitimate children, including Sir Thomas Butler, the lame Prior of Kilmainham, by an unknown mistress, and four sons by Katherine, daughter of Gerald the Poet, the 4th Earl of Desmond. However, he also had two legitimate sons by the daughter of Lord Wells – James, his successor, and Sir Richard Butler of Knocktopher, the ancestor of the present Lord Ormonde.

James, the 4th Earl, known as 'The White Earl', was Governor of Ireland several times. He was a seasoned warrior and served under Henry V. He was a benefactor of St Canice's Cathedral, Kilkenny. A robust man, he died of the plague at the age of sixty-two and is buried in St Mary's Abbey in Dublin. By his first wife, Joan Beauchamp he had three sons, each of whom successfully inherited his Earldom and each died without having a son. The eldest of them, the 5th Earl, spent most of his time in England where Henry VI created him Earl of Wiltshire, Knight of the Garter and Lord Treasurer. He partook in the War of the Roses and after one battle at Towton, Yorkshire, he was executed and his head was sent to London Bridge for all to see. He was forty. The fortunes of the family were at a low ebb when Edward IV came to power, but Edward recognised the character of the 6th Earl, John and recalled that 'if good breeding, nurture and liberal qualities were lost in the world, then they may be found in the 6th Earl, John'.

The first English Parliament of Henry VII followed suit, and the 7th Earl, 'the Earl of Wool', was one of the wealthiest of the King's subjects in England. In 1489, he was created Lord Ormond, a barony in the peerage of England, which on his death fell into abeyance between his daughters. The son of the other daughter was father of Anne Boleyn. The 7th Earl died in 1515.

The Earldom of Ormond then passed to his male heir, Red Piers, great-grandson of Sir Richard Butler of Knocktopher. Sir Richard's sons 'were not brought up after the English fashion' and may have been none the worse for that. Edmund MacRichard, who built Black Castle in Thurles to guard the passageway over the River Suir, led the Butlers to disaster in 1462, when he was captured at Piltown, Co. Kilkenny, while fighting the Desmond Geraldines. To be released he had to surrender to his captors his Book of Carrick and his copy of the Psalter of Cashel. His eldest son was father of Piers.

Piers and his wife Margaret Fitzgerald, daughter of the 8th Earl of Kildare, were a determined couple. Slowly, over time they weaved their way back into contention, Piers himself became Ormond's agent. In 1529, King Henry created Thomas Boleyn, Earl of Ormond and made Red Piers Earl of Ossory, but ten years later, when the Boleyn's fell out of favour, Piers emerged with two Earldoms in Ormond and Ossory. He died the following year in 1539. He was the first of the Earls of Ormond to be buried in St Canice's Cathedral. Piers and his wife are recorded as having founded Kilkenny College.

Red Piers was succeeded in his Earldoms by his thirty-five-year-old eldest son, James who was brought up at the Court of Henry VIII, who had high regard for him and created him Viscount Thurles. The King's policy was to create equal influence for each of the rival houses of Butlers and Fitzgeralds. For fourteen years James was Lord Treasurer of Ireland. In 1546, at the age of forty-two, he and his servants went to be entertained at a party when he was poisoned and died. The confusion created by his will gave rise to the founding of the Irish Public Record Office. By his wife, Joan he had seven sons, and Black Tom, who succeeded him, had no surviving son.

Black Tom, the 10th Earl of Ormond, was about fifteen when he succeeded his father and was he was eighty-three when he died. Throughout his adventurous life he was devoted and loyal to his cousin, Queen Elizabeth I and he defeated the Earl of Desmond at the Battle of Affane in 1565, the last private pitched battle in the British Isles. At the age of sixty-nine Black Tom was taken prisoner by the O'Moores for two months, during which time he is said to have been converted by Fr Archer to Catholicism. He is buried in St Canice's Cathedral, Kilkenny.

Black Tom was succeeded by his nephew Walter, MP for Tipperary and son of John Butler of Kilcash. A devout Catholic, he was known as 'Walter of the Beads'. His claim to the family estates was thwarted by James I. Walter died in 1633, and is buried in St Canice's Cathedral. His grandson James took over and did very well.

(D) THE THREE DUKES, 1617-1758

James, with his father drowned and his grandfather in jail, was made a royal ward and, unlike his parents or brothers or sisters, was educated a Protestant. At twenty-three, when he succeeded his grandfather as Earl, he was made a Councillor for New England (USA), one of the first mentions of America in the Butler family, but by no means the last. In 1642, he was created Marquess of Ormonde. He refused the garter, fought against Cromwell, shared the privations of exile with Charles II and then, after the Restoration, was created both a Duke in Ireland and in England. Further he had the unusual distinction of sitting in the English House of Lords with his three sons, the eldest of whom was also a Knight of the Garter. He was Lord Lieutenant of Ireland and Chancellor of Dublin, as well as Oxford University. He procured the incorporation of the College of Physicians in Dublin and founded the Royal Hospital at Kilmainham.

His second son, James, 2nd Duke of Ormonde, fought for William III at the Battle of the Boyne and succeeded Marlborough as Commander-in-Chief in Flanders. But there was mutual distrust between him and George I and he eventually backed the Jacobites. He died after thirty years in exile and is buried in Westminister Abbey.

While the 2nd Duke was in exile, his estates were bought in 1721 by his brother, the Earl of Arran, and settled first on their sister Lady Amelia Butler and secondly on John Butler of Kilcash, the representative of Richard, younger brother of the 1st Duke. The Earl of Arran was therefore the 3rd Duke of Ormonde but the dukedom became extinct in 1758. His Irish Earldoms of Ormond and Ossory and Viscounty of Thurles then devolved on his cousin John Butler of Kilcash.

(E) EARLS AND MARQUESSES OF ORMONDE, 1758-1965

John succeeded to Kilkenny Castle and the other family estates but never assumed the Earldoms to which he was entitled. Having died childless in 1766, he was buried at Kilcash and was succeeded by his first cousin, Walter, then aged sixty-three. He promptly moved from Garryricken to Kilkenny Castle, where he died in 1783.

Walter's only son, John, known as 'Jack of the Castle', succeeded his father at the age of forty-two, having married the daughter and sole heiress of the Earl of Wandersford, by whom he had eight sons and two daughters.

His eldest son, Walter, then succeeded him at the age of twenty-five. In 1811, he received the tidy sum of £216,000 as compensation for the Crown's resumption of his hereditary right to the presage of wines. Walter died in Kent, where he is buried, and was succeeded by his forty-five-year-old brother James as the 19th Earl of Ormonde. James died in 1838 in Dublin, where he is buried in St Mary's church. He had ten children, of whom John was the eldest.

John was twenty-nine when he succeeded his father as 20th Earl, having being educated at Harrow and an MP for Kilkenny. He was vice-president of the RDS and, with Revd James Graves, he arranged the vast collection of Ormonde manuscripts in Kilkenny Castle. Unlike some landlords during the potato famine of the 1840s, he helped his tenants by reducing their rents or agreeing to forgo them altogether. He had six children with his wife, the daughter of General Sir Edward Paget. He died in Wexford in September 1854, aged forty-six years. He did not leave an enemy behind him, according to the then Bishop of Ossory.

His eldest son, James, was not ten years old when his father died. He married and had two daughters. He owned 27,000 acres of land in Kilkenny and Tipperary. He died at seventy-five years old in Kilkenny and was succeeded by his seventy-year-old brother, James Arthur. Arthur married Ellen and lived until the age of ninety-four, when he was succeeded by his eldest son, George. George retired from the army in 1920 when wounded in the First World War. In May 1922, as Earl of Ossory, he was living in Kilkenny Castle with his wife Sybil when the castle was occupied by the Republicians and besieged by the troops of the Free State. After a two-day siege, the garrison surrendered. When he died in 1949, aged fifty-nine, he was succeeded by his brother Arthur. When Arthur died in 1971, he was succeeded by his cousin Charles Butler. Charles had two daughters. From then on, regarding the many descendants of John Butler of Kilcash, 3rd son of the 9th Earl of Ormond, the male line seems likely to be extinct.

THE MALE LINE FROM THE 9TH EARL OF ORMOND

The discussion continues and we in Clonboo are not in the reckoning, but several other branches of the family can be reviewed, including the Paulstown branch, where we are said to have originally come from. We will pick up some more information on the Paulstown branch of the Butler family later.

A brief overview of the different branches is as follows:

The Mountgarret branch, from 1550, descended from Richard, second son of the 8th Earl of Ormond, who was created Viscount Mongarret by Edward VI in 1550.

The Paulstown branch, from 1500, would be next in the line of succession after the Mountgarret branch. They would be the descendents of Walter Butler of Paulstown, Co. Kilkenny, the paternal uncle of the 8th Earl of Ormond. He was ancestor of the four successive Butler baronets of Paulstown and one of his great-grandsons was Pierce, father of Count Walter Butler, who, in 1634, was the principal actor in the momentous murder of Wallenstein, to quote Hubert Butler of Maidenhall. Colonel Walter's first cousin on his father's side was Thomas Butler, of Clonmore, Co. Carlow. (It is only a coincidence that we currently live in Clonmore, Co. Tipperary, but a funny one all the same!) One of Thomas Butler's grandsons, Edmund Theobald, was created Count Butler von Clonberg of the Holy Roman Empire. He married a countess of Bohemia and had descendents who inherited, through a marriage of 1771, the estates of the Counts of Haimhaussen in Bavaria.

Next would come any surviving male descendents from Richard of Boelick, Co. Tipperary (brother of Walter of Paulstown), and the Butlers of Agerte and Cowleshill, Co. Tipperary, who were descended from John, a younger brother.

There are then some Kilkenny branches dating from 1400. After the male lines from Walter of Paulstown and his brothers, the next heirs to the Ormond Earldom would be the descendents of younger sons of the 2nd Earl, of whom Theobald was ancestor of the Butlers of Tipperary on the Suir, bordering Tipperary and Kilkenny, and Pierce was ancestor of the Butlers of Kiltorcan and Knocknelly, Co. Kilkenny.

The Carrick branch, from 1300, as heirs to the Chief Butlership, though not the Earldom, would be the descendents of the younger brothers of the 1st Earl of Ormond, of whom John was ancestor of the Butlers of Lismalin, Co. Tipperary and Callan, Co. Kilkenny and Thomas was said to be ancestor of various Butlers of Galway. One interesting fact emerged from this branch. From their common ancestor, John, the younger brother of the 1st Earl of Ormond, Pierce (eight generations in descent) was created Viscount Ikerrin in 1629 by Charles I. His grandson, the 3rd Viscount, acquired Ballyinch Castle through marriage, which is now known as Mount Julliet, in Co. Kilkenny.

The Dunboyne branch, from 1300, would be next. In the unlikely event of the extinction of the male line from Edmund, the Earl of Carrick, the succession to the twelfth-century Chief Butlership would fall to the Dunboyne branch. Their ancestor was Thomas Butler, third son of the 4th Chief Butler.

Other branches from various locations are noted, including Butlers from New Ross, Butlers from Cahir, Butlers from Ballintemple in Co. Carlow, Butlers from Galmoye, and others far and wide.

4. CLONBOO AND BEYOND

It is very difficult to get back to 1177 when the Butlers first came to Ireland, almost 830 years ago. A lot of the information is in the form of historical opinions and even the changing of the name from Fitz Walter to Butler and MacRichard and then back to Butler is unclear in terms of actual dates. The other complication, in my opinion, is that some descendants would have held onto the surnames of Fitz Walter or MacRichard or reverted back to these surnames for very good reasons, namely protection from persecution or evading imprisonment as a result of religion or assistance to the nationalists in their resistance against the Crown rulers.

In any event, I am a Butler, and I have managed to go back to around the early 1700s, about 300 years ago. The major difficulty that currently exists for anyone doing searches for information about ancestors or relatives is that loads of valuable archive information was lost at various times throughout our history. There were major fires in the Records Office, and several offices were burned and demolished by all sides during the 1916 Rising and also during the Civil War. We lost many records due to carelessness concerning our documentary heritage, particularly as a result of the destruction in 1922 of the Public Records Office of Ireland.

Tracing back is easy at the start, due to the fact that most of the initial couple of generations are still alive, Thank God. As you delve further back it is necessary to get as much information and facts as you can. In most cases I have received two sources of information about certain people, which hopefully helps to prove that there is a much better chance that the information is, in fact, correct.

The concentration in retracing our roots has been on the Butler name, but the wider family has also been touched on in relation to the female surname. During my own research the following surnames emerged and some information is also included about their ancestors: Doolan, Whelan, Farrell, Shanahan, Delaney, O'Mara, O'Dwyer, Bowe and Bourke.

To draw a simple line back from my own children, the following are their Butler ancestors:

1st: Children Aoife, Sean and Sarah.
2nd: Father Jack Butler and Mother Anne Phelan.
3rd: Grandparents Johnny Butler and Mary Doolan.
4th: Great-grandparents John Butler and Catherine Whelan.
5th: Great-great-grandparents John Butler and Catherine Shanahan.
6th: Great-great-great-grandparents John Butler and Julia Delaney.
7th: Great-great-great-great-grandparents Timothy Butler and Mary O'Dwyer.
8th: Great-great-great-great-great-grandfather Theobald Butler.
9th: Great-great-great-great-great-great-grandfather John Butler (b.1718, d.1768)

With regard to Theobald (8th above), I could not find out if he had brothers and there is the possibility that if he had a brother then he might be the father of Timothy (7th) rather than Theobald. However, it was Theobald that erected the gravestone for his father John's grave in Moyne graveyard, with no mention of other children. Also, in the tithe applotments of 1824 for the civil parish of Killavinogue, Toby (Theobald) Butler is listed in the entries for the Clonbough townland.

It is probably simplest to look at each generation of ancestors separately.

MY GRANDFATHER'S GENERATION

I have covered the current crop of Butlers among the Houses and People between the crosses, and now we will go back to my grandfather's generation where there were nine children: Patrick, Kathleen, Thomas, Matthew, John (my grandfather), Matthew, Denis, Julia, and Mary.

PATRICK (PADDY) BUTLER

Paddy Butler was born in 1893, he married Mary Fitzgerald from Rossmore. Paddy was at the time living with his aunt-in-law Mrs Shanahan. Paddy's mother was Catherine Shanahan; her brother Johnny married Katie Maher from the Borrisbeg area (outside Templemore). When Johnny died they had no family and Paddy went to live in Lisdownley to manage and run the farm. Paddy lived here and the farm was left to him when his aunt-in-law died. This was the farm and house where his mother Catherine Shanahan had come from.

Paddy and Mary married and they had two sons, Eddie and John Joe. Eddie married Mary Moore from Moyne and they have two sons, P.J. and Eamonn. They went to live in Lisduff, Urlingford. They live in the county of Tipperary, close to the border with Kilkenny. The few yards are important. The locals in Urlingford sat that they are so close to the county border 'that they can piss into Tipperary'.

P.J. is married to Martina Ryan and they have two children, Rachel and Adam. Eamonn is married to Catherine Loughlin and they have three children: Shay, Mark and David. Eddie Butler was telling me that Eamonn's boys go to school in St Kieran's Kilkenny, a great hurling nursery to match any of the other great hurling schools around the country. Shay took the frees for St Kieran's and would have been a good addition to the Tipp Minors in 2008, as several of his teammates in Kieran's were on the winning All-Ireland minor team of that year.

John Joe is not married and lives in the home place in Moyne. He is a keen card player and a regular visitor to Clonboo.

KATHLEEN BUTLER

Kathleen (Katie) Butler was born in 1890, and she married John Maher from Killough, Killea. They had two sons, John and Tommy, both unmarried. John died on 22 June 2001. Tommy is still alive.

THOMAS BUTLER

Thomas, born in 1883, died at a young age in 1905. He was twenty-one years old when he passed away on 23 July 1905. He is buried in the old graveyard in Moyne. I'm not certain of the cause of death, but Eddie Butler and my own father have similar recollections of what happened. Eddie told me that his father Paddy Butler told him that Thomas was a good hurler and played a hurling match one day where he got a few belts and was concussed during the game. Thomas made nothing of the injuries when he got home. The following day, he went out to train a horse and after a while when he did not come back, somebody went out to look for him. They found him dead in the stable. Nobody knew for certain what happened; some thought he might have got a kick from a horse while others thought that the hurling injuries from the previous day might have had something to do with the tragedy.

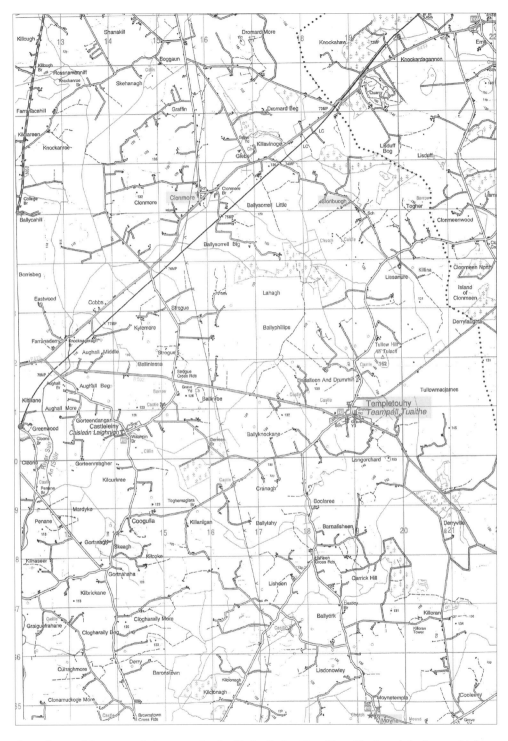

General map of the areas and places associated with the Butler Clan. Note Clonbough in the top third section of the map and Clogharaily More near the bottom left section.

MATTHEW BUTLER

Matthew died at a very young age. He was only five months old. I could find no confirmation on the cause of death or if he had been sick from birth.

JOHN BUTLER AND CATHERINE WHELAN (My Grandparents)

John, my grandfather, was born in 1878. He married my grandmother Catherine Whelan, from Kyle, Rathdowney in 1931. Catherine was a daughter of Edward and Margaret Whelan. Catherine's mother (my great-grandmother) died on 9 February 1921, aged sixty-nine years, while her husband Edward (my great-grandfather) died on 5 November 1924, aged seventy-one years. Catherine had one brother, Dan who died on 1 April 1967, aged eighty-two years. He was not married. Catherine also had three sisters: Margaret, Julia and Mary.

I remember my grandmother well and especially the later years of her life, when she lived with us in Clonboo. She died on 9 July 1973, aged eight-two years. I remember the day she died. I was ten years old, and although I had been to several funerals and wakes in houses, this was the first close family member that I remember dying. She died at home in Clonboo. I had been at school and had got an injection that day for some vaccination (measles, I think). When I was crying during one of the rosaries, I remember someone saying, 'Ah, the poor fella, it must be the injection he got today, it must be hurting him.' Being a tough man, I agreed at the time, but I was really crying because of my granny. We always called her Granny Butler, and my other grandmother Nanna Doolan. It was the way of telling them apart. Also Granny Butler was always referred to as Mrs Butler, and to this day, if anyone called her Mrs Butler, my own mother would say that she wanted to be called Mary, as there was only one Mrs Butler in the house.

I don't remember Julia Whelan, as she died in 1964, when I was less than two years old, but there was an incident in which I was allegedly involved. My grandaunt had some people in the house in Kyle and was giving the visitors some whiskey in the parlour when an unwelcome man arrived at the door. She did not turn him away as the man was a neighbour but she did not want to be giving him some of her good whiskey and offered him a bottle of stout, saying that all the whiskey had just been drank. At this point I intervened to remind her that, 'No, it's not all gone, remember the bottle that you put behind the chair in the corner of the room.' Julia was not at all impressed with me. I could not understand, as I thought I had been so helpful!

Margaret Whelan did not marry. She died on 25 June 1966, aged seventy-eight years. Julia, who had earlier emigrated and worked in America for years, came back to Kyle to retire, and she died on 30 June 1964, aged eighty-two years. The other sister, Mary married Dan Bergin from Errill and they had eight children, four girls and four boys: Kathleen, Mai, Peg, Nan, Dan, Pat, Ned and Jim.

Kathleen was a nun. She became Mother Vicar General of the Mercy Order of nuns. She was born on St Stephen's Day 1906 and died on 2 September 1987. Mai emigrated to America, where she worked. She died in New York during the week of the terrorist attack on 11 September 2001. Anne and I visited her in New York before we got married. She was a lovely woman.

Peg, who went to New Zealand, married a widower who had a family but she had no children of her own.

Nan married Martin Carroll of Castleflemming, Errill. They had two sons and one daughter: Donie, Nancy and Martin. Donie is a professor in Terenure College and Nancy is a nurse. Martin is married in Mountrath and has four children, Damien, Ronan, Marina and Raymond. Damien is married to Catherine Walters from Wexford and they have two sons, Jamie and Jack. Ronan is married to Elaine Byrne from Monaghan and they have a son and a daughter, Max and Mia. Marina and Raymond are not married. Nan Carroll died on 1 May 1984, aged sixty-six years, while her husband, Martin died on 29 June 1983, aged seventy-nine years. I remember Martin and Nan well as we would often visit Bergin's when I was young and during daytime visits someone would walk down to Carroll's with me, as they lived down the road from Bergin's. Nan always had a big smile and a jolly way about her.

Dan and Ned Bergin worked in England most of their lives, in the Birmingham area for most of the time. Neither got married. Ned died on 14 November 1984, aged seventy years. He was always a bit of a rogue, but a likeable rogue. Toby Maher often knocked great craic out of Ned Bergin. Dan moved back to Errill about five years ago and is getting close to his ninetieth birthday.

Jim married Peggy Keyes from Errill. They lived and worked in America. He also died there. They had two daughters, Mary and Kathleen, along with one son, Danny.

Pat Bergin married Peg Grey from Dromard, Clonmore. They had one daughter, Monica who is married to Sean Dunne from Errill. They live in the home place and have five children, four girls (Marguirette, Catriona, Siobhan and Bridget) and one son, Patrick James, who tragically died on 15 August 2001. The girls all live around locally to Errill with their own families.

Pat Bergin and my grandmother Sarah Doolan were my godparents. We visited Bergin's a lot when I was very young. At that time, Bergins was not a house for children. There were never too many children in the house. The kitchen had a smaller kitchen or scullery off it and this was a great room for rummaging and finding things as a young child. There was always a problem to stop me going into this room and the solution was found when they discovered that I was afraid of Pat Bergin's hat. The hat was put on the knob of the door and that was the end of my rummaging for a while, at least until I got used to the hat or they forgot to put it on the door knob.

John Butler, my grandfather, was born in 1879 and died on 6 March 1961, aged eighty-two years. Catherine, his wife, was born in 1891 and died on 9 July 1973, also aged eighty-two. They had one son, Johnny, my father, who was born on 28 September 1932.

MARY BUTLER

Mary (b.1884) married Jim Kirwin from Kylelanigan, Castleiney. They had four children: Matt, Catherine, Maureen and Anne (Ciss). Jim Kirwin died in the late 1930s and his wife Mary died soon after.

Matt left Ireland in the early or mid-1940s and never came back. I was unable to find any record of him. Maureen and Anne both became Sister of Mercy nuns and are based in Cornwall, Wales. Catherine married Dan Maher from Dromard, Clonmore. They had two children, Michael and Maura. Michael married Noeleen Dunne from Ballymackey, Nenagh. They live beside Maher's home place in Dromard and they have twin boys, Rory and Dan. Maura married Jim Fitzpatrick from Dareens, where they live. They have two sons, Joe and Donal. Jim Fitzpatrick now runs the farm in Kylelanigan.

Dan Maher was one of the regular card players on Christmas nights in our house. He always added a bit of character to the game. He often created diversions and often got the more 'serious' players going to good effect, sometimes leading to walk-outs. The walkout would only be to the kitchen from the parlour for a half hour or so to have a cup of tea, a kind of cooling off time, so to speak. When Dan Maher died, some years ago, Jim Fitzpatrick, his son-in-law, took his place at the cards on Christmas night.

JULIA BUTLER

Julia Butler (b.1882) married James Maher from Toher, Templetuohy. Julia was born in 1883 and died on 4 January 1974, aged ninety-one years. Her husband James died eighteen years earlier on 5 January 1956, aged seventy-nine years. Both are buried in the churchyard in Drom. They had nine children: Toby, Jimmy, Dan, John, Michael, Katie, Mary, Bridie and Julia. They are all now dead except Jimmy.

James's parents were Toby and Bridget. Bridget died on 20 January 1909, aged sixty years. They had a daughter, Mary who died on 20 November 1877 at one year old.

Toby married Mary Kate Meehan from Dromard, Clonmore. They lived in Lissanure and had two sons. Jim lives at home. Mick married Ann Marie Brennan from Thurles. They live in the village of Templetuohy and they have three children: Paul, Catherine and Claire.

Toby was a character, and another of the 'famous nine' – the Christmas night card players who would make up the nine to play 'Twenty-five' in Clonboo. But Toby would be a regular visitor to our house, probably on two or three nights a week. He hated people who parked cars in an abandoned fashion and several people got a tongue lashing when he arrived or tried to leave but was unable to do so because he was blocked in! He always had a great interest in my progress through college doing Construction Studies and later, Quantity Surveying. There are a lot of good stories and yarns about Toby and they often involved Patrick Clarke and Johnny Butler. Toby died on 30 August 1992, aged seventy-nine years. Mary, his wife, a lovely, gentle woman, died on 31 August 1981, aged sixty-one years.

Jimmy married Mae Holohan from Johnstown. They live in Toher and have three daughters and one son: Julie, Breda, Kathleen and Seamus. Julie married John Quigley and they live near Nenagh. They have two girls and one boy: Ann-Marie, Katie and Jamie. Breda married Donal Delaney and she lives in Portlaoise. They have three children: Isabel, Roisin and Daniel James Jeremiah. Kathleen married Noel Doughan from Toomevara and they have four children: Christopher, Claire, Katrina and James. Seamus married Siobhan Rainsford on 22 September 2000. They have a son James and they live in Toher. Seamus runs the home place. At different times I was in both Kathleen's and Breda's class in primary school in Toher.

Dan Maher married Sile Flood from Cavan. They had seven children and moved to England. The children, as far as I know, are as follows: Seamus, who married Maureen Shaw; Anne, single; Phyllis, married with four children; Brendan, married to Karen with two children, Kelly and Shaun; Arthur, married to Jill, two children, Catherine and Stuart; Julie, married to Liam, three children; Sile, married to Ben, with three boys.

John Maher married Eileen Drennan from Borris-in-Ossory. They did not have a family and Eileen died on 8 January 2007.

Michael Maher died on 23 July 1938, at the young age of twenty-three years.

Katie married Paddy Phelan from Mannin, Pike of Rushall, Borris. They have four children: Mae, Paddy, Tom and Shem. Mae married Donal Bowe from Cappolinane, Durrow and they have five children: Kathleen, Julie, Donal, Thomas and Patrick. Paddy married Briege from Ballinasloe and they have three children: Michael, Brian and Carmel.

Tom married Bonny Janes from Toronto, Canada, and they have one girl called Brenna. She is not married and lives in the home place in Mannin.

Mary Maher married Tim Meehan and they lived in Clontaffe, Killea. Tim Meehan was a brother of Mary Kate Meehan, Toby Maher's wife. So a brother and sister married another brother and sister, which was quite unusual. Both sets of children are first cousins on the double. Tim and Mary Meehan had seven children: Joan, Sile, Seamus, Pauline, Michael, Timmy and Denis. Tim Meehan was a gifted musician and was well known near and far as a superb fiddle player. He often played in our house for the 'Yanks' when they came home and came to Clonboo for a get-together of the clan. He used always play a tune called 'The Cuckoo', and as he played you could hear the sound of a cuckoo from the fiddle. He was often backed up on the accordion by Jim or Mick Maher (Toby's sons).

Tim and his wife Mary, along with all the children, were a lovely family. Growing up, I was friendly with Pauline, Seamus and Timmy. Seamus was in my class in the CBS, while Pauline and Timmy had a similar circle of friends. I always enjoy meeting Pauline. The time I met her at my brother Matt's wedding we were talking about times gone by, and she mentioned that she was there representing the Meehan family. This is something that we all do, represent our families, and it always means a great deal to us. Tim Meehan died on 23 June 2001, aged seventy-six years, and his wife Mary died on 14 January 1997, aged seventy-three years.

Seamus lives in the home place in Clontaffe. Joan is married to Hubert Durkan and lives in Nenagh. Sile married Pat Sullivan. They live in Kildare and have three children: Joan, Marie and Donnchadh. Pauline married Eamonn Burke and they have three children: Kathleen, Daniel and Eddie. They live in Killea. Michael married Margaret Lucey; they live in Cork and have two children, Maria and Padraig. Timmy is married to Conchita and they have one girl, Ashling and a baby son, Timothy James. Timmy and Conchita now live in Dromard. Denis married Helena Vasconcelos and they live in Opporto, Portugal, where they have two boys, Mark and Michael, and one girl, Marie Carolina.

Bridie Butler married Tommy Costello. They first lived in Ballyheen and then moved into the Mall, Templemore. They did not have children. Tommy was a great character and had a great hearty, funny laugh. I will always remember his laugh. He was always very interested in the cousins who came home from America and they always enjoyed his conversation and his company.

Julia Butler died at the very young age of fourteen on 3 March 1936.

MATHEW BUTLER

There was a second Mathew in the family. Mathew married Louise De Lane (French). They emigrated to the States from Liverpool, having earlier emigrated to England. Mathew emigrated to the USA in 1914. He died on 3 May 1930 and his wife Louise died on 23 June 1946. They had two sons, John and Desmond. They also had a baby girl named Catherine who died after just twenty-two days, on 23 November 1908. She is buried in England. John also had a twin sister, who sadly died at birth on 16 June 1912. Desmond was born on 31 October 1907 and died on 16 September 1988. Both Desmond and John were regular visitors to Ireland. They had a deep love and passion for Ireland and always considered it home. Both held strong republican views and never lost the opportunity to express them. They always enquired about the latest developments and monitored progress on the peace process. Thankfully, John lived to see real progress and hopefully an end to the senseless killings of the Troubles, along with the hopes of a permanent solution to the conflict.

When we once visited John and Mary in Astoria, New York, I was left in no doubt of his love and devotion to the cause of a united Ireland. His front door had a sign which had a green map of Ireland with the simple mathematical statement underneath, '26 + 6 = 1'. I thought it was so simple and clear.

Sadly John passed away on 23 June 2006. John's daughter Eileen pointed out to me that John's mother Louise also died on 23 June, in 1946. John's wife, Mary died on 2 September 2007. Both John and Mary lived to the great age of ninety-four, and were really lovely people. I remember a good story about John. He was an excellent tour guide of New York City. He knew his way around and he knew his stuff about each of the places. He was some talker and kept pumping out the facts and the history all day long. He was extremely well read, and a regular, cover-to-cover daily reader of *The New York Times*. We were standing outside the Stock Exchange and John was showing us the damage caused by bullets to the wall outside, when this couple from Texas, who were listening in to John's explanations, asked us where we got our tour guide. The lady said, 'He's pretty good.' The same couple asked us where we were from and they got a great thrill when they found out that they had met people from Ireland. It made their first trip to New York all the more special and an added talking point when they returned back to Texas. I am amazed at the number of Americans that have never left the country and who do not even have a passport, some 80 per cent as I understand.

John married Mary O'Connor and they had three children: Louise, James and Eileen. Louise married Paul Sayer and they have two children, Janice and Gloria. Janice married Joseph Dodge and they have three children: Joseph, Jamie and Jaclyn. Gloria married Robert Eddins and they also have three children: Philip, Samantha and Crystal. Sadly, John and Mary's son James died on 5 January 1972. Eileen married Charles Linek and they have two children, Mathew and Kathryn. Her mother tells me that Kathryn is affectionately called Katie by all who know her. I must ask her mother if she has heard of that Mary Black song, which is a particular favourite of mine, 'Come running Home, again Katie'?

Desmond married Margaret O'Leary and they had four children: Francis Xavier, Des, Joseph and Margaret Mary. Desmond died on 16 September 1988 and his wife Margaret died seven years earlier on 28 October 1981. Joseph died in infancy, and Margaret Mary married Frank Cassidy, a Galwegian. They live in Philadelphia and as far as I know have always lived there. They have three lovely daughters: Kathleen, Donna and Maureen. Margaret Mary and Frank have always remained close to their Irish roots and love putting on a great Irish party whenever I visit the east coast of America (sadly not too often in recent years). I have fond memories of my time in their home there. Frank still has family back in Galway. Kathleen is married to Eric Wolfgang Ziegast and they have two children, a boy and a girl called Aidan James and Margaret Lenore (who also goes by the name of Maggie Lynn). They live outside San Diego, California. My brother Pat has visited there and was always well looked after. Donna is married to Thomas Peter Rossi III and they have one girl, Kara. They live near Philadelphia, close to Donna's parents. Maureen is married to Jon Janaka and they have two daughters, Tulsi Lou and Annalee Alla.

Francis married Helen McGarrigle from Philadelphia and they had seven children: Terrance Francis, Kenneth Francis (who died at about three years of age), Helen Michelle, Eileen Patricia, Bruce Francis, Brian Norman and Cornelius (Neil) Desmond. Francis and Helen separated and Francis married Louise. Sadly Francis died in the mid-1980s and Louise died during the summer of 2010. Terry informs me that he has eight children and currently ten grandchildren, with another due shortly. The children are Beth, Heather, Lisa, Mary, Elia, Lynda M., Linda L. and Terry Jr.

Des Butler, to me, is the 'Yank' who has remained a close ally across the pond over the years. I was going to write a few words about him and his life travels and his love of all things Irish. Instead I asked him to give me an American perspective, which I am happy to include and I thank him for doing so. Partly because of his father's devotion to the 'auld sod', Dessie often came to Ireland, and he became the most common link to the States, hence he is the 'Yank'. This is his story:

Born in south Philadelphia, 2 January 1941, the second son of Desmond Roe Butler and Margaret Butler (*née* Leary), I grew up in a very Irish enclave. My parents had met on a ship going to Ireland in the 1920s. While conversing on board they discovered that her father in Philadelphia, Cornelius O'Leary, sent funds to support the cause of Irish Independence to his Dad, Mathew Butler, then living in New York.

Both of my parents, like their own parents, were devoted to the republican opposition to the English oppressor and the Free State collaborators. Matt Butler had been living in Liverpool at the start of the Great War, but fled to America when he was warned that his activities supporting the IRA and opposing conscription were about to cause his arrest. Of course, he neither had proper papers to leave England nor to arrive legally in the United States. At the end of the war, my grandmother Louise DeLane Butler and her two sons, Desmond Roe and John Patrick, arranged to legally migrate to New York and join Matt and his brother Denis, who had also 'escaped' to New York and was active in support of Irish Independence.

When the liner that was taking my future parents to Britain docked, the new friends agreed to meet in Thurles at the Munster Final. She would spend her holidays in Mallow, Co. Cork with her family, while my Dad would travel to Clonboo. Both went to the match but were unable to find each other due to the huge crowds. Dad went to Mallow a few days later to find the girl he would marry. In time, they married in Philadelphia and she came with him to make a home in New York. However, within a year the couple moved back to the bride's hometown. The O'Learys were very active in the Irish movement and Margaret had been a much-admired single girl. Her new husband was at first seen as an interloper from New York and folks who found out he was born in Liverpool, called him 'the Englishman', to which he replied to his dying day that 'Being born in a stable does not make you a horse.'

My brother Francis Xavier was born in 1932. Rather than have him educated at the local parish school, he was sent to a nearby Italian Catholic school because the nuns were all Irish Franciscans. South Philadelphia was very Catholic; the whole city was over 40 per cent Catholic. In addition to the diocesan parishes, we had 'national' churches for Italians, Greeks, Polish and Spanish. I don't think Philadelphia ever had an Irish church, since the Irish were the Church. Even today, sections of the city are best known by the names of the local Catholic church.

Despite, or because of, the large number of Catholics, especially the Irish, local Protestant ascendancy often displayed virulent anti-immigrant prejudice. The Philadelphia Cathedral of St Peter and Paul was built without windows at ground level, since the 'know-nothings' were in the habit of breaking reachable windows. 'No Irish need apply' signs reminded my parents and grandparents that for them, this was not the Promised Land. As a child, I often heard my elders wish that they could go home to the dear land they were forced to leave. Irish and

Irish-American music was heard throughout the city, and most certainly in the homes of all my parents' friends. When we visited my father's people in NYC, as we often did, there were the same conversations about Ireland and the same music, which I still love! They may have left Ireland physically, but *never* emotionally.

I was raised in a household full of love, music and books. Education was prized by both my parents. They each had more than 'normal' schooling for their times. Dad started high school before, leaving in his mid-teens to start his career in the grocery business. He was managing a store in Manhattan before finishing his teens. Mom took secretarial courses and had what were referred to as 'good jobs' in Philadelphia before her marriage. My brother was an excellent student and had a year of college before he married and started a family.

I felt the call to the religious life but had no desire for the priesthood. I was taught by what are known in Ireland as the De La Salle Brothers and in the States the Christian Brothers. At the age of sixteen I entered the Order and benefited from a first-rate education, for which I remain grateful. At eighteen I took vows as Brother Brian Malachy, FSC. I received a BA in American History/Education from De La Salle (Phila.) and was sent to teach (and coach) in Canton, Ohio. After several years of teaching, at the age of twenty-five, I was invited to take final vows. During the thirty-day retreat, prior to accepting entry, I concluded that if, after all the time I spent in the Order, I was not solid in my commitment, it was proper to decline. I was given council and support in my decision by my religious superiors and even help in looking for a job. I was fortunate to find a vacancy that had just occurred in Mt Holly NJ. I was employed and given credit for three years teaching experience. The salary was $4,800, more than twice what the Ohio diocese was paying for my services (which pooled with the other seventeen Brothers was sufficient). I could not afford to live on my own so my brother, who had a home in Levittown, PA, took me in for a year. The next year I moved back with my parents in Philadelphia.

With the solid education I had received, I found it easy to receive grants to study various subjects at different universities. Over the years, I have taken courses at La Salle, Temple, University of Pennsylvania, Georgetown, Indiana (PA), Villanova, West Virgina State, UCLA, UC Santa Barbara, and Stony Brook (NY). I have also benefited from grants to study at the NYSE and in Poland and Israel (Yad Vishem).

My upbringing stressed the rights of man to decent treatment. I involved myself to a mild degree in the Civil Rights Movement, especially in registering minorities who were likely to vote against the war in Vietnam. I became very active in various anti-war organisations and actively participated in many of the larger events on the east coast.

During my years as a Brother I had automatic respect from students, parents and the wider community. I soon found that that was not so normal a condition in public education. By the end of my first year at Rancoras Valley Regional High School, I had become an advocate for teacher rights. I objected to being expected to do extra work, especially at night or at weekends. I observed that aloud at such functions; the police were paid; the janitors were paid; the band or DJ were paid; vendors were paid – only teachers were expected to be present without compensation. I informed the Principal that I could not justify driving from Philadelphia to Mt Holly under those conditions. I was confident that I was an asset to the school and could easily land a better job. My peers soon asked me to be on what was then a salary committee, but was soon to be recognised as negotiations education. I also became involved in the efforts to change some state laws affecting education and in efforts to elect legislators favourable to education. For the rest of my career I was an involved leader at local, state and national levels.

My first trip to Europe, including Ireland, was in the summer of 1971. I was about a week in Ireland, travelling with a cousin on my mother's side, Dan Harty. I believe we made a brief stop in Clonboo, but it would have been more of a 'drive by' than a proper stay. In 1978, I took the second of what has turned out to be many visits. At my mother's insistence, my then-wife Charlotte and I properly visited the home where my grandfather Matt was born, the home where my father spent many joyful holidays as a lad. But we did not plan to stay at the cottage. Being proper American tourists, we booked a room in Thurles and drove out for what we expected to be a brief obligatory meeting. Charlotte's travel diary of 7/18/78 says, '…then to Butler farm at Clonboo. Spent great evening with Johnny & Mary & Jack, Ned, Catherine & Pat. (Mary is expecting another baby also.) Bridy & Tom Costello were there. Jim & May came in and Catherine & Dan. We stayed up till 2a.m. talking and singing on tape. Bridy & Tom invited us to stay with them next time and John & May wanted us to stay with them. Next time we will have to stay a few days. Mary said we should visit the school & church.'

Well since then, there have been many visits; on one occasion I remember a terrible drought and I mistakenly flushed the toilet which was, in those circumstances, not necessary. Johnny said not to worry, 'The boy [Ned or Pat] will fetch some water.' I said, 'how far' and the response was, 'about a mile'. I was delighted, when I returned in a few years, that the boys were still glad to see me. Often when I visited, relatives, friends and neighbours would drop in for a drink, some conversation and often a sing-along. For a couple who were not 'drinkers' themselves (Johnny never drank and Mary had the occasional drink), the house always had a ready supply and they were not afraid to pour it out. In those days, I was quite fond of the 'creature' and took many a glass full of Jameson or Powers, and, being a good guest, complimented the host by asking for and receiving seconds!

Towards the end of my father's life, I accompanied him 'back home' about every other year. When he would appear tired of life as it was, I would say, 'Let's go to Ireland this summer' and he would perk up. It was his idea to include my brother Francis on one of those excursions and what a grand time was had by all. Even his becoming seriously ill on one trip to Ireland did not stop our enjoyment of our time in Clonboo.

One would think that a person who has travelled to forty plus countries would have no difficulty finding his way to Butler's in Clonboo, but on several occasions I found myself asking directions, only to be cheerfully told that all the neighbours knew that a Yank cousin would be visiting and that I was on the right road as long as I …

Clonboo, Templetuohy and the Templemore area are an essential part of my life. I am proud of my ancestors who lived and died near the Suir. My grandfather Matt and his brother Denis brought a love for that area with them and passed it along to their heirs. We are all proud of Jack Butler for his efforts to let others know a part of the happiness we associate with the Clonboo road.

Des Butler, May 2010

DENIS BUTLER

Denis (b.1886) was affectionately known as 'Uncle Dinny' by the folks in Clonboo. Like his brother Mathew, he emigrated across the 'big pond' to the United States. (The 'small pond' is the Irish Sea between Ireland and England while the 'big pond' is the Atlantic Ocean between Ireland and North America.

Denis Butler married Anne Smyth and they had five sons: **Brian**, **John**, **Thomas**, **Denis** and **Matthew**. Denis died on 4 November 1972 and his wife Anne on 13 March 1951. There is a large clan of Butlers in this family, with more than sixty relations in all. I have tried to be as accurate as possible with the names and connections, but there may be errors and omissions. If so, I apologise from the outset.

1. **Brian** was the oldest of the five boys, born on 7 July 1920, and he died on 17 November 1996, a retired NYPD Officer. On 12 June 1948, he married Mary Murphy (b. 3 July 1925, d. 19 January 2004) and they had eight children: **Brian**, **Denis**, **Kathleen**, **Kevin**, **William**, **James** and twins, **Michael** and **Patrick**.

Brian Jnr (b. 1949) married Maureen Begg on 26 September 1970. They have three children: Brian, Megan and Sean. Brian, thirty-four, married Angela Rosano on 10 December 2005 and they have twin boys, Vincent and Jack, who will be two years old on 15 September 2010. They live in Stamford, Connecticut, where Angela is a teacher and Brian is a Police Officer. Megan, thirty-one, lives in Hoboken, New Jersey, is single and works for Lehman Brothers (now Barclays Bank). Her Dad told me she was intending to run in the New York City Marathon on 1 November 2009. Sean (twenty-seven on 27 September 2010) is the youngest, is also single and lives in Jersey City, New Jersey, where, like his brother, he is also a Police Officer

Denis (b.1951), a lobbyist for New York Federation of Teachers, married Carol Burke in March 1984. They had one daughter, Breanna, who was born in 1988 and during 2009 was in the final year at University of Rhode Island. Sadly Carol died in June 2003 at forty-six years of age. Denis later married Connie Gallup.

Kathleen (b.1952), a nurse, married Jerry Bartone in April 1974. Sadly Jerry died in October 2004, aged fifty-one years. They have three children: Christopher, Scott and Katie. Christopher (b.1978) married Allyson in March 2006 and is living in Springfield, Massachusetts. Christopher is a fireman and his uncle Brian told me that they were expecting their first child in January 2010. Scott (b.1981) is single, a stockbroker and living in Stamford, Connecticut. The youngest, Katie (b.1984), is single and lives in Albany, New York. She is completing her Masters in Biology and plans to teach.

Kevin (b.1954), a Divisional Commander/One Star Chief of FDNY, married Christine Cognitore in November 1982. They have three children: Sarah, Christina and Matthew. Sarah (b.1984) is an architectural technician, is single and lives in the Bronx. Christina (b.1986) is also single; she lives in Astoria and works in a New York City finance company. Matthew, the youngest, was born in 1991.

Bill (**William**) (b.1958) was a manager of Computer Services for New York State Assembly. He married Janet (Jan) Waller in July 1984. Bill retired and moved to a

285-acre farm in Pigeon Falls, Wisconsin. The couple have one son, Tim, who was born in 1990 and attends college at University of Wisconsin.

Jim (b. 1962), a retired member of FDNY, married Donna Ferraro in July 1987. They have two children: Samantha, who attends Clemson University and was born 1989, and her brother Brendan, who was born in 1993. Jim owns and runs a pub/restaurant on Long Island aptly named 'Butler's Publick House'. I must get over to visit it some day soon, as I hear it contains lots of Irish memories along with a photo of the house in Clonboo.

Mike (b. 1968), retired from the US Army, married Meike from Germany and they live there. They have two children: Vanessa, born 1990 and attending University in Hawaii, and her brother Brandon, who was born in 1992. Mike is now a civilian contractor and has now been in Iraq over a year. Our thoughts and prayers are with him.

Pat, Mike's twin, married Donna in November 2004. Pat works in the Jersey City Police Department. They have one son, Finbarr, who was born on 25 September 2007.

2. **John** married Winfred Leinan in June 1944. John was born on 27 December 1921 and died on the same date, 27 December, in 2003. They had three children: Kathleen, Thomas and Anne. When Winfred died in May 1979, John married Mildred Gallagher. Kathleen married Robert Polito and they have two children: Michael, who is married to Jennifer, and Tracy, who is married to Jim Gray. Thomas, the next child of John and Winfred, married Andrea (who has sadly passed away) and they have two children, Josh and Amanda. The other daughter, Anne, married Fred Hughes and they have two children, Jennifer and Tim.

3. **Thomas** married Margaret (Peggy) Galvin in October 1951. Tom was born on 23 November 1924 and he worked in a large cosmetics firm, Helena Rubenstein, as a Traffic Manager. He and Margaret did not have a family, and Tom died on 9 August 1996.

4. **Denis** married Mary Kerr in June 1961. He was born on 26 July 1927. He is a retired New York State Assemblyman; a Democrat who was re-elected on several occasions. They had three children: Kathleen, Denis and Tom. Kathleen (b. 1962) has a daughter called Deihlia. Denis was born in 1965 and is a New York City Judge. Thomas, the youngest, was born in 1968 and is married to Lisa. They live in Stamford, Connecticut, where Thomas works in a public relations firm. They have three children. At eighty-two, Denis is the last surviving son of Denis and Anne.

5. **Mathew** (b. 23 July 1934) married Catherine (Kitty) Sheen in June 1962. Matt worked with Con Edison Electric and died on 7 May 2004. He and Kitty had two sons, Mark and David. Mark married Keri Karvetski in September 1998 and they have two children, Eleanor and Luke. David lives in Colorado.

In September 1968, Denis (or Dinny) Butler wrote a twenty-page account of his life, which is a great record of him growing up. It gives a fabulous insight into the two brothers, Dinny and Mathew, who moved from Clonboo, firstly to Dublin, next to Liverpool and finally to America. He explained that he put the information together because many children born in America whose parents are foreign born, know very little of their ancestors. At the time of writing, four of his family (brothers and sisters) were still alive: Denis himself was eighty-one; Julia was eighty-five; Katherine was seventy-seven, and Patrick was seventy-five, along with John (my grandfather).

Desmond Roe Butler (Matthew's son and Dinny's nephew) is credited as the person who suggested that Dinny write down his recollections. It contains a fantastic amount of information, especially considering that Dinny was eighty-one years of age at the time of writing. It certainly filled in a lot of gaps and answered a lot of questions for me. My mother and father had a copy, and I think most of the cousins also have a copy. Some extracts about Dinny's parents and growing up in Clonboo follow, taken directly from Dinny's recollections, with only the odd comment here and there from me, by way of clarification:

> We owned a farm of about forty acres and also four houses in Church Street, Templemore, left to my father by his father. In my days, the houses in Templemore were old and the weekly rents were small. Some years ago (early '60s), the town council took over the property in that street and they took over the four houses. Compensation was given for same.
>
> We cultivated about fifteen acres of the land: corn, oats, potatoes, turnips, cabbage, beet and an assortment of other vegetables. My father did most of the plough work in early spring and was admired for his 'perfect drills'. [That ploughing would have been done with a horse pulling the plough.] The remaining twenty-five acres were grazing land for cattle and sheep. He did not let the tillage go stale by repeating the same crop annually. He alternated the usage of the land from year to year.
>
> My mother had a great task to perform with nine children. My mother, while attending to her duties, was strict with us. Often when one of us was slow in learning our prayers, she would get us to repeat the prayers while she was doing her work. She was perfect with needle and thread; she could mend a patch on clothes, knit our socks and repair them.

This was called 'darning' socks, a custom long gone as good clothes are now thrown out if there is the slightest defect. I remember wearing jumpers with leather patches on their elbows, it was a trendy fashion at one time!

> All the children would help out at home helping their mother and father on the farm. Our one great advantage was that we had more than sufficient turf-fuel for heating and cooking. The bog was near the house and we were able to sell about twenty-five pounds every autumn to men from the mountains seven miles away, who had no turf. The price of coal was always too expensive.

Growing up in the country at the time might appear lonesome, but, as Dinny explains, the contrary was the case:

> We had football, hurling and other games. In our parish, Clonmore, there were two bands; fife and drums. There was dancing on Sunday evenings at various crossroads during the summer. In the autumn when the farmers had the threshing of the corn, the girls were invited to the houses at night and the men who worked at the threshing stayed on. All danced and sang 'till the late hours, with all food and drink provided by the owner and his family of the farm where the threshing took place. All the kitchens in country houses in those days were very large and well suited for dancing.

Dinny's brother Matt left home in Clonboo at fourteen years of age to go to Dublin to serve his time in the grocery business. He stayed in a cousin Maher's house in Harold's Cross and worked for two years, which was the normal amount of time spent as an apprentice. His only pay for that time was his board and lodgings. Matt stayed there for about two years after his apprenticeship ended. Dinny came to Dublin approximately two and a half years after Matt to the same business. All clothes and petty cash had to be sent from Clonboo, but Dinny says that Matt was good to him during his two-year apprenticeship.

Matt went to Liverpool after about four years and worked in the grocery business there. He then got into the insurance business and he married Louise De Lane. Her father was French born but her mother was from Co. Louth.

Dinny spent five years in Dublin and had about £30 saved when he decided to go to America via Liverpool. At the time, Matt told him that an opportunity existed in the insurance company. Dinny took the job and made a success of it. All thoughts of going to America were parked for a while. Matt and Louise then had a son, Desmond, and when Louise's parents were unable to carry on working, Matt, Louise and Desmond moved back and took over the De Lane's restaurant business. Matt also kept the insurance job going.

Dinny met his future wife, Annie Smyth, in one of the Irish movements and societies which were all over Liverpool and every large population centre throughout England at the time. Annie Smyth was from Kells, Co. Meath.

In 1915, the insurance business was very bad in England. With his savings, Dinny decided to go to America. He left Annie and Matt and his family behind, on the basis that Annie would follow as soon as Dinny got settled with a good job. First he stayed in Philadelphia and he got a job in a warehouse for $8 a week for seventy hours work. Before long he got a job with a taxi firm and he stayed there for eighteen months. Dinny then moved to New York. After working for over eight months, a strike put them all out of work again. At this time, Matt came to New York and they both got jobs driving taxis in the city. When he was established he sent Annie the money to come over, which she did. They got married on 2 June 1919.

At this stage, Matt, Louise, Desmond and another son, John, were now in America and lived in New York at 204 East 25th Street. Dinny got an apartment across the road from them.

Dinny eventually came back to Tipperary after an absence of over forty years. He reflects:

> I found crowds of nephews and nieces who were not born when I left home. My two brothers and two sisters were in perfect health. A change for the better was visible in every place I visited. The farmer was then secure on his farm. The people were well dressed which is one of the standards of living well. Almost every farmer has an auto. My nephew (Johnny Butler) took me three times in his father's car to Templemore about five miles away. There were electric lights all over. However the farmer depends so much on the crops, they often suffer when the harvest time becomes wet. Dublin and other cities are all up to date and well stocked in the various shops, as they call them.

Dinny stayed ten weeks in Ireland at that time and returned again in 1958 with his son Denis.

MY GREAT-GRANDFATHER'S GENERATION

There were ten children in the family. My great-grandfather was John Butler, who was born on 19 May 1845. He married my great-grandmother Catherine Shanahan on 4 November 1877, and he died in 1936 at the age of ninety-one years. They had nine children, six boys and three girls: Patrick, Mathew, Denis, John (my grandfather), Thomas, Mathew, Kathleen, Julia and Mary. As you can see there were two Mathews, the first of whom died at five months old. (It was common to name a second child with the same name if a child died young.)

CENSUS OF IRELAND 1901
This census was taken on 31 March 1901. The instructions and headings on the form were different to what they would be nowadays. Under the heading of 'Education', the instruction was to 'state here whether he or she can "Read and Write", can "Read Only", or "Cannot Read"'. The religious profession had to be stated.

At home in Clonboo on the Sunday night of 31 March 1901, the following entries were made in the census filled out by my great-grandfather.

NAME	RELATION	EDUCATION	AGE	OCCUPATION
John	Head of Family	Read and Write	55	Farmer
Catherine	Wife	Read and Write	50	

John	Son	Read and Write	22	Farmer's Son
Julia	Daughter	Read and Write	18	Farmer's Daughter
Thomas	Son	Read and Write	17	Farmer's Son
Mary	Daughter	Read and Write	16	Farmer's Daughter
Denis	Son	Read and Write	14	Scholar
Kate	Daughter	Read and Write	10	Scholar
Patrick	Son	Read	8	Scholar

They were all noted to be Roman Catholic and to be all born in Co. Tipperary. The census form was signed by John Butler as 'Head of Family' and the signature of the enumerator was Patrick Clarke.

My great-grandparents' marriage was registered in Templetuohy parish, as this was the bride's home parish. They got married on 4 November 1877. The marriage witnesses were John Maher and Johanna Manton, the best man and the bridesmaid. As Catherine had a sister named Johanna it is fair to assume that Manton was her married name.

My great-grandfather was born on 19 May 1845 and his baptismal record shows that his godparents were Patrick Brennan and Catherine Delaney. His mother was Julia Delaney, so the chances are that the Catherine Delaney that stood for him at baptism was his mother's sister, his aunt.

John had six brothers and three sisters. I will go through these one by one with the only details I have about them: their baptismal records. They are all my great-granduncles and great-grandaunts:

1. **Denis** was the oldest, born on 20 February 1828. His godparents were Pat Brennan and Margaret Long. Denis must have died young as his younger brother, born 24 February 1950, was also named Denis.

2. **Mary** was the oldest girl and was born on 18 January 1830. Her godparents were Darby Maher and Mary Butler. Her mother's name was Julia Delaney and her father's name was John Butler. I could only find a brother for her father and no sister, so the Mary Butler was not her aunt. Her grandmother was also Mary, so she could have been the godmother. It is possible and would not be at all unusual. My own godmother was my grandmother Sarah Doolan. Nowadays godparents are younger and this is a good idea, as it gets young people involved with the Church from an early age. Her godfather, Darby Maher, who was married to her aunt Mary Butler, was, I reckon, Thady Maher's great-grandfather.

3. **Tobias** was next, born 14 February 1832. His godparents were John Rourke and

Margaret Laffan. I don't know the connection to Margaret Laffan, but John Rourke must have been one of the Rourkes that lived down where Thady Maher now lives, in Clonboo.

4. **John** was born on 13 June 1834. His godparents were Thomas Delaney and Anne Rourke. Anne was probably another of the Rourkes of Clonboo and the Thomas Delaney was likely a sister of his mother, Julia Delaney, and so his uncle. This John Butler must have died young, as another brother, born in 1845 (my great-grandfather), was also named John. As was often the custom, if a child died young, another child born after the death would be called the same name, part in memory of the dead infant.

5. **Judith** was born on 19 June 1836. Her godparents were Joseph Delaney and Judith Fogarty. Joseph was likely to have been an uncle and a brother to her mother, Julia Delaney.

6. **Anne** was born on 24 September 1838. Her godfather's name is not recorded, but her godmother was Catherine Laffan. I do not know what the connection or relation was to Catherine Laffan; it may have been on my great-grandmother's side, because Catherine is the second of the Laffan family to stand for this generation of Butlers (the other was Margaret who stood for Tobias).

Anne Butler married Ned Brennan from Ballinroe, Castleiney and they had four children: (a) **John**, (b) **Edward**, (c) **Mary** and (d) **Julia**.

(a) **John** married Mary Guider and they had three children: Edward who married Kathleen Joyce, Michael who married Josie Carroll and Sean who married Nell Maher.

Sean and Nell had four children: (i) John, (ii) Anne, (iii) Kitty and (iv) Mary.

(i) John married Bridget Broderick and had a daughter, Aisling.

(ii) Anne married William Bergin from Templemore and they had seven children: Joe, John, Anne, Marion, Bernadette, Joan and Catherine.

Joe married Bernadette McHugh and had five children: Joe, Daniel, James, Aine and Marie. John married Margaret Foley and had children Billy, Maura, Kate and Ann. Anne married Willie Quaney and they had four children: Mary, Michael, Julie and Ann. Marion married Pat Crone and had five children: William, Miriam, Thomas, Pauric and Sinead. Bernadette became a nun. Joan married Michael Ryan and had eight children: Seamus, Mary, Siobhan, Michelle, Willie, Elizabeth, Michael and John. Catherine married Sean Maher and had four children: Caitriona, Ailish, William and Patrick.

CENSUS OF IRELAND, 1901.

(Two Examples of the mode of filling up this Table are given on the other side.)

FORM A.

No. on Form B. 14

RETURN of the MEMBERS of this FAMILY and their VISITORS, BOARDERS, SERVANTS, &c., who slept or abode in this House on the night of SUNDAY, the 31st of MARCH, 1901.

No.	NAME and SURNAME		RELATION to Head of Family.	RELIGIOUS PROFESSION.	EDUCATION.	AGE.		SEX.	RANK, PROFESSION, OR OCCUPATION.	MARRIAGE.	WHERE BORN.	IRISH LANGUAGE.	If Deaf and Dumb; &c.
	Christian Name.	Surname.				Age last Birthday.							
1	John	Butler	Head of Family	Roman Catholic	Read & Write	55		M	Farmer	Married	Co. Tipperary		
2	Catherine	Butler	Wife	Roman Catholic	Read & Write	50		F		Married	Co. Tipperary		
3	John	Butler	Son	Roman Catholic	Read & Write	29		M	Farmer's son	Not Married	Co. Tipperary		
4	Julia	Butler	Daughter	Roman Catholic	Read & Write	18		F	Farmer's Daughter	Not Married	Co. Tipperary		
5	Thomas	Butler	Son	Roman Catholic	Read & Write	17		M	Farmer's Son	Not Married	Co. Tipperary		
6	Mary	Butler	Daughter	Roman Catholic	Read & Write	16		F	Farmer's Daughter	Not Married	Co. Tipperary		
7	Denis	Butler	Son	Roman Catholic	Read & Write	14		M	Scholar	Not Married	Co. Tipperary		
8	Kate	Butler	Daughter	Roman Catholic	Read & Write	10		F	Scholar	Not Married	Co. Tipperary		
9	Patrick	Butler	Son	Roman Catholic	Read	8		M	Scholar	Not Married	Co. Tipperary		
10													
11													
12													
13													
14													
15													

I hereby certify, as required by the Act 63 Vic., cap. 6, s. 6 (1), that the foregoing Return is correct, according to the best of my knowledge and belief.

Patrick Cooke (Signature of Enumerator.)

I believe the foregoing to be a true Return.

John Butler (Signature of Head of Family.)

(iii) Kitty married Bob Stakleum and they had three children: Noreen, Mary and Paddy.

Noreen married Dominic Foran and had three children: Claire, Lisa and John. Mary married Luke Larkin and had three children: Kathryn, Christine and Eva. Paddy married Mary Harty and had three children, Kathryn, Paula and Bobby.

(iv) Mary married Edward Ryan and they had two children, Mary and Michael. Their daughter Mary married Paddy Joyce and they live in Clonmore where they have three children: Philip, Mary and Eamonn. Paddy Joyce loves playing cards and regularly goes to card games with my father, usually on a Sunday night. Michael married Frances Maher and they have two children, Shane and Edward.

(b) **Edward**, the second child of Anne Butler and Ned Brennan, married Josie Sheppard and they had two children Eddie and Anne.

Eddie married Angela Fahey and they had two sons, Eamonn and Peter. Peter, who was full back on the winning Templemore CBS Harty team, was ordained a priest, while Eamonn married Angela Everard. Anne married Mick Russell from Longorchard, Templetuohy and they had three children: Liam (RIP), Ned and Margaret.

(c) **Mary,** the third of Anne Butler's children, married Jim Ryan from Lisheen, Moyne and they had eight children: (i) Jack, (ii) Edward, (iii) James, (iv) Kitty, (v) Annie, (vi) Mary, (vii) Shelia and (viii) Theresa:

(i) Jack married Joan Fogarty and had five children: Tim, Jim, Mary, Margaret and Joan.

(ii) Edward (Ned Ryan from Toher) married Annie Holohan and had two children, Jim and Bridget. Bridget married Barry Gorman.

(iii) James married Maura Hayes (RIP) and had three children: Suzanne, Michael and Joan.

(iv) Kitty married Jim Moloney.

(v) Annie married Paddy Ryan and had four children: Bridget, Mary, Seamus and Con.

(vi) Mary married Billy Corcoran.

(vii) Shelia married John Harte.

(viii) Theresa became a nun.

(d) **Julia** was the fourth child of Anne Butler and Ned Brennan. Julia married John Hartigan and they had five children: Ned, Sean, Tom, Teresa and Anne.

6. **Michael** was born on 24 September 1840 and had the same birthday as his sister Anne, but was two years older. His godparents were James Roorke and Bridget Ryan. Although the spelling of the Roorke surname is different than the previous Rourke, it is probably the same family who lived at Maher's in Clonboo.

7. **William** was born on 25 April 1843. His godparents were Patrick Ryan and Bridget Maher. Patrick Ryan could be some relation of Bridget Ryan who stood for Michael (brother or husband).

8. **John**, my great-grandfather, was the next to be born. As noted above, he was born on 19 May 1845 and was the second son to be named John. His godparents were Patrick Brennan and Catherine Delaney (probably his aunt).

9. **Thomas** was born on 29 March 1846 and his godparents were John Clarke and Bridget Maher.

10. **Denis** was born on 24 February 1850 and his godparents were John Clarke and Margaret Clarke. My father maintains that Denis became a Christian Brother and that Matt also became a Christian Brother. One of them went to Australia. There

is no Matt listed in the baptismal certificates for this generation, however, and so the obvious thing to think would be that the Christian Brother was Michael and not Matt. However in my great-grandmother's death notice, as published in *The Nationalist* on 27 November 1907, a Brother Gerard Butler, Christian Brother, Dublin (brother-in-law) is named among the mourners. It could well be the case that similar to the nuns at the time, the Brothers changed their first name to that of a chosen saint.

MY GREAT-GRANDMOTHER'S GENERATION

There were eight children in the family. My great-grandmother was Catherine Shanahan. She was born on 20 December 1848 and she married my great-grandfather John Butler on 4 November 1877. She died on 18 November 1907, at the age of fifty-nine years. The following announcement was published in *The Nationalist* newspaper on 27 November 1907. Such announcements were normal for the day, and we have a copy of the original extract. It does provide an insight into the way of life at the time and throws up a lot of very useful information and family connections:

DEATH OF MRS JOHN BUTLER, CLONBOO, CLONMORE

With feelings of the deepest regret I have to announce the death of the above named esteemed lady, at her residence, on Friday the 18th inst., at the age of 59 years, after an illness of some weeks duration. Deceased had been ailing for some time, and despite all that medical skill and loving nursing could do, she passed away to her eternal reward, fortified by the rights of the Holy Catholic Church, of which she was a devoted member. During her illness and almost up to the hour of her death she had the happiness and consolation of being regularly visited by her clergy who were untiring in their attendance on her. She belonged to an old respectable family, and her quiet, gentle and unobtrusive manner won for her the respect and esteem of all creeds and classes, which was fully testified to by the large and representative cortège – upwards of 200 cars and carriages which followed her remains to the family burial ground at Moyne. Revd W. Purcell CC and Revd C. O'Riordan CC officiated at the grave. The chief mourners were John Butler (husband); John Butler and Pat Butler (sons), Julia, Mary and Katie (daughters), John and Matthew Shanahan (brothers), Mrs Fanning (sister), Brother Gerard Butler, Christian Brother, Dublin (brother–in–law); Mrs Shanahan (sister-in-law); Edward Bowe, Longfordpass; John Bowe, do; Patrick Norton, do; Edmond Dwyer, do; Mrs Dwyer, do; Edward Bowe, Leigh; John Lanigan, Kilcooley; Mrs Lanigan, do; Timothy Bowe, Loughmore; Tobias Maher, Toher; James Maher, do; Jeremiah Maher, do; Philip Maher, do; John Maher, Clonboo; Mrs Blake, Moyne; James Blake DC, Moyne; Andy Brennan, Kilemakill; Miss K. Brennan, do; John Brennan, Castleliney; Miss M. Brennan, do; Andrew Hynes, do; Miss J. Hynes, do; Mrs Mullally, Hotel, Templemore; Michael Whelan and Mrs

Whelan, Baw [?]; Mrs Michael Shanahan, Kileake; Thomas Carroll, Killanigan; Donie Kirwan, do; Mrs Everard, Boularea; Thomas Everard, do; Mrs Long, [?]; Mrs Davy, Ballyknockane; Joe Davy, do; John and Mrs Fogarty, Killeran; Frank Moore, do; Miss H. Moore, do; James Russell, Killea; Miss Corcoran, do; Pat Kennedy, College Hill; Mrs T. Meagher, Templemore; Joseph Maher, Shanakill; Mrs J. Murphy, Doreae [?] (cousins).

On the Shanahan side, both of Catherine's brothers, John and Mathew attended as did her sister a Mrs Fanning. Edward and John Bowe also attended; they would have been first cousins. A James Russell from Killea is also mentioned among the list of mourners. This lends weight to Mary Russell's claim that she is related by a connection through my great-grand-aunt Ann Butler. Mary has been a close and great friend of the family in Clonboo for many years. We must be related alright.

My great-grandmother was born on 20 December 1848 and her baptismal records show that her parents were Matthew Shanahan and Mary Bowe. Her godparents were Matthew Shanahan and Ellen Bowe. The chances are that the godparents were an uncle and an aunt, being brother and sister to Catherine's parents. Catherine was the first to be born, and it was usual that the first godparents would be close family members, and often the best man and bridesmaid from the wedding.

She had four sisters and three brothers: Mary, Matthew, Johanna, John, Michael, Ellen and Bridget. All the baptismal records show their parish to be Templetuohy, as they lived in Lisdownley, Moyne. Catherine's brother Johnny had the home place, but when he died his wife asked her nephew Patrick (Paddy) Butler, Catherine's son, to help her run the farm. Paddy did this and eventually got married out of this farm. He had two sons, John Joe and Eddie. John Joe is still in Lisdownley where he continues to farm the land.

The surname of Shanahan is recorded in baptism records but in the 1911 census the surname is recorded as 'Shanaghan'. As for Catherine's brothers and sisters, Mary was born on 22 February 1850 and her godparents were Pierse Bowe and Judith Shanahan. More than likely, they were Mary's uncle and aunt. Matthew was born on 27 September 1851 and his godparents were Edmund Bowe and Catherine Shanahan. Johanna was born on 20 October 1852 and her godparents were Dennis Dunne and Ellen Brennan. Johanna married a Fanning and when the 1911 census was taken, she was a widow and had moved back to the home place. John was born on 10 June 1855 and his godparents were Daniel Scott and Ellen Bowe. Ellen could have been an aunt to John. Michael was born on 28 September 1856 and his godparents were Matthew Dooley and Mary Dooley. Ellen was born on 18 May 1858 and her godparents were John Bowe and Mary Bowe. Her mother was also Mary Bowe, so I'm not sure who this Mary Bowe could be, unless a grandmother to Ellen. Bridget was born on 3 October 1859 and her godparents were James Fogarty and Ellen Dunne.

MY GREAT-GREAT-GRANDPARENTS

My great-great-grandparents were John Butler and Julia Delaney. John was born on 28 March 1810, but I could not confirm when Julia was born. John had a brother called Patrick who was older than him, having been born on 24 August 1804. There may also have been at least three older sisters, named Bridget, Joanna and Mary. Baptismal records are not available from the Cashel & Emly diocese prior to 1800.

It is fair to say that the Delaneys that stood for John and Julia's children were more than likely Julia's brothers and sister. They were Thomas, Joseph and Catherine Delaney. A Mary Butler also stood for one of the children. I could not find any children other than John and Patrick. Mary could have been a sister, but I think she's more likely to be an aunt or grandmother.

John Butler was born on 28 March 1810 in the parish of Loughmore. His godparents were John Fogarty and Mary MacCormack.

His brother **Patrick** was born on 24 August 1804, also in the parish of Loughmore. His godparents were John Meagher and Mary MacCormack. It is possible, although unusual, that both had the same godmother, or it could be a case of two people with the same name.

Bridget Butler married Thomas Davy on 19 February 1816. Denis Deegan and John Maher were witnesses at the wedding. Bridget and Thomas had twelve children, five boys and seven girls: John, born 9 February 1817; Toby, born 23 January 1819; Mary, born 7 February 1821; Ellen, born 4 October 1822; Michael, born 22 September 1824; Catherine, born 5 December 1825; Thomas, born 11 April 1828; Martin, born 29 October 1832; Bridget, born 4 July 1834; twins Catherine and Johanna, born 23 November 1836, and Anne, born 2 April 1839.

My grandfather was apparently very friendly with Tom Everard. Tom's grandmother was the above-mentioned Bridget Butler, who married Thomas Davy, and their daughter Catherine married Michael Everard, who was Tom Everard's father. Tom married Mary Hackett in 1914, and they had eight children: Michael, who married Agnes Moloney; Catherine, who married Jim Cusack; Edward, who married Catherine Collier; Mary Bridget; Margaret (Rita), who married Danny Cahill; Thomas, who married Anne Cantwell; Ellen, and John Everard, who married Josephine Costigan.

Joanna Butler married James Healy on 7 February 1826. The witnesses at the wedding were Thomas Davy and John Quill. Thomas Davy was probably Joanna's brother-in-law, married to her sister Bridget.

Mary Butler married Darby Maher from Drom on 2 march 1828. The witnesses at the wedding were John Butler and John Rourke.

The Butlers came to Clonboo in 1820 from the Islands (or Clogharaily), Loughmore. Prior to that, they came from Paulstown, just outside Kilkenny. The Kilkenny connection ties in well with the origins of the Butler Castle still standing in Kilkenny.

ENECLANN

Primary Valuation of Ireland

Family Name: Butler
Address: Civil Parish of Killavinoge, Co. Tipperary
Date: 1st April 1851
Order Number: ENE4451362053

County: Tipperary
Parish: Killavinoge
Town or Townland: Clonbuogh

Lot Number	Name	Immediate Lessor	Type of Holding	Content of Land	Net Annual Value of Land	Net Annual Value of Buildings	Total Net Annual Value
7a	John Butler	Earl of Carrick	House, offices and ladn	58a.0r.23p.	£24.15s.	£1.15s.	£26.10s.

Eneclann Ltd , Unit 1, Trinity Enterprise Centre, Pearse Street, Dublin 2, Ireland
Tel: +353 1 6710338   Fax: +353 1 6710281   info@eneclann.ie   www.eneclann.ie

The Butlers that came to Clonboo first were Timothy Butler and his wife Mary (*née* O'Dwyer), with their two sons John and Patrick. It appears that John got the outside farm, nearer the road. He married Julia Delaney, and it is from this brother that our family descended.

A number of tithes were levied against various people in each townland, and Mary Heaphy recorded these in *Tipperary Genealogy*. There is a copy of the extract below. There is a John Butler included in the list for Cloghereally More in 1825. I wonder if, when Timothy Butler came to Clonboo in 1820, he did leave his brother (John) behind in Loughmore? Timothy's son John would have only been ten years old, so this John Butler is not him, unless Timothy's father was still alive and named John. There are no baptismal records prior to 1800 in the Cashel and Emly dioceses, so I don't even have Timothy's records. I found his name from his sons' baptismal records.

When they came to Clonboo, the farm was approximately seventy-five Irish acres. There is no definite sequence as to how or why the farm was split other than John got the outside piece of approximately thirty-six acres and the inside farm of thirty-nine acres was given to one of the other children. The outside farm was smaller as it had road frontage, which was of benefit and of greater value. They built two houses, one on each farm, in 1824. The outside farm and house is where we were born and grew up. It is where my mother and father live today. It is also where my grandfather lived, along with his eight brothers and sisters, and where my great-grandfather lived with his nine siblings.

The inside farm and house now belongs to Thady Maher. A few things might have happened. The other son that we know of, Patrick, might have got the inside farm, as usually the sons got the farm land. Patrick might not have married, or if he did maybe he did not have children. What did happen was that his sister Mary Butler got the inside farm. It may have been that the farm was left to her by her father, after all she was the youngest and maybe she had stayed at home to mind her parents. Alternatively, Mary's brother Patrick may have left her the farm in the event of him not marrying or not having any children. Mary married Darby Maher from Drom and this is how Mahers own this farm today.

This is my theory on the matter, others may differ and I can't be certain in any event, but there are some facts supporting my theory.

Going back to the Loughmore area and the townland of Clogherally More, *Tipperary Genealogy* by Mary Heaphy shows the contributions in connection with tithes levied against various people in each townland. In 1825, the entries for Cloghereally More are as follows:

Calinan, Michael
Cormuck, Andrew
Cormuck, Widow
Ryan, John
Cormuck, Widow
Carroll, Denis
Ryan, Denis
Davy, Thomas Jun.
Butler, John
Cormuck, Widow Margaret
Cormuck, Wm Jas
Cullen, Wm Jas
Shelly, Elenor
Cormuck, Widow Mgt

The surname Cormuck may have been intended to be Cormack, and there is still a Cormack family in the area.

Another townland, Old Bawn, shows a number of names, including Denis Deegan and a William Butler. The Deegans, as noted earlier were also from the area of Loughmore known as the Islands.

GREAT-GREAT-GREAT-GRANDPARENTS

From the baptismal records of John Butler and his brother Patrick, their parents are recorded as Timothy Butler and Mary O'Dwyer. There is no secondary record of proof on this generation, other than that both children fit the conditions. Age wise the children fit, as does the Loughmore connection. The Butlers came to Clonboo in 1820, with at least two sons and at least three daughters. There could of course have been other Butlers in Loughmore at the time, and there is no address recorded.

There is no birth or baptismal record for Timothy Butler or Mary O'Dwyer, as parish records expire at 1800 in the Cashel and Emly Dioceses. If the two sons were born in 1804 and 1810 respectively, it could be estimated that Timothy and Mary were born between 1770 and 1780, making them between twenty-four and thirty-four when their first son was born, which sounds like it was very much a possibility!

GREAT-GREAT-GREAT-GREAT-GREAT-GRANDFATHER

I have established John Butler as my great-great-great-great-great-grandfather. He was born in 1718 and died in 1768, aged fifty years. I was unable to find his wife's name. He is buried in Moyne Cemetery. They would have lived in Loughmore parish but his burial in Moyne is explained by the closeness of Moyne to the Islands in Loughmore where they lived. The Islands, or more properly the townland of Clogharaily More, is very close to the end of Lisheen Lane in the parish of Moyne–Templetuohy. The chances are that the Butlers living in Clogharaily More would have gone to Mass in Moyne over the years and therefore would have more allegiance to Moyne parish. When I went over with my father to Loughmore to see the approximate location of the site where the previous generations lived, Phelim O'Dea pointed across a field to where the parishes of Moyne and Loughmore met.

John Butler had a son, Theobald. I don't know if he had other children and no records or dates for Theobald have yet been found. His baptism predates available diocesan records. Putting John at twenty-five to thirty when Theobald was born would date Theobald's birth between 1743 and 1748. If this was fact and Theobald was the only child or only son, then it is possible that he could have been Timothy's father. Theobald would have been in around his mid to late twenties when Timothy was born.

There is no hard evidence for the above sequence. Theobald could have had other brothers and any of these could have been Timothy's father. However, Theobald erected the headstone for his father's grave (as stated on the headstone), which maybe adds weight to the case that he could have been an only child or only son. Headstones are often erected by the family of the deceased and individual children are not usually exclusively named without the other siblings, wife, etc., unless they are only children.

DOOLAN

My grandfather was Ned Doolan. I never knew him as he died on 16 December 1942. My mother was only two years old when he died, so she didn't know him either. He married my grandmother Sarah Farrell on 5 June 1929. Ned was fifty-eight years old when he got married and Sarah was thirty-two. They had one child, my mother Mary. The rest of the Doolan family that we can trace are as follows.

Paddy Doolan (b. 1831) married Mary Meara (Mara) from Moyne. They lived in Clonboo and had three daughters and we think three sons. The only ones that I have information on are Edward (Ned), Johanna, Margaret (Maggie), Paddy and Mary.

One son, **Paddy**, had a pub or two in Dublin. A nephew of his from Moyne worked with him in the pub. Paddy had the severe misfortune to be killed by a runaway horse while out walking in the Phoenix Park. He was a young man and unmarried when he died. He left the pub to the nephew that worked with him.

Another son went to America and never returned, as far as we know. It was a sad but all-too-common occurrence that young people went abroad in search of their fortune as there was no work at home for them. It was always intended that they would return home but more often than not they never returned and were never heard from again. Unlike current-day modes of air transport, the only means of transport to long-distance locations was the ship. It took a few weeks to get to America and the poor condition of the ships' accommodation, coupled with the whole ordeal of the journey, was a major undertaking before even getting an opportunity to earn a living. The sorry and sad event called 'The American Wake' is separately discussed.

The third son was **Ned** (b. 1873), who was my grandfather.

One daughter, **Margaret** (b. 1879), worked as a housekeeper to a Bannon family in Ballycahill. She never married and died around 1950 or 1951 and is buried in a Doolan plot in Galmoy graveyard.

Johanna Doolan (b. 1878) married James Greed. They had one son, Jimmy and three daughters, Mary, Bridget and Lizzie. Of the four children only Lizzie married. She married Paddy Meade of Dareens and this is separately detailed with the Greeds, in the Houses Between the Crosses.

The third daughter, **Mary** Ann Doolan, married Jeremiah Ryan of Rosemary Street, Roscrea. They had a shop there and they had three children: (i) **Margaret** (Madge), (ii) **Paddy** and (iii) **Martin**.

(i) **Margaret** (died 12 November 1993, aged eighty-five) married John Haugh (died 4 July 1963, aged sixty-four). They had two children, James (Seamus) and Margaret. Seamus married Bridget Walsh from Rosenallis, Laois, and they have one daughter, Mairead, who is eighteen years old and studies Arts in Mary Immaculate College in Limerick. She hopes to qualify as a secondary school teacher, just like my brother Pat, who attended the same college. Margaret married in England and had four children, Anne, Denis, Patrick and Noelle. Anne is expecting her first child in September 2010 with her partner John. Denis is married to Melinda and they have two children, Thomas (four) and Lara (two). They live in Australia, where Denis works in insurance and Melinda is a social worker. Patrick and his partner Gemma have three children, Lauren (five), Charlie (three) and Eevie Violet. Patrick is a train driver in London. Noelle moved back to Ireland. With her partner Gary, she has a daughter Ava (four). They are expecting their second child in October 2010. Margaret also moved back to Ireland and now lives in Borrisokane, County Tipperary.

(ii) **Paddy** (b.1907) married Margaret Moran, a nurse from Athlone. They had one girl and three boys, Olive, Gerry, David and Patrick. Olive inherited the pub and married a Burke, who was a teacher in the Monastery, but they are now divorced. Olive suffered a stroke and is in a nursing home in Shinrone. Gerry worked as a teacher in Dublin but sadly died in 2005 from a heart attack. He was not married. David is a quantity surveyor living in England and he is not married. Patrick is married with three children and is living in Gorey, County Wexford, where he works as a laboratory technician.

(iii) **Martin** (b. New Year's Eve 1905) married Margaret (Peg) Sharpe (b. 27 September 1922) from Roscrea and they had a big family of ten children: three boys and seven girls. Peg died on 27 September 2003 while her husband Martin died on 12 May 1991. Of Martin and Peg's children, **Margaret** (b.1947), a doctor in America, married Daniel Todd. They had three children, Danielle, Martin and Shane. Danielle is also a doctor. **Aileen** (b.1948) married Hugh McCarthy. Their son Gareth is married to Jean and they have five children, Jean, Elaine, Aishling, Andrea and Andrew. **Irene** (b.1949), a secondary school teacher, married Noel Corrigan. Sadly Noel died a few years ago. They had two sons, Paul, who is a pilot, and Mark, who owns a company that makes Solus bulbs. **Dermot** (b.1950) married Jacqueline and they live in Thurles. **Rosemary** (b.1952), a solicitor, married Errol, but they are now divorced. They have one son, Cormac Errol, who is a barrister. **Marion** (b.1954) married Frank Mulroney and they have three children, Karl, Brian and Erika. **Martin (Jr)** (b.1958) is a solicitor. He married Niamh Lennon and they have three children, Aoife, Cronin and Cathal. **Yvonne** (b.1959) lives in Dublin. Brendan (b.1960) is an accountant. He married Patrona and they have two sons, Matthew and Daniel. **Dorothy** (b.1960) worked in the bank. She married Michael Keating, a sergeant in Nenagh, where they have one son, Darragh.

DOOLAN/MARA (MEARA)

My great-grandfather Paddy Doolan was born in 1827. He married my great-grandmother Mary Mara from Moyne. On the O'Mara side of the family, Mary had one sister, Bridget, and three brothers, William, Edward and Thomas. Her parents, my great-great-grandparents, were Edward and Mary O'Mara.

William was born in 1836 and he died on 13 October in 1907, aged seventy-one years. His wife Mary died on 29 December 1918, aged seventy-four years.

Mary, my great-grandmother was born in 1839 and died on 16 October 1886, aged forty-seven years. She married Paddy Doolan. They had three children: Edmond (b.1872), Johanna (b.1878) and Margaret (b.1880). Other children included Patrick who was killed by a runaway horse in Dublin.

Edward was born in 1846 and died at the young age of twenty-three years on 31 March 1869.

Thomas was born in 1850 and died on 23 September 1896, aged forty-six years. His headstone notes his address as No.22 Aston Quay, Dublin.

Brigid was born in 1853 and died on 12 December 1923, aged seventy years. Her married name was Cavanagh but her husband's first name is not known.

There is a large headstone in Moyne graveyard, the old graveyard as opposed to the new graveyard, which contains the above information. The headstone dominates the graveyard due to its size and ornate detail with a statute of Our Lord. The tombstone was erected at the request of Thomas O'Mara, 22 Aston Quay, Dublin, and it was reported to have cost £1,000, which was a vast amount of money in those days. There is also a daughter buried in the grave named Katie, who died on 10 November 1921, aged thirty-nine years. It is assumed that this is Thomas's daughter, although his brothers and sisters are also buried there. Katie has the O'Meara surname, while other members of the family have the Mara and O'Mara surnames.

The same Thomas who erected the tombstone in Moyne died on 23 September 1896. His death and details of his funeral were reported in *The Irish Times* and *Irish Independent* on 24 and 26 September respectively. The *Irish Times* notice was short and announces the details of the funeral arrangements, while the *Independent* carries very useful information about the funeral itself:

The Irish Times, 24 September 1896

O'Mara

September 23rd at his residence 22 Aston's Quay, Dublin, Thomas O'Mara aged 47 years, son of the late Edward O'Mara, Boulabeha, Moyne, Co. Tipperary. Office and High Mass tomorrow Friday morning at Adam and Eve's Church Merchants Quay at 9.30. Funeral will leave the church at 10.15 for Kingsbridge Terminus for 11.30 train to Thurles for interment in the family burial place in Moyne, R.I.P.

Irish Independent, 26 September 1896

Funeral of Mr Thomas O'Mara

Yesterday the funeral of the late Thomas O'Mara, 22 Aston's Quay, Dublin, took place amidst scenes of impressive mourning, which testified to the esteem in which the deceased gentleman was held. Mr O'Mara was a well-known figure in Dublin commercial life. He was for years a member of the committee of the Dublin Licensed Grocers and Vintners' Protection Association and he took a prominent part in the working of the central committee of the Liquor Trade of Ireland, while as a nationalist his actions was always consistent and energetic in promoting the interest of the world in which he resided, as also in the larger sphere of furthering his country's welfare. The remains were removed on Thursday evening from Mr O'Mara's late residence 22 Aston's Quay to the Franciscan Church, Merchant's Quay where they were received by the Fathers of the Community and yesterday Solemn High Mass was sung for the repose of his soul. The church was thronged with the friends and acquaintances of the deceased. The celebrant of the High Mass was the Very Revd Fr Hyland; deacon Very Revd Fr Cassidy; and sub-deacon Very Revd Fr Cleary. On the conclusion of the religious ceremony the funeral cortege was formed for Kingsbridge, whence the remains were conveyed by train for burial in the family burial place in Moyne, Thurles, Co. Tipperary. The string of carriages was one of the largest seen in Dublin for many years, while the list of names appended, which is necessarily imperfect, proves how universal is the regret felt by Mr O'Mara's early demise.

The chief mourners were Messrs Michael O'Mara and William O'Mara, brothers, Jas Doolan (nephew), Patrick Cahill, Thos Dwyer, Hugh McDonnell, Wm Carroll and Ed Sweeney.

Amongst those present were the following: Messrs Daniel Talton, TC, chairman of the Central Committee of the Liquor Trade of Ireland; Peter O'Hara, TC, chairman; Joseph Delahunt, vice-chairman; P.J. Lennox, BA, secretary; Staniclaus Murphy, BA assistant secretary, Dublin Grocers' and Vintners' Protection Association. John Behan, Daniel L. Bergin, James Bowe, Alderman Daniel Burke, Thos Davy, Wm Delaney (PLG), James Dodd (PLG), Patk Dolan, Chas Dowling, Moses Doyle, Patk Doyle, John Fogarty, Francis Gibney, Michael Hayden, James Hennessy (PIG), James Kavanagh, James Kelly, Thomas Kennedy (TC), Wm Kenny, Thos Keogh, Philip Little (TC), Patrick Martin, Michael Nugent and Richard Wall representing the committee of the Dublin Licienced Grocers' and Vintners' Association. Alderman Michael Kernan, John Garrett, John J. Jones, R. Malone, T.J. Brennan, G.M. Dudley, Denis Healy (Bray), John Fanning, M. Fanning, Rd Fanning, Patrick Fanning, W.P. Aungier, P.J. O'Reilly and C. Cregan (Cassidy & Co. Monasterevan). M. Delaney, T. Donnelly, James Rochford, W.J. Edwards (L. & E. Egan). J.A. Fagan, Sylvester Delhaunt. James McDermott, M. Duffy, Patrick Hall, James Taylor (George Roe & Co), D. Tracey, W.H. Spinks, J. Cassidy, J. Delhaunty, W. Quinlan, P. Byrne, C. Devenish, T. Kennedy, W. Fitzpatrick, W. Hogan, T. Dooley, J.T. Durkin, P. Kennedy, J. Hewitt, J.J. Allen, A. Dowse, J. Nolan, W. Simpson, Abraham Lyon (secretary), Family Grocers' and Purveyors' Association; E.P. Monk, Alderman John Reilly, A. Whittaker, J. Hickey, A.J. Keogh, James Lyle, Sterling; T. King, L. Marks, M. Morkan, M.J. Morkan, W. Taylor, L. Doolan, George Washington, M. Ryan, P. Butler, Denis Finn, J. Kennedy, J. Powell, Wm Davy, David Byrne, Dr Dockerey, A. Clancy, W.H. Beerwood, D. Meagher, B. Milind, C. Grimes, B. Cahill, T. Mulqueen, M. Connolly, T. Mackey, J.J. Corry, J.P. Conroy, Patrick Byrne, P. O'Neill, Thomas Long, Jas Kennedy, P. Blake, T.R. Byrne, Michael O'Meara, James Tuohy, D. Ryan, J. Curran, M. Cassidy, J.P. Brennan (John Taylor & Sons), John Ryan, M. Kennedy, J. Kennedy, W. Maher, T.W. Ryan, John Clinton, Tom Higgins, J.C. Brennan, Philip Meagher, P. Hooley, W. Kinsella, S. McGrath, W. McGrath, Ed Hackett, J.P. Butler, P.J. Molloy, J.

McGowan, Daniel Ryan, T. Butler, P. Leech, Joseph Beehan, W.E. Right, T. Cahill, Pierce Ryan, John Perkins, J.J. O'Mara, E. Horton (Kingstown), M.J. Cantwell.

    A number of the more intimate friends of the deceased accompanied the remains to Thurles.

From my own children, on my mother's side, on her father's side, I have gone back five generations – nearly 200 years – to the early 1800s, to their great-great-great-grandparents, Edward and Mary O' Mara.

Next we will look at the Farrell side, where I have also gone back five generations, from my own children to their great-great-great-grandfather Michael Farrell, who was born in Borrisoleigh in the early part of the 1800s.

FARRELL

My grandmother Sarah Farrell married my grandfather Ned Doolan. Sarah Farrell came from a large family of thirteen children: seven girls and six boys. They came from Garrangrena, Borrisoleigh.

Sarah's father and mother were James Farrell (b.1855) and Anne Bourke (b.1867), my great-grandparents. They were married on 9 February 1891. Anne was a Bourke from Glanbreeda, Borrisoleigh. They were married in Borrisoleigh church by Fr Michael Finn CC. James's father's name was Michael Farrell (my great-great-grandfather on my great-grandfather's side), while Anne Bourke's father's name was Richard Bourke (my great-great-grandfather on my great-grandmother's side). James and Anne's seven girls were Mary, Anne, Sarah, Mary, Margaret, Katie and Johanna, and the six boys, Mick, Ned, Richard (Rick), Paddy, Jim and Phil.

My grandmother Sarah Farrell was a cousin of Dan Gleeson, a famous Tipperary republican. Dan's father was a small farmer and a blacksmith, but the Fenian tradition came from his mother's side. Her maiden name was Bourke and this is where the connection to my grandmother is. There were six boys and six girls in Dan's family. His eldest brother, Patrick, was the most politicised, and he was shot from behind while under arrest by Free Staters in 1923. Dan supported the republican movement, and was an activist from the age of fifteen. In 1987, a commemorative publication was produced to record Dan's seventieth year as a Volunteer of North Tipperary Óglaigh Na hÉireann. In it, he recalls his childhood memories, which included the harshness of the time growing up, when his family faced eviction, to the days when he enjoyed the simplicity of rural life, running and playing hurling. The hurling heroes of his boyhood days were the Toomevara team 'the Greyhounds' (1912).

Recollections of the 1916 Rising were limited because of the brief reports of it in the local press at the time. The Rising and subsequent executions created an atmosphere for the growth of a mass movement. In October 1917, after playing hurling, Wedger Maher (captain of the Greyhounds) and James Devany recruited Dan into the Volunteers. At that time he took an oath to the Republic and pledged his life to that objective and to the Republican Movement. Not until 1918, when Britain threatened to impose conscription, did the ranks of the Volunteers swell. Thereafter, action was taken to perfect a proper military machine through training classes, raiding for arms, intelligence, and arranging dumps, supplies and transport. In 1919, the Volunteers became known as the Irish Republican Army.

It is fair to say that politics has always played a dominant and integral part of the Butler and Farrell households. As I was going through an old biscuit tin of memory cards (USA biscuits, as I recall), which my Mother gave me, I came across an original memory card for Michael Collins. Whichever side or 'colour' we are, there is strong Republican blood in the Butler veins.

The children of James and Anne Farrell were as follows:

Mary Farrell, the first child, died at eight months old from the whooping cough.

Anne Farrell (b.1893) married Tim O'Callaghan from Kilballyowen, Bruff, Co. Limerick. They had five children: Bridie, Mary, Michael, Annie and Noelle. 'Aunt Anne's' was a place I knew well, as I spent a few weeks there in the summer for four or five years. Bridie lived close by Aunt Anne's in Knockainy and her son Michael also lived nearby. Aunt Anne was my mother's aunt and my grandaunt, but she was always known to me as Aunt Anne as I have no aunts or uncles. My mother and father are both only children, so I have no aunts, uncles or first cousins.

Aunt Anne would come to Clonboo for a few weeks during the summer and stay with her sister Sarah, my grandmother. I remember her often staying for more than a few weeks and sometimes I think she stayed for a few months. She liked the place, and it was great for Sarah and Anne, because they both lived on their own. Her son Michael would bring her up and then I would go back to Killballyowen/ Knockainey when she went back home. It was the place that I heard that a 'tram' of hay was also a 'vine' of hay. I will come back to my holidays in Co. Limerick later, in the section on hurling.

Going back to Anne's children, Bridie married Jed Barron from Killballyowen and they had seven children before Jed passed away. Sadly, four of the children, Anne, Michael, Timmy and Pat, died. Marie, Gerard and Anthony are the other children. Marie is married to Richie Enright and they have five children: Sinead, Shelly, Annette, Sarah and Shane. Shelly is married to Michael Harty and they have one boy, Daragh. Sinead also has a daughter, Amy. Gerard is married to Eileen Lees and they have two children, Aoife and Padraig. Gerard was a good hurler in his day and played for Limerick at intermediate level. He has kept fit, and was still hurling a few years ago, because I saw him play for the Limerick masters' team, over forties, when they beat Tipperary in Thurles. Tipperary won the senior game that day. My own son Sean wore two jerseys that day; he wore the Limerick jersey during the masters' match and the Tipp jersey during the senior match. He is really a Tipp man but has to keep his mother and grandfather happy by wearing the green colours now and again. Anthony is married to Tina O'Toole and they have four children: Tim, Anthony, Michelle and Yvonne. Yvonne is married to Patrick Power.

Mary married Jack Troy from Drom. They lived in Drom, located between Templemore and Borrisoleigh. They had two daughters and one son: Margaret, Anne and Thomas. Margaret teaches in Tipperary Town. Thomas is in the home place in Drom. Anne married John Corcoran and they lived in Geashill, Co. Offaly. They have four children: Colm, Sarah, John Andrew and Maria. Sadly, Anne died on 23 March 2009.

Jack Troy died when the children were at a young age and I don't remember him, but I remember Mary well as she often visited my grandmother Sarah Doolan, and she would always be over when her mother Anne came up to visit Sarah during the summer.

Annie O'Callaghan married Jimmy Wallace from Garryowen, Limerick. They have four daughters: Kathleen, Anne, Bernie and Sheila. Kathleen, Anne and Sheila live in the States. Anne is married with one daughter, while Sheila is married to Jim and they have two boys. Bernie lives in Limerick City; her married name was Byrne and she has two boys, Adam and Stephen.

Michael O'Callaghan married Anne Hurley, on 22 March 1975. They have one son and two daughters: Tim, Aine and Patricia. Tim works in Croatia and is married there. Patricia (Trisha) is married to O'Maonaigh and has one boy, Cathal. Michael was very good to me when I stayed with his mother during my summers in Co. Limerick. He showed me that there were real hurlers outside Tipperary when we used to go to county championship matches in Limerick. This was during a heyday period in Limerick hurling during the early 1970s.

Noelle O'Callaghan, Michael's sister, married Basil Quinn and they lived in Cookstown, Co. Tyrone. Basil passed away. They had six children: Sheila, Deirdre, Michael, Cathal, Annette and Sean. Like me, a couple of the girls used to go on holiday to Aunt Anne's during the summer. I was often there at the same time. I remember Sheila was one of the girls who used to visit there. The northern accents used to fascinate me as I never would have met anyone from Northern Ireland until then. Sheila eventually moved down to Co. Limerick and married Gerard Moloney. They have four children: Geraldine, Anne, Sharon and Kevin. Sharon is married to Noel Corbert. Deirdre is married to Noel O'Neill and they have two girls Ciara (or Kiera) and Sinead. Michael is married to Geraldine and they have four children: Marie, Paula, Cathal and Christopher. Cathal is married to Angela and they have three children Amy, Kerry and Seamus. Annette is married to Bobby McLaughlin and they have two children Conor and Killian (or Cillian). I don't think Sean is married but I'm not entirely sure.

Sarah Farrell (b. 20 August 1897) married Ned Doolan on 5 June 1929 and they lived in Clonboo/Toher. They were my grandparents. All details under Doolan.

Mary Farrell (b.1895) was the second Mary; the other Mary died at eight months old from the whooping cough before this Mary was born. As seen in other families covered separately, it was a common occurrence that when a child died very young, a subsequent child often bore the same name. Mary went into the convent in 1916. She joined the Sisters of Mercy in Cork. She was known as Sister Christina and I remember her as a very holy person, dedicated to her faith. It was expected by the Church that every family would send a child to a religious vocation, either as a Christian Brother, a nun or a priest.

Johanna Farrell (b.1907) became the second nun in the family. Johanna entered the Convent of the Sisters of Providence, Rome, in February 1929. She was known as Sister Philomena. In those days, girls who entered the convent always took a second name, usually a saint's name, which must have been confusing, especially for her family. I always knew her as Sister Philomena.

Katie Farrell (b.1903) married Paddy Carroll of Killaghan and they had seven children: Gerry, Jim, Bridie, Paddy, Michael, Annie and Margaret. Paddy died in 1941. In 1993, at the time of Katie's ninetieth birthday celebrations, her sister Maggie, aged ninety-four, and brothers Jim, aged eighty-six, Paddy, aged eighty-four, and Ned, aged eighty-eight, were all still alive. Katie died in 1996. Katie and Paddy Carroll's children are outlined below.

Gerry and Michael lived in the home farm place and were not married. Gerry was born in 1927 and died on 9 April 2007. Michael was born in 1934 and he died in March 1996.

Jim (b.1929) is married in Co. Meath to Tess Murray from Clonard, Co. Meath. They live in the Royal County and they have four children: Padraig, Tommy, Colleen and Dorinda. Padraig is married to Maire Hegarty from Donegal. They now live in Dublin and have one son, Graham. Tommy married June Colly from Dublin. They live in Wexford and have four children: Sinead, Aisling, Roisin and Liam. Colleen married Pat McGurl from Co. Meath, where they live, and they have four children: Padraig, Ciara, Janie and Hannah. The youngest of Jim and Tess's children is Dorinda, who is married to Ciaran O'Connor from Co. Meath, where they live. They have two boys, Eoin and Jessie.

Paddy Carroll married Peg Ely from Moyne. They have two children, Edel and Vern. Paddy passed away on 24 October 2008.

Bridie married Tom Quinn from Co. Clare. They had seven children: Joe, Kathleen, Noreen, Paddy, Deirdre, Philip and Lorraine. Tom Quinn died on 26 February 1974 at the young age of thirty-seven years and is buried in Newmarket-on-Fergus, where he and Bridie had lived. After Tom died, Bridie came back to Drom with her family. Bridie died on 23 June 2005. Joe Quinn is married to Claire Stapleton and they have four children: Rachel, Linda, Owen and Brian. Kathleen is married to John Russell from Borrisbeg, Roscrea Road, Templemore. John was a good friend of mine when we were going to the Christian Brothers' second-ary school in Templemore. I often spent weekends at Russell's. John and Kathleen have two boys, Darren and Shane. Noreen married Stephen Morrissey and they have three children: Lorraine, Thomas and Christopher. Paddy married Caroline McGann and they have three children: Paul, Rebecca and Kim. Deirdre is not mar-ried and works in Dublin. Philip married Martina Mockler and they have a boy and a girl, Amy and David. Sadly Lorraine died on 31 January 1988.

Annie married Joe Larkin from Glasscloon, Coolderry, Roscrea. Joe passed away on 17 May 2000. They had four children: Pauline, Joan, Michael and Claire.

Pauline married John Bowe from Grogan, outside Errill and they have five chil-dren: Kieran, Jacqueline, Shane, Lisa and Holly. Joan married Thomas Creagh from Harristown, Rathdowney. They live in Rathdowney and I met their two friendly chil-dren, Jake and Sarah, when I called down there one evening. Michael is married to Paula Quinn from Ballygar, Co. Galway. They have four children: Aine, Niamh, Theresa and Joe. Claire, an electrician, is not yet married.

Margaret Carroll married Jim Maher from the Orchard, Shanakill, Clonmore, and they have two children, Tim and Catherine.

Margaret (Maggie) Farrell (b.1899) married Tommy Fitzgerald from Killballyowen, Bruff, Co. Limerick. They had one daughter, Eileen. Maggie sepa-rated from Tommy Fitzgerald soon after Eileen was born and came home to live in Drom. Maggie died on 27 December 1995. Eileen was born deaf and dumb. She went to a school in Cabra in Dublin and met Michael O'Reilly from Coole, Co. Westmeath, who was also attending the school as he too was deaf and dumb. They had one son called Patrick who was born without any problems with speech or hearing. Patrick is married in England and has four children.

Mick Farrell married Katie Ryan from Knockanure, Upperchurch. They did not have a family.

Rick Farrell (b.1901) died in the 1930s. Rick contracted an illness, believed at the time to be melengitis. He lived for three weeks and died at home. He was not married and had a small farm in Drom, which he left to his sister Maggie. She lived there and farmed the land for a number of years.

Phil Farrell married Lillian Kelly from Dublin. They had no family. I will come back to Phil later when outlining his love of hurling and the association of the Farrells to Faughs hurling club in Dublin. Phil won a senior All-Ireland hurling medal with Dublin. Phil and Lily lived for many years in Clonmore, beside the hurl-ing field in Graffin.

Paddy Farrell (b. October 1911) married Stella Brennan from Castlepollard, Co.

Westmeath. They had one daughter, Concepta, who married Arthur. They have two boys and one girl. The girl's name is Sarah; she works for Aer Lingus and lives in Griffith Avenue, Dublin.

Jim Farrell (b. 1910) married Moira Dwan and they did not have a family. Jim died on 24 July 1999 and his wife Moira died on 6 November 1978. Jim was a Sweet Afton man. I knew him well and I was often over in his house out past the creamery in Drom, down a long lane where you would have to get out a few times to open and close gates. I would always be brought when my mother or father went up to Jim's and I was the one who would have to get out to open and close the gates. Across the field from Jim was where Maggie lived for a while. This must have been the small farm that Rick left Maggie when he died. Why people lived in such long lanes is hard to understand as it must have been very lonely during long winter nights. Remember, there was no television, no electricity and often only a poor radio, which, if you were lucky, got one radio station for a few hours a night. Of course courdeekin' was a regular activity. People who lived in long lanes often had neighbours who were also living in a long way from the main road, but pathways across the fields connected their houses. Jim also had a strong love of all things patriotic and was also a good hurler with Faughs.

Ned Farrell (b. 1905) married Lily Halford. They had two sons and two daughters: Henrietta, Richard, Edmond and Anne. Ned had a pub in Bray called 'The Coach and Hound'. He also played hurling.

Henrietta married Jimmy Flemming. They lived in Grosvenor Place, Rathmines, and they had three girls and two boys. I remember the house because she was very good to put us all up there when we went to see Pope John Paul II when he visited Ireland in September 1979. It was a great day; there were over a million people in the Phoenix Park (The Forty Acres). A large white cross was erected on the spot where the Pope celebrated Mass that day. It is still there and we go there with our own children now and again. It was a great time for religion in Ireland; the whole country got a lift as the economy was going so well. The number of yellow and white flags hanging in every part of Ireland put out a strong and unified message of Christian belief and goodwill towards each other. That was an aspect of life which is not as evident in modern Ireland; people fill their daily lives with pressure and strife, with the drive to grab commercial goals, and with ambitions that constantly get more difficult and demanding.

Richard, Edmond and Anne all got married. Anne lives in Blackrock. She married Paul Healy and they have three children – one son and two daughters.

FARRELLS AND FAUGHS GAA CLUB

Jim, Ned and Phil Farrell all played hurling with Faughs in the 1930s and 1940s. Jim was captain of the junior team between 1935 and 1937. He also played with the senior team, as did Ned, but Phil is named as one of the greats that ever played with Faughs.

Faughs is one of the oldest GAA clubs in the country, having being founded in November 1885. Fag-a-Bealach or Faugh-a-Ballagh is from the old battle cry, 'Clear the Way'.

On 1 November 1884, the GAA was founded in Hayes Hotel, Thurles by a small group which included Michael Cusack. Cusack was one of the most active and passionate individuals in the GAA. In 1885 the association rapidly grew throughout the country, but the development was not as fast in Dublin. Success for the GAA would mean that those in charge of athletics would lose their monopoly there. Michael Cusack had worked and lived in Dublin for the previous ten years and had been actively involved in outdoor sports of rowing, athletics, football and hurling. From his own premises at 4 Gardiner Place, now The Dergvale Hotel, he began setting up clubs to be associated with the new sporting organisation. In December 1883 he founded the Metropolitan Hurling Club, and when the clubs began affiliating to the recently established GAA, the 'Mets' were the first hurling club to join. It was not until the end of 1885, when the GAA was firmly established in the rest of the country, that Cusack turned his attention to organising his adopted county of Dublin. In November 1885, the Michael Davitts Football Club had, at the suggestion of Cusack, been formed by the Grocers' Assistant Association. That same month also saw the formation of the Faugh-a-Ballagh Athletic Club, ever since popularly known in Dublin, as Faughs.

In the past century many of contemporary clubs (including the Mets) have gone, but the Faughs are still going strong, having won twenty-eight Dublin championships in 100 years. Their yellow jerseys, with a green diagonal strip, are well known. My own son Sean has played against them a few times for Lucan Sarsfields under-ten and under-eleven hurling. They have a fine club house which was built in the early 1990s, I think.

Like a great deal of other Dublin clubs in those days, the lads from the country made up most of the teams. They were young fellas that came to Dublin for work and they brought their love of football and hurling with them to their adopted county. There was no going back home for training, so most of them settled down to play with Dublin clubs, and ultimately with the Dublin county teams, if they were good enough. The lists of *The Giants of the Faughs Club* include lads from all over the country, including:

Pat Cullen from Loughmore, Tipperary.
Danny McCormack from Borrisoleigh, Tipperary.
Jack Cleary from Kilruane, Tipperary.

Harry Boland from Dublin. A close associate to Michael Collins and Éamonn De Valera, Boland was a prominent hurler, referee and administrator.

Larry O'Toole from Dublin.

Jim Nolan from Roscrea, Tipperary.

Paddy Hogan from Horse and Jockey, Tipperary.

Jack Quane, originally from Galbally, Limerick and later Arravale Rovers, Tipperary.

Tim Gleeson from Lisboney, Nenagh, Tipperary.

Jack Connolly from Ballypatrick, Thurles.

Tommy Moore from Ballyragget, Kilkenny.

Johnny Callanan from Co. Galway.

Andy Harty from Tipperary.

Jim 'Builder' Walsh from Mooncoin, Kilkenny.

Michael Neville from Rathkeale, Limerick.

Phil Farrell from Borrisoleigh, Tipperary.

Dan Devitt from Kilcommon, Tipperary.

Pat Farrell from Athboy, Meath.

Billy Dwyer from Foulkstown, Kilkenny.

Harry Gray from Rathdowney, Laois.

Bob Mockler from Horse and Jockey, Tipperary.

Ned Wade from Boherlahan, Tipperary.

John J. Rooney from Dublin.

Jim Prior from Borrisoleigh, Tipperary.

Timmy Maher from Aghaboe, Laois.

Mick Gill from Ballinderreen, Galway.

Charlie Downes from Roscrea, Tipperary.

Mick Butler from Kilkenny.

Eamonn Rae from Limerick.

Phil Farrell had a great love of the game he played so well. He was a great hurler and played at the top level in the game during the 1930s and '40s. He played for Faughs on the full-back line and at centre field, but he dominated the centre-back position during the late 1930s and early '40s. How badly we could have done with him in Tipperary at the time. If he was here today and in his prime he would surely fill that pivotal position of centre-back, which Tipperary have struggled to fill with any degree of consistency over the past twenty years. Nobody has dominated that position in Tipperary like Tony Wall or Mick Roche.

Phil Farrell's hurling career brought him success at club level and at county level, when playing for his adopted county Dublin and his adopted province, Leinster. Dublin has won six All-Ireland hurling titles: 1889, 1917, 1920, 1924, 1927 and 1938.

The 1920 All-Ireland was won by Faughs, who represented Dublin, as in the early years the All-Irelands were played by clubs representing their respective counties.

The 1920s was a glory decade for Faughs and the 1920 county championship title was the first of four in a row. They also won three in the 1930s and five in the 1940s.

Phil Farrell was centre-back on the Dublin All-Ireland winning team of 1938. Dublin beat Waterford (in their first appearance) on a score line of 2-5 to 1-6. Army Metro, who had succeeded Young Irelands as 1938 Dublin champions, provided the backbone of the Dublin team. It also had four leading Faughs players in pivotal positions: Mick Butler at full back; Mick Gill at right half-back; Phil Farrell at centre half-back, and Harry Grant at midfield. A month earlier, the Cusack Stand had been formerly opened. Akin to the story of Tommy Doyle keeping Christy Ring scoreless, Phil, playing with Dublin in the 1937 Leinster championship, kept the great Mick Mackey scoreless. I have spoken to people who saw Phil playing and who saw him on that day in 1937. Their description of his hurling pedigree and ability says everything that fits the complete hurler: skill, speed, determination and courage. We hope that the bloodline that links back to Phil Farrell and to that ultimate prize of a senior All-Ireland hurling medal is strong enough to carry the current crop of Butlers, Stamps, Carrolls, Callaghans, Quinns, Barrons and all the cousins that have a love of the hurling code.

The Giants of the Faughs Club describes Phil Farrell as follows:

A native of Borrisoleigh, Co. Tipperary. On Faughs junior and intermediate selections in 1932; centre-back on Dublin team in Leinster JHC of 1933. On Faughs and Dublin Senior teams for many years from 1933, at centre half-back position. With Faughs, Phil won six Dublin SHL medals (1937, 1938, 1939, 1942, 1944 and 1946) and numerous Grocers tournaments. He won seven Dublin Senior Championship medals (1936, 1939, 1940, 1941, 1944, 1945 and 1946). Phil was vice captain from 1938 to 1942 and he was captain of the club senior team in 1943, 1944 and 1945. Phil was centre-back on the Dublin team that won the All-Ireland senior hurling title in 1938 and won three senior hurling Leinster medals with Dublin. He also played several times at centre-back on the Leinster Railway Cup teams. Phil was elected Vice-President of Faughs at the 1949 AGM.

Overleaf: The road between the crosses.

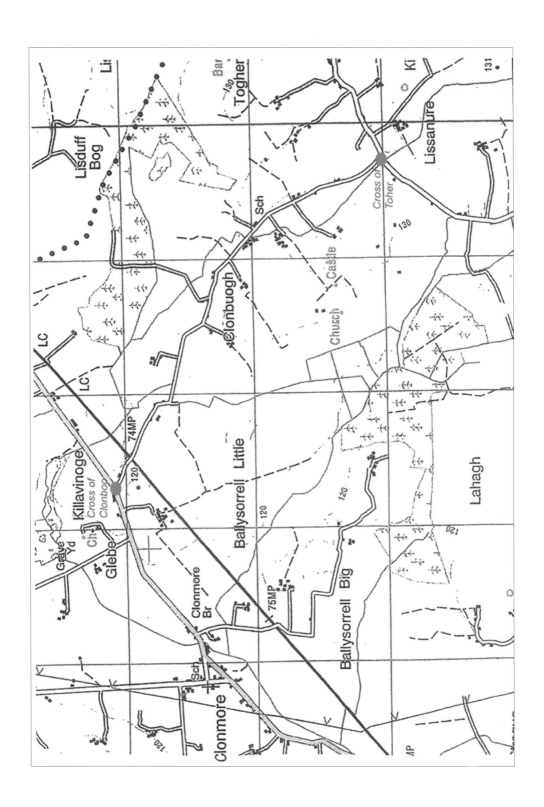

CONCLUSION

SUMMARY OF LIFE

When all the world is young, lad,
And all the trees are green;
And every goose a swan, lad,
And every lass a queen;
Then hey, for boot and horse, lad,
And round the world away;
Young blood must have its course, lad,
And every dog his day.
When all the world is old, lad,
And all the trees are brown;
And all the sport is stale, lad,
And all the wheels run down;
Creep home, and take your place there,
The spent and maimed among:–
God grant you find one face there,
You loved when all was young.

From *The Water-Babies* (1862–3), Charles Kingsley

There is a time to be young and it should be enjoyed; a time for responsibility when we should do our best to shoulder it; and if we are lucky there is a time to be old. We should not only accept it but be thankful for it because many never reach it.

EVENTS OF 1962/1963

Having been born on 30 December 1962, this is a summary of Irish and World events of the time around 1962 and 1963. Most of this information is now on the Junior Cert History curriculum, so we all grow old. Someday a History question may relate to the year the iPad was invented!

At the time, all those years ago, Éamonn De Valera was President, a position he held from June 1959, when he resigned as Taoiseach and offered himself as a candidate for President, until May 1973 when he retired. He was seventy-five years of age when he became President, and eighty-four when he retired.

In July 1962, RTÉ transmitted the first edition of *The Late Late Show*, presented by Gay Byrne.

In October, the Second Vatican Council met and President John F. Kennedy stunned the world by announcing that Russia were building secret nuclear missile bases in Cuba, just ninety miles from the Florida coast. The standoff that ensued became known as 'The Cuban Missile Crisis'. Ultimately, Russia backed down and withdrew the missile bases, having initially thought wrongly that Kennedy was a weak President, having been in the job a short while at the time. This event marked a bright day for the Kennedy administration and the Kennedy family legacy in general. His brother Bobby, along with Vice-President Lyndon Johnston, shared the glory.

Nelson Mandela was jailed for five years in South Africa in November 1962 and Marilyn Monroe was found dead in August 1962 at the age of thirty-six.

It was a cold December in 1962 and there was snow on the ground, but I had loads of blankets, thank God. In January 1963, one of the worst blizzards in living memory brought the country to a halt. The army managed to get supplies to families who were isolated for weeks in some parts of the country, due to huge snow drifts.

In 1963, Pope John XXIII died and Pope Paul VI was elected as the new Pope. Ian Paisley led protests to City Hall in Belfast against the tributes being paid to the Pope that died.

In June 1963, President John F. Kennedy visited Ireland in a memorable occasion for the country, as he was the great-grandson of a Co. Wexford emigrant who had done well for himself.

However, the country was again in shock when the news of JFK's death was announced on 23 November 1963. He had been in office for two years and ten months when the President was shot by an assassin as he drove in an open-top car through the streets of Dallas. He was forty-six years of age at the time of his death. Several stories and conspiracy theories have emerged over the years, and even up to the current day, about the death, including that there was more than one gunman, that the Russians were involved, that his own people were involved, about how the route of one of the bullets through the President's body was shown to have been 'a magic or golden bullet' if it travelled from the observatory window where the single assassin's gun was shot from, etc., etc.,. Lee Harvey Oswald was suspected of the killing but he himself was shot while in police custody and was never convicted.

The Beatles came to Dublin to perform in the Adelphi Cinema and caused havoc as fans thronged the city streets to see the Fab Four. They are considered the inspiration for modern day pop-music artists and they were four guys from Liverpool who took the music world by storm onto a whole new level. The Rolling Stones played the same venue two years later in 1965.

A census revealed that the population of the Republic of Ireland was 2.88 million.

In December 1962, one newspaper headline read, 'Deaths from Smog reach 60 in London'.

That's probably enough about the Golden era of 1962/63, but it is a good reminder of how the years fly by and how ancient we can make ourselves feel. However, it also marks the tremendous progress we have made as a country and the changes that each generation contributes. I remember my grandmother, over and over, using the words 'well I never thought I'd see the day' to describe how she felt about something new like a television or teabags or a calculator or the telephone. There is no chance you could convince her that radios can be put into watches.

That reminds me of a story about an Irishman sitting in a hotel Jacuzzi with an American and a Japanese man. There is a bleeping sound and they are wondering where the noise is coming from, when the Japanese man says, 'Oh excuse me, that's my message bleeper from the office, it's a microchip in my arm.' A few minutes later there was another buzzing sound in the Jacuzzi and this time the American says, 'Oh excuse me, but that's my phone ringing, the microchips are in my thumb and index fingers, I'll just take the call.' At this stage the Irishman is feeling very inadequate, so he gets out of the Jacuzzi and goes to the bathroom. As he walks back, the American notices that a short length of toilet roll is sticking out of the Irishman's backside, so he says, 'What's that at your rear end?', to which the Irishman replies, 'Oh sorry lads, I must be getting a fax.'

HOW DID WE ALL SURVIVE?

Taking editorial privilege, and for the benefit of the younger generation, I have put in this section on 'days gone by'. It may be difficult to comprehend how we survived at all but we did. I remember my grandmother Sarah Doolan telling me about her childhood and also telling me how they were totally self-sufficient. A friend of mine from Cork, Michael Healy, sent me a list of things that happened to us which would nowadays be considered dangerous, health hazards, strange and weird … unbelievable really. I have added a few more to the list and I'm sure some readers could add several others:

First, we survived being born to mothers that drank and/or smoked.

They took aspirin, ate blue-cheese dressing, and tuna from a can and didn't get tested for diabetes.

Then, after that trauma, our baby cots were covered with bright coloured lead-based paints, which we chewed with our gums and cut our first notch into with our new teeth.

We had no childproof lids on medicine bottles, doors or cabinets and when we rode our bikes, we had no helmets, not to mention the risks we took hitchhiking.

As children, we would ride in cars with no seat belts or airbags.

Riding in the back of the boot on a warm day was always a special treat.

We drank water from the hose and not from the bottle.

We shared one fizzy drink with four friends from the same bottle and no one actually died from this.

We ate buns, white bread and real butter and drank drinks with sugar in them, but we weren't overweight because we were always outside playing.

We could leave home in the morning and play all day, as long as we were back when the lights came on.

No one was able to reach us all day, and we were ok.

We would spend hours building go karts out of scraps and then ride them down the hill, only to find out we forgot the brakes. After running into the bushes a few times, we learned to solve the problem.

We did not have Playstations, Xboxes, iPods, Nintendo DSs, iPhones, no 200 TV channels or DVDs, no Surround Sound, no cell phones, no laptops or personal computers, no internet or Bebo or chat rooms. We had friends and we went outside and found them.

We fell out of trees, got cut, broke teeth and bones, and there were no lawsuits from these occurrences, which were otherwise known as 'accidents'.

We ate worms and mud pies made from dirt, and the worms did not live in us forever.

We were given cowboy guns for our tenth birthdays, made up games with sticks and tennis balls and although we were told it would happen, we didn't poke out very many eyes.

We rode bikes or walked to a friend's house and knocked on the door or rang the bell, or just walked in and talked to them!

The local club, mainly GAA, had team trials and not everyone made the team. Those who didn't had to learn to deal with disappointment. Imagine that!

If we had a ball to play hurling with, we were lucky, and if we lost it we would get stung with nettles and briars to find it, because it was our only ball. Afterwards, dock-leaves would be the only ease for the pain of those stings. No complaining, though, because you would get a clip on the ear with no sympathy for losing the ball in the first place. The ball being lost was enough punishment.

If the ball wasn't found, an empty bean can or a small plastic measuring jug that we used for sheep dip would have to do until we found the ball. We lost loads of balls over the years, in the high nettles in the haggard at the end of the yard. When winter came and the nettles and briars died off we would walk straight out and find loads of the balls that were lost during the summer.

The idea of a parent bailing you out if you got into trouble was unheard of; they actually sided with the teacher most times.

This generation, our generation, has produced some of the best risk-takers, problem-solvers and inventors ever. The past forty to fifty years have been an explosion of innovation and new ideas. We had freedom, failure and responsibility and we learned how to deal with it all.

If you are one of them, well done. You might want to share this with others who have had the good luck to grow up as kids, before the lawyers and the Government regulated our lives for our own good, and while you are at it, tell your own kids, so that they will know how brave their parents were!

ALL ONE HAS IS LEFT BEHIND

I live for those that love me
For those that know me through
For the Heavens that smiles above me
And awaits my spirit too
For all human ties that bind me
For the task my God assigned me
For the bright hopes left behind me
And the good that I can do.

I live to learn their story
Who suffered for my sake
To emulate their glory
And follow in their wake
Bards, martyrs and patriots
Nobles and sages of all ages
Whose deeds crowd history pages
And those times great volumes make.

I live for those that love me
For those that know me through
For the Heavens that smiles above me
And awaits my spirit too
For all human ties that bind me
For the task my God assigned me
For the bright hopes left behind me
And the good that I can do.

For the cause that lacks assistance
For the wrong that needs resistance
For the future in the distance
And the good that I can do.

Jack Butler 2010

THE BROTHER

BY MATT BUTLER

History is something that is of great interest to all of us, as we are all continually a part of it whether we want to be or not. Jack has undertaken an extremely difficult venture with this book but it is one I am very happy he has put his mind to. Clonboo is a wonderful part of the country and it will be great to have a small part of it preserved in print for future generations to appreciate.

Clonboo was a wonderful place to grow up in, and it's a place I will always associate with great neighbours and friends. My wife Niamh and I have recently received planning permission to build a house in Clonboo and we can't wait to live there again. It will be great to raise our two girls, Kiera and Zoe, there, as I think there is no better place to be brought up.

Jack is the eldest in my family and despite the several decades in age between us, we have always got on well. He is left Clonboo a long time now, but a big part of him will always remain there. He has always been a very focused and driven individual, so I honestly believe he is the best man to see a project like this through. Speaking of driven, a very early memory of Jack that I have goes to prove the lengths he will go to in order to get the job done. Or to put it another way, the lengths he will put other people through to get it done! When Jack was in college he had to do a project based around before-and-after refurbishment, so he chose me to be a part of this. It involved taking me up the fields and getting me the dirtiest a child has ever been. A photo was taken at this stage for the 'before', and I might add there were parents present who were none too pleased at the sight of what they presumed was their youngest underneath all the muck. I was then cleaned to within an inch of my life for the 'after' picture. So take it from me, Jack definitely has the drive and focus to do this book justice.

Jack was born on 30 December 1962, the eldest of five children. Parents, Johnny and Mary Butler (*née* Doolan). Primary school education at Toher National School, secondary at Templemore CBS (Christian Brothers School), third level at Limerick Institute of Technology. Studied Quantity Surveying and joined Michael McNamara & Co. from Lisdoonvarna upon completion of his studies in 1984.

He got married in 1989 (after a very long courtship) to Anne Phelan from Ashbrook, Ennis Road, Limerick. They have three children, Aoife aged nineteen, Sean aged sixteen and Sarah aged ten. After seven years living in Maynooth, they moved to Lucan in 1996.

Jack is a sporting enthusiast, with a particular love for hurling and especially any involvement from the Premier County. He has now seen Tipp win five All-Irelands, with hopefully many more to come. He enjoyed playing the game, but is still a bit bitter of the fact he wasn't born two days later, for hurling and age group purposes. He is still proud to this day that he was involved with Clonmore when they won the County Intermediate Final in 1987.

After the summer hurling season is over you will often see Jack following his next favorite sport, rugby, and Munster in particular. Horse racing is also a favour-ite with Jack, but probably less so now after a venture in racehorse ownership did not finish in the multiple race wins hoped for. Jack was also involved in setting up Clonmore FC, who back then played a better brand of football than Jack's beloved Leeds United. He still looks up their results with optimism every week, a habit which can't be shaken off even with countless disappointments. Golf is also some-thing Jack enjoys playing and watching.

Along with sport, Jack has a keen interest in politics and political discussion, which he couldn't really get away from, being from the Butler household. He also has a great appreciation of history and its importance, along with a respect for the ways of old and traditional Ireland. Music, film and books are added value to all of the above interests and hobbies.

Recently he became a writer, but I will leave it up to all who read this book to decide if he has succeeded!

Matt Butler